Contemporary Worldviews

In this book, Mikael Stenmark identifies and explores several prominent religious and secular worldviews that people in contemporary society hold. Three nonreligious worldviews are highlighted: scientism, secular humanism, and transhumanism. These are contrasted with four religious worldviews: Abrahamic theism, Buddhism, the new spirituality (the so-called spiritual but not religious individuals, SBNR), and religious naturalism. Some challenges facing each of these worldviews are discussed toward the end of each chapter. The book offers a unique study of several key secular outlooks on life that go far beyond previous studies of atheism, nonreligion, and religious "nones." It also provides a rare insight into the beliefs, values, and attitudes that secular and religious thinkers consider essential to our identity and place in the world, as well as what we should deeply care about in life.

Mikael Stenmark is Professor of Philosophy of Religion at Uppsala University. His books include *How to Relate Science and Religion*, *Rationality in Science, Religion, and Everyday Life*, and *Scientism: Science, Ethics, and Religion*. He is a leader of the Centre for Multidisciplinary Research and Society at Uppsala University, which focuses on religious and social processes of change. He is the recipient of the Oscar Prize (1998) and the Torgny Segerstedt medal (2022).

Cambridge Studies in Religion, Philosophy, and Society

Series Editors

Paul K. Moser, *Loyola University, Chicago*
Chad Meister, *Bethel College, Indiana*

This is a series of interdisciplinary texts devoted to major-level courses in religion, philosophy, and related fields. It includes original, current, and wide-spanning contributions by leading scholars from various disciplines that (a) focus on the central academic topics in religion and philosophy, (b) are seminal and up-to-date regarding recent developments in scholarship on the various key topics, and (c) incorporate, with needed precision and depth, the major differing perspectives and backgrounds – the central voices on the major religions and the religious, philosophical, and sociological viewpoints that cover the intellectual landscape today. Cambridge Studies in Religion, Philosophy, and Society is a direct response to this recent and widespread interest and need.

Recent Books in the Series

Charles Taliaferro and Jil Evans
Is God Invisible?: An Essay on Religion and Aesthetics

David Wenham
Jesus in Context: Making Sense of the Historical Figure

Paul W. Gooch
Paul and Religion: Unfinished Conversations

Herman Philipse
Reason and Religion: Evaluating and Explaining Belief in Gods

Phillip H. Wiebe
Religious Experience: Implications for What Is Real

Norman Russell
Theosis and Religion: Participation in Divine Life in the Eastern and Western Traditions

Amy E. Black and Douglas L. Koopman
Civil Religion and the Renewal of American Politics

Lenn E. Goodman
God and Truth

David Shatz
Judaism and the Philosophy of Religion

Mikael Stenmark
Contemporary Worldviews: A Comparative Study

Contemporary Worldviews

A Comparative Study

MIKAEL STENMARK

Uppsala University

CAMBRIDGE
UNIVERSITY PRESS

Shaftesbury Road, Cambridge CB2 8EA, United Kingdom

One Liberty Plaza, 20th Floor, New York, NY 10006, USA

477 Williamstown Road, Port Melbourne, VIC 3207, Australia

314–321, 3rd Floor, Plot 3, Splendor Forum, Jasola District Centre,
New Delhi – 110025, India

Cambridge University Press is part of Cambridge University Press & Assessment,
a department of the University of Cambridge.

We share the University's mission to contribute to society through the pursuit of
education, learning and research at the highest international levels of excellence.

www.cambridge.org
Information on this title: www.cambridge.org/9781009745086
DOI: 10.1017/9781009745079

When citing this work, please include a reference to the
DOI 10.1017/9781009745079

First published 2026

A catalogue record for this publication is available from the British Library

Library of Congress Cataloging-in-Publication Data
NAMES: Stenmark, Mikael author
TITLE: Contemporary worldviews : a comparative study /
Mikael Stenmark, Uppsala University.
DESCRIPTION: Cambridge, United Kingdom ; New York, NY, USA :
Cambridge University Press, 2026. | Series: Cambridge studies in religion,
philosophy, and society | Includes bibliographical references and index.
IDENTIFIERS: LCCN 2025048045 | ISBN 9781009745062 hardback |
ISBN 9781009745079 ebook
SUBJECTS: LCSH: Religions – History – 21st century
CLASSIFICATION: LCC BL98 .S74 2026
LC record available at https://lccn.loc.gov/2025048045

ISBN 978-1-009-74506-2 Hardback
ISBN 978-1-009-74508-6 Paperback

Contents

Preface

Ninian Smart writes that an "educated person should know about and have a feel for many things, but perhaps the most important is to have an understanding of some of the chief worldviews that have shaped and are now shaping human culture and action."[1] Maybe he is right. Anyway, it is definitely essential to understand some of the outlooks on life that influence our contemporary culture. This is the book's central focus. We will explore seven of the most influential worldviews, both religious and secular, in our time. One distinctive feature of this book is that it identifies and analyzes some of the secular alternatives to religion emerging in modern society.

Professor Anders Jeffner introduced the study of worldview in Sweden during the 1970s. I am grateful to him and Professor Carl Reinhold Bråkenhielm for their inspiration and guidance over the years. I dedicate this book to these pioneers of worldview studies. Sections of the text have been presented at many international conferences, and I appreciate the comments and helpful suggestions I received from attendees at these events. Most of all, I thank the members of the research seminar in the philosophy of religion in Uppsala. Being part of that critical and constructive environment makes philosophical research enjoyable and rewarding! As a member and, more recently, a leader of the Center for Multidisciplinary Research on Religion and Society (CRS) at Uppsala University, I have gained a deeper understanding of the various ways researchers approach and understand religion, as well as what many of them refer to as "nonreligion." These insights have allowed me to

---

[1] Ninian Smart, *Worldviews*. Prentice-Hall, 1995, p. 5.

write a significantly better book than I would have if my peers had only been philosophers.

The book draws from revised parts of some of my recent essays and articles: "Att filosofiskt studera religioner och livsåskådningar," in *Filosofiska metoder i praktiken*, edited by Mikael Stenmark, Karin Johannesson, Ulf Zackariasson, and Francis Jonbäck (Uppsala Studies in Philosophy of Religion 5, 2018); "Scientism and Its Rivals," in *Scientism: Prospects and Problems*, edited by Jeroen de Ridder, Rik Peels, and René van Woudenberg (Oxford University Press, 2018); "Worldview Studies," *Religious Studies* (58) 2022; "Att välja livsåskådning," *Filosofisk Tidskrift* (4) 2022; "Secular Worldviews," *European Journal for Philosophy of Religion* (14) 2022; "Choosing a Worldview," *AGATHEOS – European Journal for Philosophy of Religion* (1) 2024; and "Worldviews and Science," *Zygon: Journal of Religion and Science* (59) 2025.

I

Introduction

In the Western world, we can see changing attitudes toward traditional religions. People are less inclined to accept the traditional teachings of their home religion and instead prefer, to a greater or lesser extent, to decide for themselves which of these beliefs they should embrace and which practices they should participate in. New forms of spirituality are also emerging among people today. Its participants aim to discover the divine within themselves, not guided by religious organizations but by self-help books, meditation courses, and other spiritual techniques. Yet another change is that more people than before – especially in the northern parts of Europe and America – self-identify as nonreligious and reject religion.[1] They want to live secular rather than religious lives. They maintain that religious beliefs are false, that moral values can be developed and defended without reference to a divine, transcendent, or spiritual dimension of reality, and that religious practices are unnecessary. The book aims to explore some of these religious and secular outlooks on life, presenting them as distinct yet coherent rival worldviews, although it is possible to combine them in different ways.

An influential theoretical framework, often a merely unstated assumption, for understanding what it means to self-identify as nonreligious is what I call the *subtraction theory*. It posits that individuals or groups who reject religion view it as unnecessary, false, or an inadequate addition to our shared view and way of life. They simply cease holding religious beliefs and participating in religious practices and organizations.

[1] Ronald Inglehart, *Religion's Sudden Decline: What's Causing It, and What Comes Next?* Oxford University Press, 2021.

They become atheists (a rejection of theism but not much of a positive statement about anything else), agnostics, religious nones, or nonreligious people. One way of stating this view is to say that religious people believe in the supernatural, whereas nonreligious people stop doing that and merely believe in the natural, as religious people also do. Religious believers add on beliefs about the supernatural, whereas nonreligious people do without this addition; they are nonbelievers and are left only with the views they share with religious believers. We can also adopt a more practice-oriented understanding of the subtraction theory and say that religious people participate in certain organized activities. In contrast, nonreligious people stop doing that so they can be adequately described as "religious nones."[2] Self-described nonreligious people are simply marking an absence or standing in opposition to religion. For this reason, many scholars have been inclined to use analytical terms that are primarily negative and talk about nonreligion, religious nones, nonreligious people, or religion's others.[3] The core idea is that we need to add nonreligion to the study of religion due to the changes we see in society today. To religious studies, we must now add nonreligious studies.

I argue in the book that we should challenge this theoretical framework and explore to what extent the *substitution theory* can be philosophically and empirically sustained instead. It recognizes that some individuals and groups reject religion but assume that they also consciously or unconsciously replace or strive to replace religion with an alternative outlook on life. As Charles Taylor phrases it, they try to develop immanent construals of human flourishing.[4] They try to come up with an alternative story of why we are here, what makes something good or evil, what provides meaning in life, and how we should live our lives in light of the key features of this alternative story. Self-identifying as nonreligious, in this sense, is assumed to be not merely a matter of being without religion but also as being with something else. For this reason, scholars need to develop analytical terms that are primarily affirmative, rather than

---

[2] Pew Research Center, "Religious 'Nones' in America: Who They Are and What They Believe."

[3] Lois Lee, *Recognizing the Non-religious*. Oxford University Press, 2015; J. H. Smith & R. T. Cragun, "Mapping Religion's Other," *Journal for the Scientific Study of Religion*, 2019, 58/2, pp. 319–335; and Stephen Bullivant, "Explaining the Rise of 'Nonreligion Studies': Subfield Formation and Institutionalization within the Sociology of Religion," *Social Compass*, 2020, 67/1, pp. 86–102.

[4] Charles Taylor, *A Secular Age*. The Belknap Press, 2007, p. 9.

negative, or terms of presence, rather than absence. They should proceed similarly to political philosophers when it comes to classifying political ideologies; they do not organize their field of research by distinguishing between, for instance, socialism and nonsocialism or socialists and non-socialists. Instead, they distinguish between socialism and, for example, liberalism and conservatism. They do not call those who do not identify as socialists "nonsocialists" but "liberals" and "conservatives" (if we limited ourselves to these three options). Therefore, I propose that we in worldview studies should talk about "secular worldviews," "secular people," "secular rituals," "secular faith," and "secular nones," or develop similar categories. Consequently, we sometimes need to distinguish between religious and secular worldviews.

I will call the academic study of both religious and secular worldviews, as well as everything in between, *worldview studies*. Since there are no clear-cut boundaries between religious and secular outlooks on life, it may also be appropriate at times to discuss semi-secular or semireligious worldviews.[5] Correspondingly, we could and should distinguish between religious, secular, and semi-secular or semireligious people. Worldview studies aim to go beyond religious studies. Their objective is not merely to understand and theorize about the world's religions but also the secular alternatives emerging in some parts of contemporary society. The idea is that conceptualizing them in worldview terms provides a better understanding and makes comparisons with traditional religions more accurate than conceptualizing them in terms of nonreligion or religious nones. According to the substitution theory, we should assume that even if not all people are religious, most people have a worldview of one kind or another. Of course, whether or not that is the case is both a conceptual and an empirical question. First, it depends on what we take a worldview to be and, second, on whether we can confirm the existence of emerging secular worldviews.

The choice of the term worldview might lead one to think that a worldview must be all-embracing. So, we expect and count only those outlooks on life that encompass a whole way of looking at ourselves and our world, or express our overall view of the nature of reality, as worldviews. Not everyone has such a comprehensive worldview. In this sense,

---

[5] Some semi-secular worldviews are discussed in Francis Jonbäck and Carl-Johan Palmqvist, "Between Belief and Disbelief, between Religion and Secularity: Introducing Non-doxasticism and Semi-secularity in Worldview Education," *British Journal of Religious Education*, 2024, 46/2, pp. 109–121.

there is evidence supporting the subtraction theory. Many, if not most, nonreligious people have not replaced Buddhism, Christianity, or Islam with some similar overarching set of beliefs, values, and practices. Do such people not have a worldview? I assert that we should resist defining and understanding the notion of worldview in such a way as to imply that they do not. Arguably, many Buddhists, Christians, and Muslims do not have a worldview in this sense either.

In Chapter 2, I will elaborate on what I consider a worldview to be and the implications of understanding it in this way. I will, in this study, assume that a *worldview* is a constellation of beliefs (or ideas), values, and attitudes that people – whether consciously or unconsciously – hold and that constitute their basic understanding of who they are, what the world is like, and what their place in it is; what they should do to live a good and meaningful life; and what they can say, know, rationally believe, or hope about these things. A great deal of research on worldviews has been conducted. In this study, I will not list or review the research. In the introductory chapter of John Valk's *Worldviews*, you can find an excellent summary of much of this scholarly work.[6] I will only add to this the Swedish research tradition on worldviews that Anders Jeffner initiated in the 1970s, a tradition to which I belong.[7] Unfortunately, most of this research is not available in English.[8] The idea was to investigate what worldview or view of life (the Swedish word "livsåskådning" would literally translate closer to "view of life" than "worldview") the already by then relatively secularized general public replaced their religious faith, primarily Christian, with – if anything.

Generally, there appear to be three distinct and often unrelated research trajectories related to worldviews: (a) the philosophical discourse about religion and naturalism; (b) the empirically oriented studies of emerging secular alternatives to traditional religions; and (c) the research conducted by scholars on religious education (RE) in countries such as Norway, Sweden, and the UK, where secular worldviews are

---

[6] John Valk, *Worldviews*. Palgrave Macmillan, 2021, pp. 2–23.

[7] My first attempt to develop an understanding of what a worldview (what I then called a view of life) is in Mikael Stenmark, *Rationality in Science, Religion, and Everyday Life*. University of Notre Dame Press, 1995, pp. 239–244.

[8] Three exceptions are Anders Jeffner, "A New View of the World Emerging among Ordinary People." In *Christian Faith and Philosophical Theology*, edited by Gijsbert van den Brik, Luco J. van den Brom, and Marcel Sarot. Kok Pharos, 1992, pp. 137–146; Anders Jeffner, *Biology and Religion as Interpreting Patterns of Human Life*. Harris Manchester College, 1999; and Carl Reinhold Bråkenhielm, *The Study of Science and Religion*. Pickwick Publications, 2018.

studied alongside religions in public schools. Notice also that terms other than worldview are sometimes used in this literature, for example, life philosophy, life stance, lifeworld, orientations, outlook, meaning-making system, view of life, way of life, and world picture.

The core idea of worldview theory is that people – whether or not they are religious – express, through their actions and what they say, a particular understanding of what the world is like, what we ourselves are like, what is most important about the world, what our place in it is, and what we must do to live a good life. While a person's understanding might be limited or partial in several ways, it is a worldview if it is still about these important issues in life. A worldview contains those beliefs, values, and attitudes that are particularly important for our self-identity and the things we fundamentally care about in life. Hence, we should not be misled into thinking that worldviews must be comprehensive; we must allow that they might merely consist of loosely interconnected attitudes, beliefs, and values central to how individuals understand and live their lives. This is so, in the same way, that we should not assume that religions have to be comprehensive to be religions. Like their religions, people's worldviews can be more or less articulated, comprehensive, and coherent.

If religious people should not be contrasted to nonreligious people or religious nones but to secular people, then we can distinguish between two types of worldviews, not denying that there are many borderline cases. Specifying the difference is challenging; I will elaborate on it in Chapter 2. Still, we could say that *religious worldviews* affirm or assume the existence of a transcendent, divine, or spiritual dimension of reality and uphold its importance for how we understand and live our lives. Religious people understand this dimension of reality in different ways. *Secular worldviews* deny or doubt the existence of a transcendent, divine, or spiritual dimension of reality, instead assuming that reality has a different makeup, and it is the basic features of this reality that are important for understanding and living our lives. Secular people understand this alternative outlook on life in various ways. I will identify and discuss three examples of secular worldviews: scientism, secular humanism, and transhumanism.

PHILOSOPHY OF WORLDVIEWS

My philosophical inquiry will center more on the beliefs, claims, or ideas of these worldviews and their rationale or grounds than on analyzing them in terms of traditions, race, class, gender, politics, institutions, or lived practices. These gendered, historical, practical, political, and social dimensions are essential, and worldview studies must encompass them all, as well as the ideas or beliefs central to the religious and secular outlooks on life. Thus, the focus is on the intellectual dimension, but we should not reduce worldviews to one-dimensional cognitive and theoretical phenomena. This is so because the issue concerns not merely what you and I should believe to be true about the universe (including us) but how you and I shall live our lives in that universe. In an alternative terminology, one could say that the focal point of the study is the first of the classical 3Bs of the sociology of religion – belief, behavior, and belonging.

Although the philosophy of religion can study a wide variety of aspects of religion, philosophers have been particularly interested in what religious people believe about the basic constitution of reality, about the nature and place of human beings in the scheme of things, about what constitutes a good and meaningful life, and about their grounds for holding these beliefs to be true. Questions of truth and rationality have long been at the heart of philosophical studies of religion. Not all religions explicitly require their practitioners to believe certain things; nevertheless, when people participate in religious practices, they presuppose that reality is a certain way. When people exhibit religious behavior, they thereby commit themselves to a view about what is the case. For some individuals, their behavior could be an instance of make-believe, but it is not feasible to assume that that is the default stance.

Indeed, most philosophers think that human action – and, consequently, religious action – involves holding certain things to be true. Therefore, to say that religious people or communities have no beliefs is to say that they hold nothing to be true, have no convictions, and make no value judgments. One reason philosophers view belief as a universal phenomenon is that to count as a person at all, we must be able to have beliefs about things, and this is also something we must attribute to others to see them as persons.[9] If not, people can never have reasons for their actions. In fact, the distinction between mere behavior and action presupposes an intention behind an action, such as voting in an

---

[9] In the chapter, "Must Religious People Have Religious Beliefs?" In Kevin Schilbrack, *Philosophy and the Study of Religions.* Wiley-Blackwell, 2014, pp. 55–81, a more detailed discussion of these questions is provided, which cannot be accommodated in this context.

election, for instance, because one believes in democracy, in contrast to merely bodily happenings, like accidentally tripping on the stairs.

Being a person means being aware of the beliefs of others and recognizing that they may differ from one's own. To cooperate or coordinate one's actions requires the ability to communicate one's beliefs and intentions in a way that is comprehensible to others. Moreover, beliefs, intentions, and reasons are of great importance for evaluating what some people do to determine whether their actions are worthy of our admiration or praise. For instance, Susan may help her old grandmother because she loves and cares about her. Susan's sister, Sarah, has no such feelings; instead, she dislikes her grandmother. Still, Sarah helps her grandmother just as much as Susan does, but she does this because she wants to inherit her grandmother's great wealth.

Another central idea behind the concept of belief is that what we hold to be true may not actually be the case. The concept of belief thus allows us to formulate a notion that truth and falsity are independent of what we happen to believe. For example, what we believe may turn out to be an expression of wishful thinking. People can think, hold things to be true, and realize that what is true does not necessarily correspond to what they believe to be true. If philosophers are correct that human behavior (or, at least, human action) involves holding certain things to be true, then it follows that secular people also believe things about the nature of reality, human nature, and what constitutes a good life. It is just that they hold partly different things to be true than religious people do.

The frequent focus on beliefs by philosophers of religion does not necessarily imply an assumption on their part that beliefs are the most essential part of what it means to be religious or to embrace a worldview, but only an assumption that religions and worldviews have a cognitive or intellectual dimension. Nevertheless, for methodological reasons, philosophers of religion often reduce religion to a collection of beliefs, claims, or ideas. One problem here is that we, as researchers, sometimes overlook the distinction between methodological and ontological reduction, or, at worst, believe that our methods can capture all of reality. We can make a methodological reduction of the phenomena we are studying without being forced or justified to make an ontological reduction, that is, assuming that phenomenon X is nothing more than phenomenon Y. Philosophers of religion's focus on the intellectual dimension of religions must not express an ontological reduction of religions to a set of beliefs or claims.

We can say that the philosophy of religion is the academic study of what people assume to be true, real, and good, and their grounds for having these commitments, when they engage in various religions, such as Buddhism, Christianity, Islam, or the New Spirituality. Now, the idea is that the *philosophy of worldviews* would go beyond that and also include the study of what people assume to be true, real, and good – and their grounds for having these commitments – when they engage in various secular ways of thinking and living, such as scientism, secular humanism, or transhumanism.

The philosophy of worldviews is also distinctive from historical, sociological, and psychological studies of worldviews because it emphasizes evaluating or assessing the arguments and evidence for or against various religious or secular worldviews. Its central analytical tools and theories are derived from different subdisciplines of philosophy, particularly ontology, epistemology, and ethics. (If you are familiar with philosophy, you could skip the rest of this section.)

We can say that *ontology* is the inventory of all the things, kinds, properties, and relations that must exist for reality to be as it is. Simplified, ontology is an account of what exists. As we will see later in this chapter, the worldviews that we examine do not agree on what exists; some assume that selves or persons exist, whereas others entail that this is just how things appear to be. Advocates of some worldviews believe that people (sometimes) have or can exercise free will – they could have chosen differently than they indeed did; others deny this. There is a profound ontological difference between a reality in which God exists, one where there is a law of karma, and one in which reality consists of physical particles and nothing more. Some worldviews presuppose that the only real causes are material ones, whereas others assume that there is also mental causation, not reducible to the former. Some things or properties are not as easily physically located as stones, trees, and rivers. However, people tend to take them for granted – things and properties such as consciousness, thoughts, intentions, beliefs, numbers, values, and human rights. Indeed, this lack of physical space could be a reason to exclude them from one's ontology. Some ontologies consider the existence of social things, such as schools, countries, and professors, to be real, whereas others view this as merely a way of speaking – there exist only natural things and natural facts; ultimately, there are no social things or facts.

Epistemology conveys our views on the constituents and various kinds of knowledge as well as the criteria for a belief to be rational, justified, and true. What does it mean to say someone knows or fails to know something? Are there different types of knowledge? How much could we know? Are there some areas of human life in which knowledge is impossible (such as morality)? Hence, epistemology focuses on theories of knowledge. Still, just as ontology encompasses not only what lies beyond physics (metaphysics) epistemology encompasses also theories of rationality, justification, truth, and intellectual virtues.

By not only distinguishing between *belief* and *knowledge* but also enriching our language with a third concept, *rationality*, we open up the possibility that our choice or embracement of a worldview is not either a matter of knowledge or a matter of mere belief or faith, that either we have proofs for what we hold to be true or that what we believe is arbitrary or groundless. A third option is that it can be perfectly reasonable or rational to believe as we do, even though we do not know if what we believe is true. Another crucial point that follows is that I do not necessarily have to share the other person's point of view to accept that it is rational to believe differently than I do on the topic. The question we must remember to ask is: "If I were in their shoes, would it be reasonable to believe as they do?" I can answer "yes" (and, of course, also "no"), even if I am convinced that they are wrong. Therefore, it is vital that we understand the difference between belief, rationality, and knowledge. Moreover, our reason, cognitive faculties, or intelligence enable us to articulate and understand these differences.

Epistemological questions arise whenever we pause to consider whether what we or others believe is true, whether our beliefs are rational or reasonable, or whether we should reconsider a particular view in light of new evidence. If epistemology concerns how we ought to conduct our intellectual or cognitive affairs, *ethics* is about how we ought to conduct our moral affairs. It is about how we should act and behave toward our family and kin, other people, living things, and nature as a whole. Ethics expresses our views about what is morally good and evil, and right and wrong. Philosophers could study what people believe is morally good and evil, and right and wrong (*descriptive ethics*). But foremost, philosophers are interested in what we should believe are morally good and evil, or morally right and wrong, as well as what norms and principles should guide us in conducting our moral affairs, and how to justify our moral stances, beliefs, commitments, or attitudes (*normative ethics*).

Philosophers develop moral or ethical theories, that is, systematic accounts of how we should view morality and how we should live our lives in relationship to one another. These theories are designed to help people make the best moral decisions, give us principles and directives, justify those, and thereby guide our actions. But they are not alone in doing this; instead, every person must, in their life, at least presuppose certain ideas about what is good and evil, and right and wrong. Moreover, in my view, a worldview must say something about these things to be considered a worldview. A worldview is considered life-oriented in this sense; it provides insight into how we should live our lives, interact with others, and engage with the world around us. Still, there is no requirement that the morality in question must be articulated, comprehensive, and coherent to qualify as a proper part of a worldview.

To summarize, what a philosophical analysis of worldview can highlight is different, and sometimes similar, answers that people give to *ontological* questions (What is real? Is reality a social construction? Do humans have a self and free will? Does God exist?), *epistemological* questions (What can we know? When is it rational to believe something? What is truth? Can we know that the law of karma operates in the world? Can we hope that God exists?), and *ethical* issues (What is right and good? Why should we act morally? Do all living things have intrinsic value? Is God worth worshipping? Are there any moral human rights and why should we think so?). A worldview, of course, contains more than answers to these kinds of questions, but not less. More precisely, a worldview includes those parts of our ontology, epistemology, and ethics that are central to understanding and living our lives. It is the constellation of beliefs, values, and attitudes that give shape and meaning to the world an individual or group experiences and acts within.

METHODOLOGICAL ISSUES

The book is a philosophical inquiry into different contemporary worldviews, some with a long history, while others are just emerging in today's society. The focus is on their current significance for people, why they embrace that particular worldview, and what they think about their rivals. The book aims to identify several religious and secular worldviews that people in contemporary Western society appear to embrace, whether or not they are aware of them.

The biggest challenge is identifying emerging secular worldviews, as they are relatively new in human history and underdeveloped, in the sense that secular people often are more certain about what they reject (religions) than what they affirm.[10] So, even if the ones we will study have been carefully thought through, we do not know how many secular people in society embrace them or somewhat similar worldviews. This points out a limitation of this study. On the other hand, a unique feature is that it identifies and analyzes the understanding of secular (and religious) intellectuals regarding their own worldviews, as well as those of others. What do some of the brightest minds on this planet believe about the big questions in life? How do they respond to existential inquiries about who we are, where we come from, where we are headed, what is good and evil, and how we should live to thrive? We will focus on intellectually elaborated versions of different worldviews or, more exactly, on some of them. The book examines the beliefs, values, and attitudes that these thinkers argue are of particular importance for our self-identity and the things that truly matter in life.

This book exemplifies a more descriptive project than is typical in philosophy because I will not assess these worldviews and provide reasons why one is preferred over the other. Still, some of the reasons the advocates of a worldview themselves give for why we should adopt their worldview over others are stated. They constitute an important part of what we can call their *internal rationale*. I will instead limit myself to stating some of the challenges a particular worldview faces at the end of each chapter, but without suggesting that the worldview in question cannot provide a satisfying answer. These challenges could provide a good starting point for a critical discussion and comparison in the classroom, seminar, or in conversation with friends.

I approach the great diversity of ways of being a Buddhist, Christian, secular humanist, and so forth, using the *method of rational reconstruction* to identify a primary alternative of each worldview. It is possible to offer other reconstructions, but I argue that mine is a reasonable interpretation of these worldviews. An account of a particular worldview is modeled as a kind of hermeneutical and conceptual tool to bring some degree of order to the complexity of human intellectual history. However, it should not be misinterpreted as a straightforward description of what we find in specific historical or contemporary sources. It is a thought construction that aims to capture important properties of a particular view and merge, if necessary, these elements into a more

---

[10] One attempt to find out what they affirm can be found in Valerie van Mulukom et al., "What Do Nonreligious Nonbelievers Believe In? Secular Worldviews around the World." *Psychology of Religion and Spirituality*, 2023, 15/1, pp. 143–156.

coherent standpoint. It is frequently used in political studies (and then referred to as "ideal types") to refine the ideas that characterize a particular ideology, such as conservatism, liberalism, or socialism, thereby clarifying and summarizing its central content without exact replication in the real world. Thus, a rational reconstruction of a political ideology, or in our case, a worldview, is neither strictly true nor false, but rather more or less useful. However, they are still intended to be approximations that are reasonably close to what can be found in real life. It is a construction that highlights the essential differences between this and rival worldviews (or political ideologies) that we think are important. The idea is to arrange the material so that its ideas' logical relations are promising, such that they do not conflict with each other and such that some generate reasons to accept others or at least naturally fit together to make them, to some extent, tenable options.

The method of rational reconstruction can be contrasted with the *method of deconstruction*, which exemplifies a different and more critical way of reading texts or interpreting discourses. It is used to examine something (such as a theory or a given "natural" state of affairs and, thus, assumed unchangeable human condition) to reveal its inadequacy or unmask hidden assumptions, power relations, binaries, and hierarchies. One can say that these methods employ two distinct kinds of hermeneutics. The method of deconstruction employs a *hermeneutics of suspicion*, as exemplified by the grand masters Marx, Nietzsche, and Freud, when examining religious or secular beliefs and practices. We should approach both religious and secular worldviews with suspicion and distrust and seek alternative descriptions or explanations of what is happening, focusing on who benefits or not from certain claims and practices. This approach is consistent with Bruce Lincoln's thesis that scholars of religion – and worldviews (my addition) – should ask "destabilizing and subversive questions" about religious and secular worldviews to discover their "inner tensions and conflicts, turbulence and inconsistency, permeability and malleability."[11]

The method of rational reconstruction instead implies that the researcher approaches the object of study with a curious and fundamentally positive attitude, a *hermeneutics of curiosity*. Is there perhaps something essential to learn from how religious people understand the world and live their lives? What can we learn from the way secular

[11] Bruce Lincoln, "Theses on Methods," *Method and Theory in the Study of Religion*, 1996, 8/3, pp. 225–226.

people live and understand life? A core principle of the methodological approach is the *principle of charity*. It says we should avoid attributing irrationality, fallacies, contradictions, falsehoods, and questionable or harmful motives to other people's views and why they hold them when a coherent, rational interpretation of the view and its grounds is available. However, if our task is to reconstruct the content of a view or an argument for that view, then we must not go beyond what, based on the evidence available to us, we may reasonably expect the advocates of that view or argument to have in mind. I think both methods are necessary to use within worldview studies, but this work exemplified foremost the method of rational reconstruction and the hermeneutics of curiosity.

The overall aim of the study is to explore some basic religious and secular outlooks on life and present them as distinct, opposing, and coherent worldviews, although it is possible to combine them in different ways. Differentiating religious worldviews can be done in many ways. The standard procedure within religious studies is to distinguish between different religions, such as Christianity, Islam, and Buddhism, and then separate subgroups of Christians, Muslims, and Buddhists within these broader religious traditions. A Christian worldview differs from an Islamic worldview in important ways, just as a Christian Catholic worldview can be contrasted with a Christian Lutheran or Pentecostal worldview.

However, that is not the approach I will take in this study. One of my reasons for distinguishing between worldviews differently is that I want to identify and contrast some basic religious alternatives to some basic options available to secular people today. So, for instance, atheism is a core element in many secular worldviews, and it is intended to be set in direct contrast to belief in God or to theism. Atheism is primarily understood as a rival stance to this particular kind of religious outlook on the world. For this reason, I will explore the fundamental features of a theistic worldview, a worldview that people can further develop in a second (logical but not chronological) step in different, sometimes radically different, ways.

Chapter 2 is structured so that I shall first explain the notion of worldview and then discuss the difference between religious and secular worldviews. In the process, it will become clear why the term *secular worldview* is preferable over nonreligion and the term *secular people* over nonreligious people or religious nones. Helpful distinctions for analyzing worldviews are introduced, including those between reflective and unreflective, articulated and enacted, folk and elite, manifest and hidden, and fragmented or comprehensive worldviews.

In Chapter 3, we will take a closer look at some of the core beliefs of the monotheistic worldview that has dominated the Western sphere and spread to all corners of the Globe for the past thousand years. The idea is to distinguish features that many theists agree on or at least recognize as central features of theism, even if they do not hold all these views themselves or accept them precisely as I express them. In some places, I will highlight the differences between Judaism, Christianity, and Islam, and also say something about what distinguishes the form of theism found in Hinduism (or in some of the religious traditions that have become named "Hinduism"). The idea here is to look at what they may, after all, have in common and to which atheism and emerging secular worldviews might be understood to be in opposition.

A Buddhist worldview is in focus in Chapter 4. Like many of the world's other great religions, Buddhism encompasses a diverse range of teachings and traditions across various cultures. I have attempted to reconstruct an engaging version that incorporates specific core ideas, which Buddhists may recognize as part of their rich religious traditions, even if they do not hold all of these views themselves or accept them precisely as I have explicated them. The aim is to identify a Buddhist worldview that differs significantly from the others considered in this study and thus constitutes a genuine alternative to them. It also provides a background for understanding the New Spirituality (the focus of Chapter 5), whose advocates often view their worldview as a form of Buddhist or Eastern mysticism.

The religious worldview we will survey in Chapter 5 lacks a generally accepted label. Specialists have called it Western esotericism. Many advocates of this outlook on life and reality would say that they are "spiritual but not religious" (SBNRs) and see themselves as embracing a spiritual but not a religious worldview. The increasing popularity of this phrase has even given rise to the acronym SBNR. The SBNRs would maintain these things, although they tend to believe in the divine or our inner divinity and that we have an inborn capacity to know the divine or the deeper spiritual realities of the cosmos. I will, for this reason, often use the term spirituality when referring to this worldview.

The worldview we will study in Chapter 6, religious naturalism, is claimed by its practitioners to be a form of religion. However, it still affirms that the physical world is all that exists and denies the existence of an unseen spiritual reality that is the source of all visible things. But, on my account, is it then a religious worldview? The answer given by religious naturalists is that it is a religious worldview because religious meaning, value, or significance can be found solely in nature. A core idea is that we should grant nature the kind of reverence, awe, love, and devotion we in the West have previously reserved for God.

From Chapter 7 onwards, we will discuss different secular worldviews. Since secular outlooks on life are not institutionalized in the same manner as major religions, the range of beliefs and values embraced by secular individuals is unclear, and it is also uncertain whether these cluster into groups, as they might in specific religions or faith traditions. However, in the book, I distinguish between three such clusters. I will articulate them in a way that makes them coherent and distinctive nonreligious worldviews: scientism, secular humanism, and transhumanism.

Advocates of a scientistic worldview maintain that secular people should rely on what science says about reality and then try to understand themselves, their lives, and society from that starting point. Science is the measure of all things. There is nothing outside the domain of science, nor is there any area of human life to which science cannot successfully be applied. A scientific account of anything and everything constitutes the full story of the universe and its inhabitants. Or, if there are limits to the scientific enterprise, the idea is that science, at least, sets the boundaries for what we humans can ever know about reality. This is the view of scientism (sometimes called scientific naturalism). In the second half of Chapter 7, we identify its core claims and discuss their consequences for morality and the everyday world you and I inhabit.

The second nonreligious worldview we will consider is secular humanism. It is the topic of Chapter 8. It is not unusual for scientism and secular humanism to be conflated and assumed to express essentially the same worldview, or at least that they are obviously compatible. However, one can be a scientific naturalist and reject the core idea of humanism of human freedom, autonomy, and dignity simply because one thinks that scientific naturalism entails moral nihilism or because one thinks that human freedom is an illusion or that persons do not exist – the carrier of dignity in a humanistic worldview.

The last secular worldview that is explored in this study is transhumanism. It is the topic of Chapter 9. Transhumanism is an outgrowth of secular humanism, yet it is more radical. It is more radical because transhumanists are actively striving to accelerate an end to the human condition as we know it. We should create transhumans and, eventually, posthumans. The transhumanist core value consists of the normative claim that, by utilizing biotechnology and AI, we should radically change, improve, or refine humanity, even to the extent of creating a new species, the posthuman. Posthuman lives are worth striving for because they, in contrast to ours, are characterized by super-longevity, superintelligence, and super-wellbeing.

In Chapter 10, I summarize, offer some concluding remarks, and suggest some challenges that worldview studies face in the future. If I am right, all of you who read this book have a worldview, whether you are fully aware of it or can articulate its content. So, I conclude my inquiry by suggesting how we, as reflective individuals, can develop an intellectually and existentially satisfying worldview.

2

Worldview Studies

With the increased secularization of certain parts of the world, there are many people who no longer see themselves as religious. Scholars of religion have been searching for alternative notions to use in identifying such people and what they replace religion with, which often have a family resemblance to the concept of religious believers and religious belief. Frequently, these scholars have used the term nonreligion and have called these individuals nonbelievers, religious nones, or religion's other.

In the philosophy of religion, another notion has often been employed, encompassing both those who identify as religious and those who do not. These philosophers have employed "worldview" as a core analytic concept. In the introduction and throughout this chapter, I will argue that the terminology used in the philosophy of religion is preferable to that typically employed in religious studies.[1] Still, philosophers of religion have not paid sufficient attention to the secular outlooks on life that have recently developed as alternatives to traditional religions, nor to the issue of how to characterize the difference between these two kinds of worldviews. These issues will be addressed in this chapter. Ultimately, I hope that the philosophy of religion can be developed to become a philosophy of worldviews. Similarly, I hope that religious studies could be widened into worldview studies.

This chapter explores the concept of a worldview and provides a helpful definition. Additionally, the differences between religious and secular worldviews are examined and explained. The issue of agnosticism and

---

[1] There are some significant exceptions within religious studies, such as André Droogers and Anton van Harskamp, eds., *Methods for the Study of Religious Change: From Religious Studies to Worldview Studies*. Equinox Publishing, 2014; and Ann Taves, "From Religious Studies to Worldview Studies," *Religion*, 2020, 50/1, pp. 137–147.

whether agnostics embrace a secular worldview is raised, and it is argued that we need to distinguish between secular and religious agnostics. Helpful distinctions for analyzing worldviews are introduced, including those between reflective and unreflective, articulated and enacted, folk and elite, manifest and hidden, and fragmented or comprehensive worldviews. It also highlights the kind of contribution philosophers of religion can make to the emerging field of worldview studies.

WHAT IS A WORLDVIEW?

Ninian Smart was one of the first scholars in the English-speaking world to emphasize the need for a more comprehensive term than "religion" and to argue for a change of focus in both the philosophy of religion and religious studies. He was, in fact, both a philosopher and a scholar of world religions. Similar developments and protagonists can be found in countries such as Germany, the Netherlands, and Sweden. As I mentioned in the introduction, Anders Jeffner developed a research program in *livsåskådningsforskning* (worldview research) in the late 1970s. It aimed to study empirically – through questionnaires and interviews – the outlooks on life that were emerging among the public in a post-Christian or secularized society such as Sweden.

These approaches share the idea that we need to develop a new theoretical framework that encompasses the world's religions as well as the views of life of people who do not consider themselves religious. Smart writes, "The English language does not have a term to refer to both traditional religions and ideologies; the best expression is perhaps 'worldviews.' ... The study of religions and secular worldviews – what I have termed 'worldview analysis' – tries to depict the history and nature of the beliefs and symbols that form a deep part of the structure of human consciousness and society."[2] Philosophers of religion write frequently about worldviews. Typically, they consider a worldview "a sort of total way of looking at ourselves and our world" or "our overall view of the nature of reality."[3] In particular, they have used the term to characterize the difference between a theistic worldview (theism) and a naturalistic worldview (naturalism).

A substantial number of definitions of worldview have also been offered. In what follows, I will build on previous research I have conducted

---

[2] Ninian Smart, *Worldviews*. Prentice-Hall, 1995, p. 2.
[3] John Cottingham, *Philosophy of Religion*. Cambridge University Press, 2014, p. 1.

to propose one that I think we should use. I will explicitly or implicitly explain why it is preferable over some of the others and what it can offer us in our study of religions and their secular alternatives. I suggest that by *worldview*, we mean:

the constellation of beliefs, values, and attitudes that people, whether consciously or unconsciously, hold and which (a) constitute their basic understanding of who they are, what the world is like, and what their place in it is, (b) what they should do to live a good and meaningful life, and (c) what they can say, know, rationally believe, or assume to be true about these things.

Thereby, two things that a worldview contains are, among others, our ontology – what we take to exist and how these things relate to one another and what properties they have – and our epistemology – what we can know, rationally believe, or merely assume to be true about these things, properties, and relations. A third requisite is that a worldview encompasses our ethical or moral stance – the value commitments we express in thought and action. Alternatively, and more precisely, a worldview contains those parts of our ontology, epistemology, and ethics that are central to understanding and living our lives. A worldview is best understood as action-oriented. One can say that a worldview's function is primarily to help people deal with their existential concerns, that is, their questions about who they are, why they exist, what the meaning of their life is, and what attitude or stance they should take toward the experience of death, suffering, guilt, anxiety, love, friendship, forgiveness, and the like. Consequently, not just any of our beliefs, values, or attitudes will do. A worldview contains those beliefs, values, and attitudes that are of particular importance for our self-identity and the things we fundamentally care about in life.

If we understand the idea of a worldview in this sense, it follows that it has a broader application than just to religion. Here, we have a notion that encompasses all religions and also encompasses people's views of life, whether or not they hold a religious outlook on the world. The basic idea is that most people are not religious, but they do have a worldview. They have, or express in their lives, particular attitudes, beliefs, and values about who they (we) are, what the world is like, what their (and our) place in it is, what they (or we) must do to live a good life and what they (and we) can know and rationally believe, or at least hope or assume to be true about these things.

By *belief*, in the definition given earlier, I mean what people claim, think, or assume to be true about the world and their place within it. One might believe that God exists or that everything that exists is ultimately made out of matter, that people have or do not have free will, that we are basically good or evil, or that there is or is not an afterlife. However, worldviews also encompass different *values* regarding what we should do or avoid to lead a good life, both on an individual and collective level. Humanists believe that human dignity and the values and duties that stem from a commitment to that dignity should shape our worldview. Transhumanists believe that posthuman lives would be better lives: We ought to enhance ourselves. Furthermore, worldviews also include *attitudes* or *stances* toward the world, other people, or oneself. We could say, roughly, that these attitudes express our emotional dispositions toward things, properties, processes, and states of affairs in the world. (Belief, on the other hand, is an epistemic attitude, so epistemic attitudes are not what I have in mind when I talk about attitudes here, as these attitudes are assumed to be emotional.)[4]

Jeffner calls this last component of a worldview a "basic mood" and says that it is intended to capture an emotion toward life that stays with us for a long time and gives a certain emotional color to the rest of our experiences: One person may be satisfied with life, the other experiences life as hopeless. Yujin Nagasawa's talk about "existential optimism" might express a similar idea: It is "the thesis according to which the world is, overall, a good place and that we should be grateful for our existence in it."[5] The definition of worldview proposed by Jeffner is, "A worldview is the theoretical and evaluative assumptions that constitute or are of decisive importance for a comprehensive picture of humans and the world, which form a central value system and express a basic mood."[6] I have chosen the term "attitude" instead of "basic mood" because it is important to note that our different stances or emotional dispositions also influence the shaping of our worldview in more specific life situations or particular areas of life and do not always affect our general mood or attitude toward life as a whole.

Perhaps it is less evident that attitudes should be an essential part of a worldview than beliefs and values should be. Therefore, let me provide

---

[4] However, they or some of them could include a cognitive element.
[5] Yujin Nagasawa, "The Problem of Evil for Atheists." In *The Problem of Evil*, edited by N. N. Trakakis. Oxford University Press, 2018, p. 154.
[6] Anders Jeffner, "Att studera livsåskådningar." In *Aktuella livsåskådningar*, edited by Carl Reinhold Bråkenhielm. Doxa, 1981, p. 12 (my translation).

some examples of what I have in mind and explain why I claim we cannot omit attitudes if we want to understand people's worldviews or outlooks on life. Thomas Nagel writes:

I want atheism to be true and I am made uneasy by the fact that some of the most intelligent and well-informed people I know are religious believers. It isn't just that I don't believe in God, and, naturally, hope that I'm right in my belief. It's that I hope there is no God! I don't want there to be a God; I don't want the universe to be like that.[7]

Nagel does not simply disbelieve in God's existence; he goes further and takes a certain attitude toward God's existence: He does not want God to exist. Nagel also wonders whether any atheist or secular person really could be indifferent. But at least some such people have stated that they do not care whether there is or is not a God. Such a view has been called *apatheism* – a stance expressing apathy toward believing in God.[8] An apatheist does not care whether there is a God or not. We can also assume that there are secular people who are atheists but regret – and do not celebrate – the "death" of God. Charles Taylor agrees and writes that, in a secular age, there will be people "who feel bound to give it [belief in God] up, even though they mourn its loss."[9] He seems to think this might primarily be due to the social pressure of a secular society. Maybe so, but another possibility is that these atheists think that there are, albeit sadly, enough good reasons to believe that there is no God, that reality does not admit of one. Such secular people are *reluctant atheists*, whereas those whom Nagel exemplifies are *relieved atheists*. Either way, attitudes shape their secular worldviews in different ways. Attitudes could also be directed toward life in general and express, in Jeffner's terminology, basic moods. During much of Nagel's life, he thought life was absurd.[10] Existentialism is a worldview famous for emphasizing how vital *angst* (Eng. "anxiety") should be in an authentic outlook on life. The form of "secular faith" that Martin Hägglund thinks we should have (instead of religious faith) is also tied to a particular attitude. He writes: "My point ... is that if you care for our form of life as an end in itself, you are acting on the basis of secular faith ..."[11]

---

[7] Thomas Nagel, *The Last Word*. Oxford University Press, 1997, p. 130.

[8] Trevor Hedberg and Jordan Huzarevich, "Appraising Objections to Practical Apatheism," *Philosophia: Philosophical Quarterly of Israel*, 2017, 45/1, pp. 257–276.

[9] Charles Taylor, *A Secular Age*. Harvard University Press, 2007, p. 3.

[10] Thomas Nagel, "The Absurd," *The Journal of Philosophy*, 1971, 68/20, pp. 716–727.

[11] Martin Hägglund, *This Life: Secular Faith and Spiritual Freedom*. Anchor Books, 2019, p. 9.

It is the sense of finitude, of being devoted to a life that will end, that is at the heart of secular faith. Devotion toward finite life is a crucial ingredient of Hägglund's secular worldview.

Religious faith is another example of the relevance of attitudes when we try to explicate people's worldviews. Most theists do not merely believe that God exists but also think that adopting a particular attitude toward this truth is appropriate. A person only has genuine religious faith, on this account, if she loves and trusts God or prays to or worships God. Attitudes toward God play a central role in how these people understand reality. It is, consequently, of utmost importance to identify this feature when describing their worldview. Jeffner suggests that many Christians' basic mood is, or at least ought to be, one of hope, because one day God will redeem us and defeat evil. In Buddhism, to be enlightened is not merely about a change in belief but includes being transformed affectively, and the lack of such transformation betrays a failure of imperfection in one's religious understanding. As Ian James Kidd points out, certain human experiences "should naturally invite, if not demand, certain affective responses – grief or joy, dread or awe – and the absence of such response should, in many cases, strike us as indicative of some failure of our emotional faculties."[12]

Attitudes, beliefs, and values are features that a proper understanding of a worldview must take into account. But, as I have already hinted, it is unreasonable to think of or construe worldviews in such a way that *all* our attitudes, beliefs, and values are included. One reason to add some constraints is that if a worldview were the totality of attitudes, beliefs, and values, no two persons would share the same worldview. Each of us would have a unique worldview. In one sense, this is undoubtedly true. Still, we would like to be able to say that when there is sufficient overlap in attitudes, beliefs, and values, some individuals share the same worldview – even if they do not agree on everything. If this were not possible, we would not be able to say that there are people who, for example, are Christians or have a Christian worldview.

Moreover, it is the centrality in a person's life and for her identity and relation to others that determines whether certain beliefs, values, or attitudes belong to her worldview. Still, it might be useful to distinguish between what lies closer to the core or center of a particular worldview and what is more peripherally located. When it comes to worldviews,

---

[12] Ian James Kidd, "Emotion, Religious Practice, and Cosmopolitan Secularism," *Religious Studies*, 2014, 50/2, p. 145.

some things lie closer to people's hearts than other things do. We could say that their *degree of concern* varies. For some people, it is God and their relationship with God that is at the center; for others, it is the environment and climate change, or women's equality and rights, or the fight against poverty and racism, or, for that matter, becoming rich and famous. For yet other people, hedonism, consumerism, or nationalism are at the core of their worldview.

Let me also say a few words about part (c) in the definition. How one understands the nature of language and knowledge (or rationality) and their limits could play an essential role in shaping people's worldviews. Some people think that science sets the limits for what we can know about reality. What science cannot discover, we cannot know anything about. Such an epistemic position drastically limits the kinds of beliefs that could be part of one's worldview. For instance, if God, the self, free will, and human rights are not within the purview of science, then we cannot know that God exists, that we have a self and free will, or that human rights exist. Moreover, some elements of our worldview may be such that we do not believe them to be true, but rather, we hope they are. We may hope that – it is a desirable epistemic live possibility – people are made in the image of God, that there is human dignity, or that people are essentially good and act on these assumptions in the life we choose to live.

Some religious individuals believe that religious language consists essentially of metaphors. They utter doctrinal sentences and participate in confessions and ceremonies where those statements find their home, but disavow any interpretation of them that implies substantive doctrines about a transcendent or spiritual reality. These *religious symbolists* could maintain that God is beyond or without being. Thus, we cannot say anything about God other than that God is the ground of being or being itself. The basic assumption is that religion provides us with stories that cannot be translated into statements about the nature of existence that can be true or false. They argue that there is no fixed interpretation of religious doctrines; we only have metaphors, images, and stories to work with (see Chapter 6). In simple terms, we can say that religious symbolists know that there is a profound truth in religion. Still, they do not know how to express it in a language that is not purely poetic or metaphorical, or they cannot translate religious claims into a nonreligious language. Thus, it becomes impossible for us to compare the claims that are part of religious people's perception of reality with those that atheists or other secular people hold to be true. Hence, both our explicit and implicit epistemology and semantics could profoundly shape our worldview.

As I have defined it, a worldview does not have to be something its adherents have consciously chosen to embrace. It might be, but many people's worldviews remain simply a background or horizon of which they are only vaguely aware, yet guide how they perceive the world and what they do and value in life. Or things might just as easily be the other way around, so people's outlook on life mirrors their behavior. The traffic goes, so to speak, both ways: not merely from what is taken to be true to action (from belief to practice) but also from how people live their lives to what they thereby take to be true (from practice to belief). A worldview, at times, must be inferred from an individual's or a group's way of engaging with the world.

Furthermore, a worldview is not something we easily and frequently change into another worldview; rather, it is part of our cultural heritage or social upbringing. This also explains why aspects of it are often hidden from us – it is simply a part of what we take for granted in life. Still, people do change worldviews: A Muslim could become a secular humanist or vice versa. Conversion is a real possibility, more than ever before. Previously, a person could go through life without much reflection, simply assuming the accepted worldview. But people are thrown back on their own resources today. What am I to believe? How should I act? Indeed, who am I? Of course, people are held back by restraints arising from their reasoning, upbringing, family, and need for stability in life. Yet the awareness that one can change one's worldview is always there; thus, the possibility is open that one might change one's choices at some point. The plurality that characterizes our contemporary society increases people's ability to choose between and among worldviews.

Additionally, changes within a worldview are also possible, and this is something we need to consider. For instance, one could change some of one's values or ideas about who we are or our attitudes to the environment. Many Christians have not abandoned their Christian faith but have rejected the anthropocentric view of nature, in which only humans are assumed to have intrinsic value, and have replaced it with a biocentric or ecocentric view of nature, in which other things besides humans have a value of their own. Many of them, over the last thirty to forty years, have also significantly changed their view on sexual minorities. Worldviews are not static but dynamic phenomena that respond to changes in society and to things in people's personal life history.

This means that we need to distinguish between *worldview formation* – questions about the origin of people's worldviews and how they are maintained over time; *worldview configuration* – questions about the specific content of their worldviews and how these things fit together; *worldview revision* or *development* – questions about how and why people change the content of their worldview; *worldview conversion* and *transmission* – questions about how and why they move (if they do) from one worldview to another and how a worldview is transmitted to the upcoming generations; and *worldview justification* – questions about how people justify or motivate their choice of or adherence to a particular worldview, or to a specific configuration of one particular worldview.

One problem with using the notion of worldview as an umbrella term to encompass both religious and nonreligious people's outlooks on life is that there is a fundamental ambiguity in how the concept is applied in contemporary society. On the one hand, people talk about a "scientific worldview," which means the picture of the universe that emerges if we combine the different theories of physics, astronomy, biology, sociology, and so on into a systematic whole. On the other hand, and in line with how the notion is used here, we can find people making statements about the embeddedness of science *within* a particular worldview, such as Christianity, Islam, or naturalism.

If, as I think we must in worldview studies, we understand the concept in the second way, it follows that science alone cannot provide us with a worldview, even though science can significantly contribute to forming or revising one. This is so because this conception entails that science lacks certain features that characterize a worldview. It is a matter of dispute what these features are exactly, but science seems to lack two elements: values and metaphysics. In this sense (and as I have defined it), a worldview tells us who we really are, what the world is ultimately like, and what we should do to live a satisfying life. It gives our life direction and meaning and thus provides us with values. However, science essentially provides us with facts, or, more accurately, nonnormative descriptions of the world, rather than values. It does not tell us how we should live or what we should ultimately value in life. If this is correct, science does not qualify as a worldview. (A deeper discussion of this issue can be found in Chapter 7.)

Moreover, no scientific discipline can tell us whether the physical universe is all there is. If scientists make such an assertion, they make a metaphysical rather than a scientific claim. Instead, a view that says that reality consists of God and all that God has created, and that we should live our lives according to God's will, is a worldview. The same is true for a view that says that, ultimately, reality consists of nothing but matter or physical particles in motion and that nothing possesses any moral value. Some advocates of scientism (as we shall see in Chapter 7) question this, arguing that the boundaries of science can be expanded in such a way that it can offer us both values and metaphysics.[13] However, this view is highly controversial and lacks scientific consensus. Therefore, we scholars should refer to it as a "scientistic" rather than a scientific worldview. This use of the analytical term "worldview" is, of course, compatible with the observation that some individuals think science qualifies as a worldview. Still, we call such a view "scientistic" because these people extend upon the current conceptions of what science is and what it provides.

Consequently, within worldview studies, we should strive to avoid talking about a scientific worldview and refrain from comparing it to a religious worldview, as they are not rivals. Instead, we can compare religious worldviews with secular worldviews and ask what relevance science has for forming, configuring, and justifying such types of worldviews. Science plays a much more profound role in some fields than in others. Some people attempt to *derive* their worldview from science (as do adherents of scientific naturalism or scientism). Others are *guided* by science in the formation and configuration of their worldview (as are liberal naturalists and religious naturalists), whereas the objective of yet others is to express a worldview that is *compatible* with science (such as secular humanists, many Christian theists, and Islamic theists).[14]

Evolutionary biology cannot then be considered a worldview, but Darwinism arguably can. Brian Baxter maintains that "many thinkers have developed from his [Darwin's] account of the origin of species, especially applied to our species, a distinctive perspective on the universe that merits the label 'worldview.'"[15] Baxter takes a worldview to be a synoptic account of the basic features of reality and how we, and what has value, are related to that outlook on life. Similarly, Daniel C. Dennett holds that Darwin's "dangerous idea" is an idea "bearing an unmistakable likeness to universal acid: It eats through just about every traditional concept, and leaves in its wake a revolutionized worldview,

---

[13] Alex Rosenberg, *The Atheist's Guide to Reality*. New York: W. W. Norton, 2011; and Edward O. Wilson, "The Biological Basis of Morality," *The Atlantic Monthly*, April 1990, pp. 53–70.

[14] For a more detailed account of how to relate one's worldview to science, see Mikael Stenmark, "Worldviews and Science," *Zygon: Journal of Religion and Science*, 2025, 59/4, pp. 925–948.

[15] Brian Baxter, *A Darwinian Worldview*. Ashgate, 2007, p. 1.

with most of the old landmarks still recognizable, but transformed in fundamental ways."[16] Both Baxter and Dennett, in their different approaches, try to develop and defend a Darwinian worldview. While we cannot properly talk about a scientific worldview, we can talk about a Darwinian worldview if we understand the term "worldview" in the way I have proposed. It would be one example of how a worldview can be configured: one that is heavily influenced by science, particularly, in this case, by evolutionary biology.

Another challenge we face, as I see it, is that the choice of the notion of worldview might lead one to think that a worldview must be all-encompassing. So, we expect and count only those outlooks on life that encompass a whole way of looking at ourselves and our world, or express our overall view of the nature of reality. This is, of course, what philosophers are particularly interested in; however, not everyone has such a comprehensive worldview. Some people have ideas about human nature and what is good in life, but they lack an identifiable overall view of the nature of reality. Do such people not have a worldview? I claim that we should resist defining and understanding the notion of worldview in such a way as to entail that they do not. Recall that the core idea is that people – whether or not they are religious – express, through their actions and what they say, a particular understanding of what the world is like, what we ourselves are like, what is most important about the world, what our place in it is, and what we must do to live a good life. While a person's understanding may be limited or partial in several ways, it is nonetheless about these important issues in life: It is still a worldview. Hence, we should not be misled into thinking that worldviews – in the sense the notion is used in worldview studies – have to be comprehensive: We must allow that they might merely consist of quite loosely interconnected attitudes, beliefs, and values central to how individuals understand and live their lives. Perhaps we should talk about "worldview fragments" or "fragmentary worldviews" in this context, as I have suggested elsewhere.[17] Jeffner expresses this idea by writing, "the worldviews of many people consist of loosely interconnected fragments."[18] But if we want to understand the notion in a similar way in both the philosophy of religion and religious studies, we must acknowledge that worldviews can be more (or less) comprehensive or more (or less) fragmented.

[16] Stenmark, *Rationality in Science, Religion, and Everyday Life*, p. 63.
[17] Ibid., p. 239.
[18] Anders Jeffner, *Livsåskådningar i Sverige*. Uppsala (unpublished handout), 1988, p. 10 (my translation).

WORLDVIEW FORMATION AND CONFIGURATION

Worldviews differ in content or configuration, and that, of course, is what makes them different. Despite this, I suggest we can distinguish between certain aspects that can constitute central elements in a worldview. However, before exploring these elements, I would like to address the importance of narratives in worldview formation and maintenance.

For most of us, presumably, our worldview does not primarily consist of a set of (more or less) interconnected beliefs and values – a product of our thinking. Instead, our beliefs and values are experienced, absorbed, and expressed in the course of life. (Even though this does not stop philosophers from identifying ideas or thought structures inferred from how people talk and live their lives.) For this reason, the narrative form of worldview is of great importance. A worldview is often transmitted to us through stories rather than through the grasping of abstract ideas. That this is the case is self-evident when it comes to religions that contain Holy Scriptures, such as Judaism, Christianity, and Islam. In these religions, narratives, for instance, of the creation of heaven and earth, of the exodus of the Israelites from Egypt, of the life, death, and resurrection of Jesus, or of God's revelation to Mohammad and his call to become God's last prophet on earth, all play a crucial role.

However, stories also play a crucial role in shaping nonreligious or secular worldviews. Edward O. Wilson maintains that when religious narratives are rejected and regarded as obsolete, evolutionary theory can replace them and play a similar role in people's lives. He writes: "the evolutionary epic is probably the best myth we will ever have."[19] Wilson believes that secular people today can and should understand themselves and their lives in the light of an evolutionary narrative, and not a narrative of creation. Mary Midgley emphasizes that scientific theories could fulfill such an existential role in people's lives. She writes:

The theory of evolution is not just an inert piece of theoretical science. It is, and cannot help being, also a powerful folk-tale about human origins. Any such narrative must have symbolic force. We are probably the first culture not to make that its main function. Most stories about human origins must have been devised purely with a view to symbolic and poetic fittingness. Suggestions about how we were made and where we come from are bound to engage our imagination, to shape our views of what we now are, and so to affect our lives.[20]

[19] Edward O. Wilson, *On Human Nature*. Harvard University Press, 1978, p. 201.
[20] Mary Midgley, *Evolution as a Religion*. Methuen, 1985, p. 1.

Other sources of worldview formation and expression include literature and film.

Martha C. Nussbaum seems ready to go so far as to say that some outlooks on life or truths about human life could be expressed only in terms of narratives.[21] Other philosophers, such as Eleonore Stump, are satisfied to point out that we cannot grasp *some* aspects of a worldview – she exemplifies with a Christian understanding of suffering – if we ignore the unique resources that narratives offer us, in contrast to abstract and isolated propositions about God, suffering, and evil.[22]

Regardless of which side we ultimately take in this debate, we must consider that people's worldviews often take a narrative form. Such a narrative expression gives them an existential or coercive power that a set of carefully defined propositions can never give, no matter how coherent. For this reason, it is crucial that we develop a narrative philosophy of religion (or of worldviews) as one of the approaches available for philosophical inquiry into religions (or worldviews). Mikel Burley defends such a view. He maintains that a narrative philosophy of religion "is the type of philosophical inquiry into religion that, without becoming a work of narrative art itself, takes seriously the contribution of narrative sources to our philosophical understanding of religion and, in the course of developing a philosophical argument, engages with such sources in a sustained manner rather than, at most, citing them only cursorily as mere decoration."[23]

We have so far considered, without me explicitly saying so, four of the six dimensions of worldview that Smart identifies. These six are (a) doctrinal or philosophical, (b) mythic or narrative, (c) ethical or legal, (d) ritual or practical, (e) experiential or emotional, and (f) social or institutional.[24] Smart is, of course, right in that worldviews can have both a ritual and a social dimension. This is self-evidently true of traditional religions such as Christianity and Islam but is a factor that some people with a secular outlook on life have also recognized as being essential. Some have tried to develop substitutes for religious rituals and organizations or associations. Secular organizations have begun offering alternatives to religious confirmation and funerals, aiming to meet people's need for belonging by establishing gatherings such as

[21] Martha C. Nussbaum, *Love's Knowledge*. Oxford University Press, 1990, p. 5.
[22] Eleonore Stump, *Wandering in Darkness*. Oxford University Press, 2010, pp. 1–81.
[23] Mikel Burley, "Narrative Philosophy of Religion: Apologetic and Pluralistic Orientations," *International Journal for Philosophy of Religion*, 2019, 88/1, pp. 6–7.
[24] Smart, *Worldviews*, p. 7.

The Sunday Assembly or The Church of Perpetual Life, and developing secular forms of spiritual practices. The secular philosopher Philip Kitcher even thinks that the roles religion fulfills in human lives in these regards constitute a severe challenge to secular worldviews. Atheists have to offer something to replace these social and experiential functions of religion and provide secular surrogates. He writes: "Religious institutions connect their members, providing a sense of belonging and of being together with others, of sharing problems and of working cooperatively to find solutions."[25] A "challenge for secularism," as he puts it, "is to provide secular forms of community and a sense of belonging that can replace the religious ones." Still, I have not included rituals in my definition of worldviews because some of them contain them, others do not. What I emphasize is merely that for something to be considered a worldview, it must have significance for how we live our lives. Practice is essential, not ritual behavior.

Scholars of various disciplines will be interested in different aspects of worldviews. Perhaps we can say that our focus could be either more practically oriented or more theoretically oriented. Typically, philosophers are more interested in the intellectual aspects of people's worldviews, while sociologists tend to focus less on beliefs and more on behavior and social belonging. In other words, we have both *theoretical* and *empirical worldview studies*.

What can we then say about the intellectual aspects of worldviews and the kinds of beliefs they contain? I suggest we identify specific clusters of questions or central topics and then use these as tools to identify the theoretical content of different worldviews. We will then be able to compare them, identify where they differ and where they overlap, and determine how comprehensive they are. These issues and topics would at least include the following:

- A view of the basic constitution of reality or an ontology. (Does God exist, or do physical particles lie at the root of everything? Is nature God's creation or God's body, or is it a brute state of affairs that exists for no reason? Are all causes material or physical, or are there also nonmaterial or mental causes in the world? What is the relation between the natural world and the social world? Is there an afterlife? Do spiritual processes and phenomena such as

---

[25] Philip Kitcher, "Challenges for Secularism." In *The Joy of Secularism*, edited by George Levine. Princeton University Press, 2011, p. 35.

reincarnation, laws of Karma, psychics, ghosts, aura, or channeling exist, or do they not?)

- A view of human nature or philosophical anthropology. (What characterizes humans in contrast to other living things? Are male and female naturally given subgroups of humans, or are they social constructions? What is the human condition? Do we have free will? Are we morally good or evil, unselfish or selfish creatures? Who is normal, and who is abnormal? Are there different races, and what, if anything, does that imply?)
- A view of society or political ideology. (When is a society well-ordered and just? What role should our worldview commitments play in the public sphere? Should the state provide welfare and health care or primarily protect our freedom and fundamental rights? Should our loyalty, devotion, or allegiance to a nation outweigh other individual or group interests?)
- A view of history. (Is time a linear or cyclic process? Is it God's will, Karma, people's ideas, or economic forces that shape historical developments? Is there a historically grounded progress in human culture and society, so we are moving toward a better world, or will the future merely repeat the past?)
- A view of the environment or an environmental philosophy. (Is nature a resource we can use in any way we want? Are humans the only species of intrinsic worth on this planet? Is nature robust or fragile? Does climate change constitute a severe threat to human society and life on earth?)
- A conception of the good or ethics. (What are good and evil? Is a good life about getting what you want, or is it a matter of obtaining happiness, living an authentic life, or establishing a personal relationship with God, or is it escaping the wheel of samsara – the cycle of repeated birth? Moreover, are values objective or subjective, something we discover, or something socially constructed?)
- A conception of the meaning of life. (Is human life meaningful or meaningless, or is life absurd? What is it that makes life meaningful or meaningless? Do we exist for a reason, or is our existence merely the result of material processes that did not or could not have us in mind?)
- A view of knowledge, rationality, and truth, or an epistemology. (Does science set the limits for what we can know, or are there other sources of knowledge besides science? Is there a difference between knowledge and rationality or reasonable belief?

What is truth? Is truth deemed important or irrelevant in our choice of a basic outlook on life?)

- A view of language or semantics. (Are words and concepts mental representations of reality, or are they merely tools for communication and coping? Is God ineffable, so our talk about the divine must be irreducibly metaphorical? Is religious language useful fiction and religious life a game of make-believe?)

I take these to be central themes or topics that contain several questions, some of which I have exemplified within the parentheses. Philosophers would likely reflect more deeply and care more about some of these topics and questions than the general public. Moreover, some themes are more central to certain worldviews than others.

Ann Taves suggests that we can narrow these questions and topics down to six Big Questions:

REALITY (ontology) – What is ultimate reality? What exists? What is real?

ORIGINS (cosmology) – Where did it come from? How did we get here? (Where is "here"?) Where are we going?

KNOWLEDGE (epistemology) – How do we know this (about ourselves and reality more generally)?

SITUATION: What is the situation in which we find ourselves? (Who are "we"?)

GOAL (axiology): What is the good (the goal) for which we should strive?

PATH (praxeology): What do we need to do to reach the goal? What path should we follow? How do we ensure that we are on the path?[26]

Perhaps this kind of reduction is possible, but we must keep in mind that a worldview, as I have described it, encompasses those beliefs, values, and attitudes that are central to how people understand and live their lives. Not just any of our beliefs, values, or attitudes will do. It contains those that are of particular importance to our self-identity and the things we fundamentally care about in life. Therefore, answers to some of these Big Questions might not even be an implicit part of some individuals' actual worldview. For instance, they might never have thought about what ultimate reality is, nor can we necessarily derive an answer to that question based on what they believe and how they behave. Moreover, some individuals may deny that they know that God exists but believe or merely hope that God exists, so we cannot reduce the epistemic dimension of a worldview to knowledge claims.

---

[26] Taves, "From Religious Studies to Worldview Studies," p. 138.

It is also unclear whether Taves thinks that people must answer all of these questions to have a worldview or if it suffices to have an answer to some of them.

Philosophers and other scholars are becoming increasingly interested in how secular alternatives to religions are understood and materialized in contemporary society. What we gain by using the notion of worldview, rather than the notion of religion, is an analytical category in which both religions and secular outlooks on life (what sociologists of religion have called nonreligion) can be studied in affirmative terms. This makes it possible for us to identify features we wish to compare critically and constructively and allows us to study worldviews or outlooks on life without worrying whether they are religious. That is a good thing, but, at the same time, we still face the question of how to distinguish between religious worldviews (or religions) on the one hand and secular worldviews (or nonreligions) on the other. Perhaps, for instance, we want to know the difference between religious humanism and secular humanism. Of course, there will always be a gray area where it will be hard, perhaps even impossible, to classify non-arbitrarily a way of life as religious or not. Where, for example, would those who say they are SBNR belong? Therefore, it might sometimes be appropriate to talk about semi-secular or semireligious worldviews.

One way of formulating the difference would be to say that a religious worldview affirms or, at least, assumes that reality has a transcendent, divine, or spiritual dimension, which, roughly speaking, could be taken to mean, as Keith Ward puts it, that:

there is a non-physical reality (or realities) that is of supreme value and that humans can become aware of through various forms of prayer or meditation. In the great religious traditions, this supreme value is said to have the nature of consciousness, intelligence, compassion, and bliss. Human awareness of it is meant to lead to the realization of those qualities in the human world and to the cessation of forms of egoism and selfish desire.[27]

William James expresses a similar idea when he writes: "Were one asked to characterize the life of religion in the broadest and most general terms possible, one might say that it consists of the belief that there is an

---

[27] Keith Ward, *The Big Questions in Science and Religion*. Templeton Press, 2008, p. 4.

unseen order, and that our supreme good lies in harmoniously adjusting ourselves thereto."[28] We then add, alongside this characterization, that in contrast, a secular worldview denies or, at the very least, seriously doubts that reality is constituted in such a manner.

One problem with this way of understanding the difference between a religious and a secular worldview is that the latter is often perceived as merely negative in content. But if people unavoidably express in their way of living an understanding of who they are, of the larger setting of which they are a part, and of what has value in life, and accordingly, how life should be lived, then it must also be possible to express secular worldviews in affirmative terms. The question is: What, more precisely, is this positive content, and what should we call such outlooks on life and those who hold them? Regardless of the terminology we use, we will encounter problems. As I have already indicated, I propose using "secular" as the contrast to "religious." Religious people should not be discussed in comparison to nonreligious people or religious nones, but to *secular people*. The worldview that the latter embraces or develops in their lives – consciously or unconsciously – ought not to be called a non-religious worldview but a *secular worldview*. If we do so, we can also talk about secular believers, secular faith, secular rituals, ceremonies, and gatherings. (I shall return to some of the problems this terminology creates.) We can then distinguish between two types of worldviews, without denying that there are many borderline cases. How to specify the distinction is not easy, but we could say roughly that:

Religious worldviews affirm or assume the existence of a transcendent, divine, or spiritual dimension of reality and uphold its importance for how we understand and live our lives.

Secular worldviews deny or doubt the existence of a transcendent, divine, or spiritual dimension of reality and instead affirm or assume that reality has a different makeup and uphold its importance for how we should understand and live our lives.

Secular people can understand this alternative outlook on reality in differing ways. The problem, however, is that we end up with a relatively empty formulation because we lack something that performs the equivalent function to the phrase "the existence of a transcendent, divine, or spiritual dimension of reality" in determining a religious worldview. But maybe that

---

[28] William James, *The Varieties of Religious Experience*. Penguin Books, 1982, p. 53.

is the best we can do for now, and only when we have identified and studied a range of secular worldviews can we develop a more substantial account.

Perhaps so, but let me offer a suggestion that many secular philosophers seem to assume describes their alternative to religions more clearly. They say they embrace *naturalism*. It involves the conviction that there is nothing beyond, before, or apart from nature, which means that everything that has existed, exists, or will exist is part of nature. It is essential to understand that naturalists emphasize that this ontology is incompatible with the existence of a transcendent, divine, or spiritual dimension of reality or nature. Instead, they argue that matter or physical particles ultimately underlie everything that exists, and that there is no plan or purpose to the existence of nature, nor is there conscious guidance to its increasing complexity over time or to the origin and development of life. Instead, these phenomena are merely the accidental result of causally chained events. Julian Baggini exemplifies it when he writes: "What most atheists do believe is that although there is only one kind of stuff in the universe and it is physical, out of this stuff come minds, beauty, emotions, moral values ..."[29] Hence, a more substantial account of what characterizes secular worldviews, in contrast to religious ones, would be the following:

Secular worldviews deny or doubt the existence of a transcendent, divine, or spiritual dimension of reality and instead affirm or assume that nature is all there is, ultimately constituted by physical matter and its unintended configurations, and uphold these features' importance for how we should understand and live our lives.

What may be worrying about such a more detailed specification is that it may capture intellectually deliberated secular worldviews (elite worldviews), but can we really assume that more popular secular worldviews (folk worldviews) have naturalism – at least as an implicit presupposition – for the understanding of reality, view of humanity, and ethical stance that they express in their lives? The Western secular worldviews we study in this book all assume that we, in this sense, live in a naturalistic universe. But what about secular worldviews in other parts of the world or those secular individuals who are better described as (ontological) idealists than materialists? There is, at least, some empirical support for the idea that naturalism (sometimes referred to as materialism) is the prevailing view among secular people, particularly those who self-identify as atheists. The Pew Research Center reports that "35 % [of religious nones]

---

[29] Julian Baggini, *Atheism*. Oxford University Press, 2003, p. 6.

express the materialist perspective, saying that the natural world is all there is. Most atheists say the natural world is all that exists."[30]

Still, naturalism is flexible and can be developed in different ways. Two of the more influential are scientific naturalism and secular humanism. *Scientific naturalists* privilege science in all areas of life and are consequently suspicious of everything else. Science alone should be our guide for understanding the world we live in and how we should live our lives. *Secular humanists*, on the other hand, reject the hegemony of science. Instead, they maintain that secular people should be guided by humanism, a belief in human freedom, autonomy, and dignity. Consequently, in their worldview formation, they emphasize culture more than the natural order discovered by the sciences. (A more detailed account of these secular worldviews can be found in Chapters 7 and 8.)

The group of worldviews that naturalists primarily reject are theistic worldviews. We could say that *theism* is the religious worldview that affirms that there is a God or an all-encompassing divine mind, who is the creator of the world, and that the highest good for human beings is to be in a proper relationship with this divine reality (see Chapter 3). Much research within the philosophy of religion focuses on how to think about the nature or content of theism and whether it is a better-justified worldview than naturalism.

Secular worldviews also reject those religions in which God plays no central role or in which God's existence is denied. Within the philosophy of religion, atheism is understood as a rejection of monotheism. If atheism were also to cover the option of rejecting gods such as Aphrodite, Shiva, or Thor, then many Christians, Jews, and Muslims would be atheists. This would complicate the philosophical discussion about the merits of theism and atheism: We would then have to keep track of those particular gods with respect to which someone is an atheist or a theist. However, within a global philosophy of religion, and certainly within religious studies, things become more feasible if we understand an atheist as someone who denies the existence of both God and gods. Naturalists go further and reject all religions, even those in which belief in gods lacks importance, such as Buddhism or Advaita *Vedānta* in Hinduism. They also reject animistic belief systems, which involve the belief in innumerable spiritual beings that are involved in human affairs and capable of

[30] Pew Research Center, "Religious 'Nones' in America: Who They Are and What They Believe." 2024, p. 48. www.pewresearch.org/wp-content/uploads/sites/20/2024/01/PR_2024.01.24_religious-nones_REPORT.pdf.

helping or harming human interests. While none of the major world religions are animistic (though they may contain animistic elements), most indigenous religions are. Animism can also be found in some forms of so-called New Age spirituality. Some philosophers of religion have proposed that, in this context, we should talk about "nontheism."[31] We would then have at least two fundamental kinds of religious worldviews – theistic and nontheistic – to be contrasted with secular worldviews, such as scientism and secular humanism.

Hence, naturalists believe that neither agents such as gods, goddesses, spirits, and guardian angels, nor phenomena or processes such as Karma, reincarnation, channeling, and auras are a part of the natural order, nor is the natural order a creation of God. According to my proposed definition, this understanding of reality is not merely a characteristic of naturalism but characterizes all secular worldviews. As naturalists like to express it, naturalism excludes not merely theism but all forms of supernaturalism (or both theism and nontheism). Mario de Caro and David MacArthur take naturalism to entail "the rejection of supernatural entities such as gods, demons, souls and ghosts," including "the Judeo-Christian God and the immaterial soul."[32] In their understanding, even a substance dualist view of the human self is incompatible with naturalism.

The distinction between atheism and naturalism is essential in two ways. The first is that if we understand atheism as merely a negating claim – an atheist denies the existence of God – then it cannot constitute a worldview. In contrast, naturalism can, since it also contains affirmative claims. The second is this: If atheism merely entails the denial of the existence of God, then an atheist might still accept the reality of gods, Karma, reincarnation, channeling, or auras. This is one reason why certain forms of Buddhism and New Age spirituality may be atheistic yet still be classified as religious. A naturalist must, in contrast, reject all of these spiritual dimensions of reality.

What about agnosticism? Where do agnostics belong? Do they embrace a secular worldview, so we have, on one side, atheists and agnostics, and on the other, theists? Some definitions of atheism entail such a classification.

---

[31] William J. Wainwright, *Philosophy of Religion*. Wadsworth, 1999, p. 10; and Paul J. Griffiths, "Nontheistic Conceptions of the Divine." In *The Oxford Handbook of Philosophy of Religion*, edited by William J. Wainwright. Oxford University Press, 2005, pp. 59f.

[32] Mario de Caro and David Macarthur, "Introduction: The Nature of Naturalism." In *Naturalism in Question*, edited by Mario de Caro and David MacArthur. Harvard University Press, 2004, pp. 2–3.

When someone claims to be an atheist in the *Oxford Handbook of Atheism*'s sense, she has failed to come to the belief that there is a God or gods.[33] Atheists can then be disbelievers, but it is enough that they are non-believers and lack a belief in God (or gods). Thus, agnostics are a subgroup of atheists, and they will consequently have a secular worldview.

However, there are at least two problems with such an understanding of atheism and agnosticism. The first is that an agnostic may maintain, as does Anthony Kenny, that there are "significant differences between the two positions, and the differences show agnosticism, if carefully defined, to be both epistemically and morally preferable to atheism."[34] So, agnostics can be just as critical of atheists as of theists. The second and more important one for our purposes is that it is quite possible to be a religious agnostic. To take one example, Paul Draper believes that there are good arguments for theism, but also good arguments for atheism or naturalism. So, neither theists nor atheists have been able to convince him that they are right. At the same time, this does not stop him from identifying with a religious outlook on life and from prayer because he regards "God's existence as a *real* possibility," so "there might be a God listening. More generally, I ought to do what I can to cultivate or at least prepare for a relationship with God."[35] The possibility of this agnostic stance is also exemplified by the recent focus within the philosophy of religion on *non-doxasticism*.[36] According to doxastic or belief-based religion, belief is necessary for authentic religious life. In contrast, a non-doxastic understanding of religion, or belief-less religion, holds that a weaker epistemic attitude, such as hope or acceptance, combined with appropriate behavior, is sufficient. But then again, the agnostic might hope that there is no God, have no desire for religious life, and thus dismiss prayer or any other religious activity. Consequently, we need to distinguish *religious agnostics* from *secular agnostics*, with only the latter having a secular worldview.

[33] Stephen Bullivant and Michael Ruse, "The Study of Atheism." In *The Oxford Handbook of Atheism*, edited by Stephen Bullivant and Michael Ruse. Oxford University Press, 2013, p. 2.
[34] Anthony Kenny, "Agnosticism and Atheism." In *Philosophers and God*, edited by John Cornwell and Michael McGhee. Continuum, 2009, p. 117.
[35] Paul Draper, "Seeking but Not Believing: Confessions of a Practical Agnostic." In *Divine Hiddenness*, edited by Daniel Howard-Snyder and Paul K. Moser. Cambridge University Press, 2002, p. 210.
[36] Robert Audi, *Rationality and Religious Commitment*. Oxford University Press, 2011, pp. 51–88; and Carl-Johan Palmqvist, "The Proper Object of Non-doxastic Religion," *Religious Studies*, 2019, 55/4, pp. 559–574.

Moreover, we should not overstate the strength of the epistemic commitment that theists, atheists, and agnostics make. It is undoubtedly true that some theists maintain that they know (or that we all can know) that God exists, some atheists think that they know (or that we all can know) that God does not exist, and some agnostics believe that they (or even any of us) do not know whether or not God exists. But we must not fail to recognize those who merely claim that it is reasonable or rational for them to believe that the central claims of their religious or secular worldview are true. For this reason, we should take a theist to be someone who believes that God exists, an atheist to be someone who does not believe that God exists, and an agnostic to be someone who simply neither believes nor disbelieves in the existence of God. Notice that we fail to identify many agnostics in our society if we neglect to take that into account. Joseph O. Baker and Buster G. Smith write that they consider "agnostics to be those who believe knowledge of god's existence or nonexistence is beyond human capacity" or believe that "theistic claims are unverifiable in principle."[37] Hence, from this viewpoint, only someone who answers a survey question about God's existence by selecting an option such as "I don't know, and there is no way to find out" is an agnostic. But this is inadequate sociology, leaving large groups of agnostics out of the picture: people who neither believe nor disbelieve in the existence of God. For some of them, it may remain a real possibility that God may exist. They might also hope to come to believe in God before their lives end and, in the meantime, participate in religious activities and even be members of religious congregations.

Religious agnosticism is about relating positively to a religious outlook on life that might, for all one knows, turn out to be true. In contrast, secular agnosticism is about relating positively to a naturalistic outlook on life, which, for all one knows, might turn out to be true. We can borrow a term from Lynne Rudder Baker and say that secular agnostics embrace *near-naturalism*.[38] This stance remains quiet about anything transcendent yet refrains from taking a stand on whether nature is all there is and ever will be, as its defenders typically believe there is insufficient evidence for such a view, while still living as if a naturalistic worldview is true. Religious agnostics, in contrast, live as though a theistic worldview is true: They embrace *near-theism*. Another option for some religious

[37] Joseph O. Baker and Buster G. Smith, *American Secularism*. New York: NYU Press, 2015, p. 15.
[38] Lynne Rudder Baker, "Naturalism and the Idea of Nature," *Philosophy*, 2017, 92/3, p. 348.

agnostics is to live as though a nontheistic worldview is true, rejecting both naturalism and theism, yet desiring that there might exist a non-divine but transcendent or spiritual dimension of reality, and thinking this to be epistemically possible. There may be a reality that encompasses the laws of Karma, reincarnation, disembodied spirits, auras, or channeling, and it is this constitution of reality that should have significance for how we live our lives. Such people embrace *near-nontheism*.

So, we have secular people who are agnostics and doubt (but do not deny) that there is a transcendent, divine, or spiritual dimension of reality but live their lives as though such a dimension lacks importance. Likewise, we have religious people who are agnostics and doubt (but do not deny) the existence of a transcendent, divine, or spiritual dimension of reality but still live as though such religious reality is significant for their lives.

Both *belief* (and sometimes weaker epistemic attitudes such as hope and acceptance) and *behavior* (people's way of living) are essential when identifying and distinguishing between religious and secular worldviews. But what should we say about the third of the "three B's" that sociologists of religion focus on in their study of religion, namely, *belonging*? I suggest we restrict the notion of "nones" to this aspect of people's worldview since a person cannot be without life-orienting beliefs and behavior. Anyone can, however, choose to belong or not to belong to a religious or secular organization or community. However, given that we distinguish, as I argue, between religious and secular worldviews, rather than between religion and nonreligion, our understanding of religious nones will need to change. Religiously non-affiliated people are those who self-identify as religious but have no affiliation with an organized religious group or community. These persons are "religious nones." Secularly nonaffiliated people are those who self-identify as secular but have no affiliation with an organized secular group or community. These persons are "secular nones." Most religious people are affiliated in some way, but most secular people are not. There are many secular nones but fewer religious nones. The group of religious nones is nevertheless growing.

Suppose we choose to name the alternatives to the religions of the world "secular worldviews" and reject the term "nonreligions." In this case, we must be quite careful in how we use the notion of secular, and to some extent, also go against current usage. For instance, a secular society or state can no longer be one that aims at being neutral with respect to the worldviews that set us apart from one another but must be a society in which secular worldviews are taken to be the default position (arguably as Sweden is today, but the USA is not). Understandably, the traditional view of the state as secular is widespread because, in the original cases, the views about which the state ought to be neutral were all religious in nature. But, and this is important, that is no longer the case. Today, there is a great variety of secular outlooks on human life, and there are many nonreligious citizens. The core idea of liberal democracy is that the state should protect individuals in their pursuit of *whatever* outlook or worldview they choose and treat them equally, regardless of their choice. Rather than using the notion of secular society in its traditional sense, we should employ it to refer to a specific change in Western society: A growing number of people in certain parts of the world do not consider themselves religious when self-identifying. When we talk about the state's relation to its citizens' worldviews, we could, instead, talk about it as being or striving to be "worldview-independent." The core idea of liberal democracy is that the state should, to the extent it is possible, be impartial with respect to the different worldviews, the conceptions of the good, or the substantive ways of life that its citizens embrace.

What about secularism? Secular people might embrace secularism, but they need not do so, that is, they are not necessarily *secularists* in the sense of having an anti-religious stance. *Secularism* comes in many forms, but I would say that all its forms aim to minimize the influence of religion on society (or on all aspects of life) and hope that religion will one day cease to be a live option for people. Secularism's core idea is that we should actively strive to minimize the influence of religion, first on politics and, eventually, on society as a whole; this is essential to the defense of science, democracy, and human flourishing. Society is better off without religion because it is not merely false or, at the very least, irrational, but is also dangerous to human well-being and a democratic society. We should, therefore, actively push history forward toward the goal of a nonreligious world.

However, secular people could, and many of them do, reject this vision of a future society without religion. They could be individuals who feel bound to give religion up, even though they mourn its loss. Or they might believe, as does the secular philosopher Jürgen Habermas, that secular Western society needs access to religious beliefs, values, and practices if it is not to cut itself off from key resources for creating meaning and identity. He maintains that what needs to be overcome is a narrow secularist consciousness, and instead, we should take religious contributions to contentious political issues seriously and not see religions as "archaic relics of pre-modern societies" and "lacking any intrinsic justification to exist."[39] So, secularists are a subgroup within the larger group of secular individuals.

DIFFERENT WAYS OF STUDYING WORLDVIEWS

Many scholars, other than philosophers, are interested in studying people's worldviews. This means they will use different approaches (anthropological, historical, psychological, or sociological) when addressing those aspects of human life and those existential questions that people strive to grapple with and respond to: Who am I? Where am I going? How do I fit into the totality of things? How should I live my life, and how should I treat other people and other living creatures? Would it be better if I (or we) lived in another way than I (or we) do? Some scholars conduct surveys, others conduct interviews, while yet others study texts of various kinds using discourse analysis, critical theory, or conceptual analysis. They also analyze different types of material, including manifestos, literature, film, art, and study how these ideas are expressed in social media – on TV, Facebook, X, or in the professional writings of scientists, philosophers, or theologians. Moreover, scholars might focus on a particular aspect of a worldview, such as its narratives, theory of human nature, conception of God, rituals, or modes of belonging.

Philosophers have mainly been interested in studying intellectually reflected or deliberated worldviews. They analyze the sorts of worldviews that their fellow philosophers, theologians, scientists, or other intellectuals have articulated and defended or criticized. If these worldviews contain contradictions or tensions of different kinds, philosophers frequently rationally reconstruct them to make them as coherent and free from inconsistency as possible, given the limitations imposed by the material. They do not conduct empirical surveys, nor do they study the kinds of worldviews people generally hold in a particular society, nor do they compare them to what a similar group of citizens thought about these issues twenty years earlier.

In contrast, the worldview of many people, perhaps most, is not something they have given much thought to. When sociologists or psychologists interview someone to identify the contours of their outlook

---

[39] Jürgen Habermas, "Religion in the Public Sphere," *European Journal of Philosophy*, 2006, 14/1, p. 15.

on life, this might actually be the first time that person has tried to articulate their worldview and express it coherently. Not only can worldviews be more or less comprehensive or fragmentary, but they can also
be more or less a product of deliberation or intellectual consideration.[40]
We have both *reflective* and *unreflective* worldviews, as well as everything in between.

Furthermore, we can study *articulated* worldviews, whether
expressed in writing or merely verbally, or be more interested in
enacted worldviews – that is, as they are performed in practice. People
frequently enact aspects or elements of their worldview without artic-
ulating them. An articulated worldview might be identical to an
enacted one, but also differ significantly. What we say and what we
do are not always the same things. It is also reasonable to think that
an enacted worldview is more fragmentary, incoherent, and situation-
dependent than an articulated worldview. A higher degree of systema-
tization, coherence, and situation independence almost automatically
follows when we start to reflect on something and express it in words.
Cognitive dissonances are easier to detect when we verbalize our ideas
and describe our patterns of behavior.

Both distinctions admit of degree: People's worldviews could be
more or less comprehensive and contain more or less discrepancy
between what is said and what is done. However, the first captures
mutually exclusive alternatives (an individual's worldview cannot
simultaneously be both intellectually elaborated and unreflective),
whereas the second does not (a person's articulated and enacted worldview can be the same).

It is common within religious studies today to distinguish between
lived and officially organized religion. According to Meredith B.
McGuire, a lived religion is "expressed and experienced in the lives of
individuals" and not constituted by the beliefs, norms, and practices
promoted by religious organizations.[41] The latter includes the sanctioned expressions of religion found in, for example, creeds, bishop
letters, and church rituals. Instead, lived religion is the concrete expression religion takes in people's lives. For example, they can be Catholics
and believe in both the triune Christian God and reincarnation, even
though the latter belief is not compatible with the official teachings of
the Catholic Church. This distinction is less relevant when studying

---

[40] See Stenmark, *Rationality in Science, Religion, and Everyday Life*, pp. 238–239.
[41] Meredith B. McGuire, *Lived Religion*: Oxford University Press, 2008, p. 3.

secular worldviews since they are not typically institutionalized and organized in the same or a similar way as religions often are. However, there have been and indeed are exceptions. The socialist–atheistic worldview of the former Soviet Union (USSR, Union of Soviet Socialist Republics) was sanctioned by the state. Still, we can assume that the way some of its citizens express this worldview in their lives diverged from the official teachings of the USSR. So, sometimes, in the study of secular worldviews, we may need to distinguish between individuals' actual worldview beliefs and practices and the official understanding or expression of those beliefs and practices, between what we could call a *lived* or *personal* worldview and an *official* or *organized* worldview.

To summarize, worldviews could be more or less articulated, comprehensive, coherent, lived, and reflected. If we are interested in studying *folk* worldviews, that is, ordinary people's outlooks on life, then we must allow them to be less articulated, less comprehensive, less coherent, and less reflected than *elite* worldviews typically are.

An academic study of worldviews also needs to consider that certain parts of people's worldviews are more or less manifest, whereas others are more or less latent or hidden. Groups of religious or secular people may want us to know only some things about the content of their worldview. Other things might become revealed if we study texts, speeches, or behavior patterns that aim to communicate adequate beliefs, values, attitudes, or ways of behaving to the in-group alone. The distinction between *manifest* worldviews and *hidden* worldviews is particularly important when studying what could be termed "forbidden worldviews," such as racism, sexism, radical forms of environmentalism (like the Earth Liberation Front), or militant forms of religion (like ISIS). These are worldviews or parts of worldviews that are neither socially or morally accepted nor legitimate to embrace in a particular society.

What, then, characterizes philosophical worldview studies and makes this discipline different from a religious studies approach to worldviews or from what I previously called empirical worldview studies? I propose that they differ in at least two ways, which makes them complementary rather than rivals. Although the second way contains (surprisingly for many philosophers) a more controversial claim. Let us start with what is not controversial. Philosophers are primarily interested in the first of the three B's, *belief*, rather than the other two, *behavior* and *belonging*. Moreover, they are particularly interested in intellectually elaborated versions of people's worldviews. These could be the secular worldviews of public intellectuals such as

Richard Dawkins or Sam Harris but are more typically those of philosophers such as Philip Kitcher or Thomas Nagel (and sometimes these categories overlap, as in Bertrand Russell or, more recently, Martin Hägglund). Researchers in religious studies are interested in all three of the B's, but when they are interested in religious and secular beliefs, the emphasis is on what people in general believe or what major subgroups of them believe. Is it the case that more people today embrace or try to develop secular alternatives to the world's religions, and if so, what do they, more exactly, believe? Having such a focus implies that the worldviews they study are often less reflected, comprehensive, systematic, and coherent than those that philosophers study. But studies of both kinds are important.

Now, to the more controversial part. Religious studies are taken to have essentially two aims: One is to *understand* the world's religions in all their diversity, and the second is to *explain* why religions (or subgroups of them) arise, how they develop and are transmitted, why they attract people, or why they decline and perhaps perish. When it comes to the aim of understanding, there is a significant overlap with philosophy, as hermeneutics and phenomenology are of great relevance. Conceptual analysis could also play a part here, but it seems less appreciated within religious studies than those other two strands.

One possible explanation for why people may cease to be religious and perhaps become atheists, and develop a secular worldview, is the increasing success of science in explaining more of our universe. This might be the correct explanation. Still, philosophers are not satisfied and want to ask: "Even if this is true, is it really a *good* reason for becoming an atheist and for developing a secular worldview?" Such a critical question indicates that philosophers are not satisfied with a form of worldview studies that fails to critically assess the content of people's worldviews and their grounds and that fails to explore the criteria we could and should use when developing our own and evaluating others' basic outlook on life. They want to complement a descriptive worldview analysis with a normative one. They view critical thinking or critical reasoning, employing logic and informal argumentation methods, as at the core of philosophy. In fact, philosophers in their inquiry presuppose that a third aim of religious studies, or, more broadly, worldview studies, should be to *critically* and *constructively evaluate* the world's religions in all their diversity and, likewise, their secular counterparts.

This objective is highly controversial in religious studies circles, with much being said about why such philosophical inquiry (in contrast to, say, hermeneutics) should not be considered a proper part of religious studies.[42] To understand the rationale behind this stance, we must consider that religious studies developed out of confessional theology and aspired to be a scientific discipline, rather than being seen as part of Christianity or any other religion. Religious studies aim to be scientific in the sense that this form of inquiry does not require a particular faith commitment on the part of its practitioners, and it accepts only the methods of the social and human sciences. Religious studies do not focus merely on the home religion. It also aims to be neutral, as it contains only descriptions and explanations of diverse religious phenomena and does not attempt to justify or reject them. Religious studies are not involved in any form of apologetics, whether positive or negative. This is understandable, but it is time to move on and fully accept the philosophical study of religions and their secular counterparts as a proper part of worldview studies. At the same time, this often very negative attitude toward critical philosophical reasoning within religious studies is difficult for philosophers of religion to grasp, who work in philosophy departments and rarely engage academically with scholars outside their philosophical peers, who would never dream of rejecting the normative elements of philosophy. In fact, if the objection is that philosophical normative analyses of religions and worldviews are not a proper part of the human sciences, then it seems that philosophy, as it is currently practiced, cannot be a part of those academic disciplines either.

In the future, much bridge-building and serious attempts to understand the other groups of scholars involved in the emerging and much-needed field of worldview studies will be required. This book aims to avoid controversy within the field of religious studies, as it primarily offers a descriptive account of the intellectual content of various religious and secular worldviews.

---

[42] An excellent discussion of these problems can be found in Schilbrack, *Philosophy and the Study of Religions*, pp. 175–204.

3

A Theistic Worldview

Western culture has been primarily based on a monotheistic worldview for the past millennium. Christianity has been the dominant religion, but the other great monotheistic religions – Judaism and Islam – have also contributed to the development of theistic worldviews; today, and in Europe, Islam is present more than ever. The dominance of theism in the Western world has been threatened in the last two centuries. Alternative religious and secular worldviews have become a live option for people. Nevertheless, I will begin this survey of worldviews by identifying and rationally reconstructing the central beliefs or core claims of a theistic worldview as they are understood by many theistic intellectuals today. The idea is to distinguish features that many theists agree on or at least recognize as central features of theism, even if they do not hold all these views themselves or accept them in exactly the way in which I explicate them. In some places, I will highlight the differences between Judaism, Christianity, and Islam and also say something about what distinguishes the form of theism found in Hinduism (or in some of the religious traditions that have become named "Hinduism"). Many books are available for those interested in learning about the specifics of these individual religions. The idea here is to look at what they may, after all, have in common and to which atheism and emerging secular worldviews might be understood to be in opposition. What are then the key features of a theistic worldview?

GOD AND SUPERNATURAL BEINGS

The emergence and development of the Abrahamic religions (Judaism, Christianity, and Islam) mark a transition in the part of the world in

which they emerged, from a worldview in which there are many different gods to one in which there is one God who is the creator of all that
exists and on whom everything depends for its existence. God is also not
limited in the same way that the gods were thought to be, localized to a
particular spatial or geographical area, but is considered omnipresent.
God is also much more powerful or much greater, *Allāhu 'akbar*, as a
Muslim would say, or maximally perfect, as Christians standing in the
tradition of Anselm of Canterbury (1033–1109) would say, than the
gods are – if they exist.

Theists maintain that since God is the creator and sustainer of all
things, God is radically different from gods and spirits in that if Shiva,
Baal, Zeus, Aphrodite, and Thor, if angels, demons, fairies, and ancestral spirits exist, they are all as dependent on God for their existence as
are humans, plants, mountains, stars, black holes, and indeed the entire
universe or the multiverse – if there are multiple universes. (The multiverse is the hypothetical set of all universes, among which our universe
is one.) God is the ground and source of all that exists. We might say
that they believe God belongs to a unique ontological category, alongside the category of natural things and phenomena, and alongside the
category of supernatural things and phenomena, such as gods, angels,
demons, fairies, and ancestral spirits. According to theists, we make a
category mistake if we confuse God with beings of these other kinds, just
as if we think that mathematical numbers belong to the same ontological category as mammals, or that both humans and processes, such as
World War II and globalization, are individuals. On this understanding,
God is not a supernatural reality but rather a "pre-natural" one, someone who exists before nature and is the ground and source of all that
exists. In this sense, theism is an expression of pre-naturalism rather
than supernaturalism.

Theists emphasize that if God is understood in this way, it means that
when someone denies or doubts the existence of God, it is not just a matter of failing to find a particular supernatural being in the world (much
like when we ask whether there is a ghost in the attic), but it requires
believing or assuming that the natural world can exist all by itself, and
not depend on God for its existence. That is, that matter, physical particles, or something similar, instead of God, is the source and ground
of everything that exists. Thus, God is not to be understood as "one
additional thing" or "another being among all other beings" that exist.

It is quite possible for theists to believe that, in addition to God and
natural beings, there are also certain supernatural beings, such as gods

or other spiritual or heavenly creatures. For example, many, perhaps most, of them have believed in the existence of angels. Within Hindu traditions, we find a variety of gods populating the natural order or cosmos, such as Vishnu, Lakshmi, Shiva, Parvati, Brahma, and Saraswati. According to Hindu polytheism, there are different gods, and it is possible to distinguish them from one another. According to Hindu monotheism, all these gods are aspects of one supreme power, a single God, who is the source of all the others and the universe itself. The major traditions of Hinduism, centered on Shiva, Vishnu, and the Goddess, are forms of monotheism insofar as they regard their particular focus as the Supreme Being, from whom other gods are manifestations. Gavin Flood writes, "Many Hindus will regard themselves as monotheists who worship one God through different forms; the many Hindu gods are articulations of a transcendent deity."[1]

We could say that a core claim of theism is as follows:

(1) There is only one God (*monotheism*).

Everything is either part of God or has its ground in God. There is no reality more fundamental or more real than God. Theists thus believe that in the beginning or always, there was something with self-consciousness, namely, what they call God, and this God is the creator of all that exists. Thus, there is an all-encompassing mind beyond the consciousness of individual humans and other beings, and this consciousness is the foundation of the universe's existence and properties, moral and aesthetic values, and our existence, nature, and purpose. Consciousness plays a central role in the story of the origin, development, and content of the world. It is not just an unexpected product that appears by chance billions of years into the story but also one that has guided or directed the process from its beginning until now. Hence, another core conviction of theism is as follows:

(2) Consciousness or an all-encompassing mind underlies everything that exists (*the mind-first view*).

The divine reality is infinitely greater, but if we are to imagine it at all, we are, according to this view, more right than wrong to think of it as consciousness or mind. Theists maintain that our understanding of God is necessarily limited, incomplete, and flawed. If we do not understand

---

[1] Gavin Flood, *Hindu Monotheism*. Cambridge University Press, 2020, p. 62.

this, theists maintain that we risk God becoming a superhuman created in our image – an idol. Still, God is best described not as "Something" but rather as "Someone"; therefore, it is adequate to use personal pronouns when talking about God.

GOD, THE UNIVERSE, AND SCIENCE

Theists believe that in the beginning or always, there was something with consciousness or awareness, namely, what we call God, and this God is the creator and sustainer of all that exists. Hence, another core belief in a theistic worldview is as follows:

(3) The world or the universe is a creation, and God is its creator and sustainer – and, if there are any, of all other worlds or the multiverse (*the creation-conservation thesis*).

It is in maintaining that the continuing existence of the world depends on God's ongoing creative activity that Abrahamic theists proclaim one of the features distinguishing their understanding of divine action from that of the *deists*.[2] God does not just bring things into existence and then take a hands-off approach to them. God continually supports things in existence, moment to moment, throughout their careers on the stage of reality. For this reason, it is problematic to say that God sometimes intervenes – as if God came in from outside somewhere – in natural processes, because God is already as fully involved as possible. God is as much responsible for the world continuing to exist for another second as God is for its existence at all.

However, there is a crucial way in which Abrahamic and Hindu theism differ regarding their understanding of creation and God's relationship to what is created. Flood writes:

If by monotheism we mean the idea of a single transcendent God who creates the universe out of nothing (*creatio ex nihilo*), as in the Abrahamic religions, then it is open to question whether or not that idea is found in the history of Hinduism. But if we mean a supreme, transcendent deity who impels the universe (whether created from nothing or not), sustains it, and ultimately destroys

---

[2] *Deism* is the view that God created the world, but thereafter God has exercised no providential care or control over what goes on in that world. The continuing existence of created things requires no activity by God beyond that of having created them in the first place. God respects the full autonomy of the world and its inhabitants and has accordingly created it so.

it before causing it to emerge again, who is the ultimate source of all other gods who are her or his emanations, then this idea does develop within that history.[3]

In Abrahamic theism, the introduction in Genesis, "In the beginning, God created the heavens and the earth," is interpreted as saying that God created the world from nothing (*creation ex nihilo*). God created the universe out of nothing, which means that before (whether "before" is understood temporarily or ontologically) God created the universe, there was nothing distinct from God or something that is a part of God used by God as raw material for the formation of this world. God is not just a molder but also an absolute maker. Moreover, the world is not an accident or a necessity. Instead, God was free to create or refrain from creating any universe at all. God created the world and its structures freely, giving its inhabitants a free and generous gift. The existence of the universe should prompt our gratitude, whereas the being of the universe should evoke our wonder. God created the world because God perceived that it would be good that such a world should exist. Therefore, the world as physical is affirmed as good within a theistic worldview.

Still, in choosing to create, theists believe that God was also free to create a different universe from our own and free to create the things and creatures the world displays in any particular way. The world, the things in it, and the properties they have are all contingent. God could have done things differently. God could also have created other worlds than ours, but we do not know whether that is so. Therefore, the reason why there is something rather than nothing and why the world or the universe exists is that God created it. The universe is not an uncaused, pure chance event, or simply a brute fact without explanation. God is the ultimate reason the universe, life, and humans exist. Theists hold that one of the most important, if not the single most important, truths about our world is that it is a created world.

God is not a very large material object, such as the universe, since God created it *ex nihilo*. God is instead supposed to be immaterial; that is, God is without a physical body. God is a spiritual reality or a pure, all-encompassing mind. As far as we know, consciousness and mental states, such as thoughts and ideas, do not occupy space, have mass, or even have a shape. In us, consciousness or mental states are related to physical processes in the brain, but not so when it comes to God. Still, God acts in the world, but not as we do through a body. God acts just by willing. God

[3] Flood, *Hindu Monotheism*, p. 2.

wills that things be a certain way, and they are that way. God said, "Let there be light," and there was light (Genesis 1:3). The Qur'an describes the divine act of creation as follows: "When He [God] decrees a thing He needs only to say: 'Be,' and it is" (Sura 3:47).

In Hindu theism, the world is in some sense divine – part of God. It also suggests that the world is necessary and, thus, eternal. God cannot exist without the universe because it is an integral part of God's being. Still, God is not identical to the universe in a similar way that we, as persons, are not identical to our bodies. The world is God's body, but God's personality or self-consciousness goes beyond the natural order of the cosmos. A central element of Hindu theism (which it shares with Buddhism) is the cyclical view of time, contrasting with Abrahamic theism's linear view of time, and the idea of an eternal and oscillating universe. The latter is the view that the world is never definitively created or destroyed; instead, through endless eons of time, the universe goes through cycles of creation, destruction, and recreation. God governs this endless cycle of the universe. God is transcendent; nevertheless, the universe emanates from God. The universe has always existed and, therefore, has no absolute beginning.

Even if these thoughts have originated within the Western tradition of process philosophy, some Christian thinkers have recently developed ideas about God's relationship to the world that are similar to those found in Hindu theism.[4] There are two elements in this so-called *process theism*: panentheism and process philosophy. Pan-en-theism means that everything (Gk. *pan*) is in (Gk. *one*) God (Gk. *theos*), but that God is more than the world as a whole. The world is a part of God, and God depends on the world for God's own existence, but God is more than the world. The creation of the world comes from God's very being as an emanation and not *ex nihilo*. Process philosophy, foremost, contains a particular ontology that posits that processes, rather than things, are the basic constituents of reality. Ultimately, all that exists in the world is not things or individuals and their properties, but processes and their properties. This ontology also applies to God, so God is best described not as a necessary being but as a necessary process.

Some theists then believe that God created the universe out of nothing by willing it into existence. Others believe that God created the world

---

[4] See, for instance, Donald Viney (2022), "Process Theism." In *The Stanford Encyclopedia of Philosophy*, edited by Edward N. Zalta, https://plato.stanford.edu/archives/sum2022/entries/process-theism/.

from something, implying that there were elements within God, such as chaos, void, prime matter, empty space, the quantum vacuum, or dark energy, that God molded into a universe. Theists differ in their views on God's relationship to the world. What I will call "traditional Western theists," or the received view in Abrahamic theism, accept the first, and Hindu theists or panentheists (whether Christians or Hindus) accept the second of the following claims:

(4) God does not depend on the world for God's existence, whereas the world depends on God for its continuing existence (*the asymmetry-dependence thesis*).

(4*) God depends on the world for God's existence, and the world depends on God for its continuing existence (*the symmetry-dependence thesis*).

No matter which religious or secular worldview we embrace, it seems like there are essentially three options we can choose from when we think about the universe's existence: (a) The universe (or the multiverse) has always existed in one form or another. (b) The universe (or the multiverse) came into existence from nothing without any cause. (c) The universe (or the multiverse) was caused to exist by something or someone else, such as God. Theism is compatible with the idea of an eternal and oscillating universe (option a) and the idea that the universe is finite and has an absolute beginning caused to exist by something or someone else, which they identify as God (option c). Theism is not compatible with option (b). Secular worldviews are compatible with either (a) or (b), but presumably not with (c).

For much of the first half of the twentieth century, the *steady-state theory* in cosmology was the dominant theory. The theory states that the universe is infinite in extent, infinitely old, and, taken as a whole, it remains the same in all directions and at all times, both in the past and the future. The universe is eternal and does not evolve or change over time. It aligns well with option (a) above, and since the universe has always existed, we require no explanation for its existence. Only contingent things and processes need an explanation. However, in contemporary cosmology, it has been replaced by the *Big Bang theory*, which states that the universe originated from an incredibly hot and dense state 13.8 billion years ago and has been expanding and cooling ever since. If the Big Bang is the beginning of space-time, matter, and energy, then there would be no prior physical stuff of any kind to cause it. Traditional Western theists claim that recent scientific discoveries support a theistic worldview, even if they do not entail it. The idea that the universe has an absolute beginning fits neatly into a theistic worldview. If there is a cause of the Big Bang, it must have been a being beyond nature, space, time, matter, and energy. Theists maintain that it is difficult to find a better candidate for such a being than God.

Moreover, scientific research has shown that the universe is finely tuned for the emergence of life. In cosmology and physics, scientists have discovered that even a marginal difference in the universe's original state would have resulted in no life at all, yet life exists in the universe. For example, a minimal increase in the initial velocity at the beginning of the universe would have made it impossible for gravity ever to pull together local islands of matter to form galaxies and stars. Instead, an equally insignificant decrease in initial velocity would have meant that the universe would have collapsed again before stars had time to form. If the weak nuclear force had been only slightly stronger than it is, there would be neither water nor sufficiently stable stars for life to evolve in the way it has on Earth, and so on. The universe seems to be fine-tuned to favor the emergence of life. Theists point out that this is not unexpected, given theism. If God intended to create human beings or other intelligent beings who are self-conscious and can act morally, then the fine-tuning of the universe is not surprising, perhaps even something we should expect. Theism, it is argued, is not merely compatible with science, but contemporary scientific cosmology supports or adds to the credibility of a theistic worldview because it is more plausible to attribute this fine-tuning of the universe to God, the creator of the universe, than to mere chance.

In that the Big Bang theory supports the belief that the universe began to exist in the finite past, traditional Western theism seems to have the upper hand over Hindu theism or panentheism, and arguably to secular worldviews too since a universe that comes into existence uncaused (a cosmic luck event) seems less plausible than an eternal and oscillating universe. The fact that an explanation for the existence of the universe is not needed is essential for naturalists because an adequate explanation cannot refer to the universe or nature itself but must be based on something beyond, before, or alongside nature.

In what follows, I will focus on traditional Western theism. These theists maintain that accepting their worldview, specifically the belief in creation and the idea that humans are created in God's image, was a crucial factor behind the development of empirical science in the

Western world. It is no coincidence that science emerges in this cultural and religious context. It is because God created the world with certain regularities and structures that creatures like us can understand it. It is because God has created us in God's image that we can understand the world. It is because God could have created the world differently (all things in it are contingent) that it must be studied empirically and cannot be known a priori. Not only is the universe orderly in itself, but it is also intelligible to us. Theists believe that by studying the created world, we indirectly learn something about God, so seeking God through creation is a form of reverence for God.

Hence, traditional Western theists believe that theism offers a superior explanation for the success of science compared to any other religious or secular worldview. The very fact of science makes the best sense in a theistic universe. Michael Peterson reminds us that, as a theist, he is not speaking about a scientific explanation here because science cannot explain itself. It is a philosophical explanation.[5] To say that theism explains a particular phenomenon, such as science, better than a rival worldview is to say that the likelihood of that phenomenon occurring is higher or much higher on the assumption that theism is true than on the assumption that the rival worldview is true. It is not blind cosmic luck (one option open to advocates of secular worldviews to embrace) that our reasoning abilities happen to yield results that conform more or less to the truth about the world; it is only to be expected if we live in a theistic universe.

According to these theists, there is a deep concord between theism and science because a theistic worldview provides a rationale for the conditions required for the development and success of science. However, they also acknowledge that there is superficial conflict, as they see it, because influential secular critics, such as Richard Dawkins, argue that the theory of evolution is incompatible with the idea that life in all its diversity is God's creation.[6] Theistic thinkers argue that a problem with this line of reasoning is that it overlooks the possibility that God may have chosen to create life and its immense diversity through genetic variation and natural selection. This is the view of Charles Darwin in the *Origin of Species*. Darwin believes that natural selection is a set of processes designed by the Creator (as he writes) to produce adaptation and improvement in the organic world:

[5] Michael Peterson and Michael Ruse, *Science, Evolution, and Religion: A Debate about Atheism and Theism*. Oxford University Press, 2017, p. 49.
[6] Richard Dawkins, *The Blind Watchmaker*. W. W. Norton & Company, 1987.

Authors of the highest eminence seem to be fully satisfied with the view that each species has been independently created. To my mind it accords better with what we know of the laws impressed on matter by the Creator, that the production and extinction of the past and present inhabitants of the world should have due to secondary causes, like those determining the birth and death of the individual.[7]

Here, Darwin states a theistic interpretation of evolutionary theory, also known as *theistic evolution*. According to this understanding of evolutionary theory, God has initiated, directed, and supervised the process of evolution; that is, God has used the laws of nature, matter, natural selection, and mutations to create and develop life on Earth. Natural selection has been directed so that more complex life forms would emerge over time, and eventually, intelligent life would evolve. To borrow a metaphor from Albert Einstein, God would have loaded the dice at the moment of creation so that it would have a specific outcome. Theists argue that an all-encompassing divine mind has exerted a pull on the world toward ever-greater complexity and species richness, which is compatible with the laws of nature and the causal mechanisms of natural selection and mutation without being reducible to them.[8]

Still, theists believe that God is far beyond our ken since God is the ground and source of the world, which means that God is qualitatively different from everything within the world. God is unsurpassable. The belief that God created and sustains the world at each moment of its existence also entails that God has immense power on an almost inconceivable scale. Therefore, God is said to be almighty or omnipotent, or at the very least, God is as powerful as one must be to create the world and sustain its continued existence. Theists disagree on how to explicate the powers necessary to create the world and everything that God can and will do in the world once it is created. But, at the very least, God must have sufficient power to create the universe and everything else that exists and sustain its ongoing existence. If God is even omnipotent,

---

[7] Charles Darwin, *The Origin of Species*. Penguin Books, 1985, p. 458.

[8] There are groups of Jews, Christians, and Muslims who do not accept evolutionary theory or essential parts of it. These theists believe that their Holy Scripture – the Torah, the Bible, or the Qur'an – teaches a particular theory of creation with direct implications for biological research. However, most Jews, Christians, and Muslims do not read their Holy Scripture as if it is intended to give us scientific information but to show us a way to God and give us guidelines for a morally good, righteous, and meaningful life. Be that as it may, in my rational reconstruction, I take theists to embrace theistic evolution, rather than the so-called creationism.

it strengthens the belief that there is only one God because there cannot be two omnipotent gods.

Being able to create and consciously plan the unfolding of the universe and the development of life also entails that God has knowledge on an almost inconceivable scale. Again, theists disagree on the extent of God's knowledge. Is God omniscient, knowing everything possible to know? And what does that mean? Does it mean that God only knows what has occurred and is occurring (present knowledge), or that God also knows all that will happen in the actual world (simple foreknowledge), or does it even imply that God knows what would happen in every situation in every possible world (counterfactual knowledge)? Moreover, theists' answers depend on whether they think God exists outside of time or, after creation, God exists in time.

Whereas, for example, classical Greek religion and Viking religion (or Old Norse religion) ascribed to the gods very human foibles, theism from Plato onward has affirmed that God is purely good and could not be the author of anything evil. Indeed, theistic Platonists usually identify God with the Good. In Judaism, divine goodness is believed to be shown, especially in the giving of the law (*Torah*). In Islam, it is understood to be manifested through divine revelation of truth, as revealed to the prophets, especially in the Qur'an. In Christianity, it is displayed in the gracious granting of Christ as the way of salvation. Theistic philosophers have suggested other roads to justify the belief that God is supremely good. For Immanuel Kant, divine goodness is known as a postulate of pure practical reason: God must be there to reward virtue and punish evil.[9] Richard Swinburne thinks that if God is omniscient, then God knows all moral truths – what is good and what is evil – and since God is completely free (and thus never has to perform actions that there are overwhelmingly good reasons to refrain from doing), God will always, since God is also omnipotent, do and be able to do what is, on the whole, the best thing to do. Therefore, God is completely good.[10] On either account, traditional Western theism strongly emphasizes God's supreme goodness.

In Hindu theism, God is also good, although God is still ultimately the source of suffering and death.[11] Generally speaking, it is more

---

[9] Immanuel Kant, *Critique of Practical Reason* (English translation). Cambridge University Press, 1997.
[10] Richard Swinburne, *Is There a God?* Oxford University Press, 2010, pp. 13–14.
[11] Flood, *Hindu Monotheism*, p. 9.

challenging to argue that God is entirely good within a panentheistic conception of God. Since the world is part of God, and no part of the world is outside of God, and the world contains evil, it appears to follow that God cannot be entirely good. The evils that form parts of the universe are also parts of God. Either way, it is definitely so that in traditional Western theism and presumably also in Hindu theism, another core belief is as follows:

(5) God is unsurpassable in power, knowledge, and moral goodness.

God is truly worthy of worship because God is unsurpassable in power, knowledge, and moral goodness and is the creator of the world and everything that exists. To say that you believe in God, therefore, means that you, as a theist, adopt a particular attitude toward the object of your faith. This means it is incompatible with theism to say: "Of course, God exists, but I do not care about that at all." On the contrary, theism entails a commitment to live in a certain way – to adopt a particular attitude or orientation toward life. However, theists hold different opinions on how this commitment should be concretely expressed in human life. Still, we can say another central element in a theistic worldview is as follows:

(6) God is truly worthy of our worship and obedience because God is unsurpassable and the creator of the universe.

Whatever else God is, God must be worthy of worship and of directing our lives toward, or be able to constitute our highest good.

HUMAN NATURE

It is a crucial part of Christian, Jewish, and some Islamic thought to see human beings as created in the image of God. The idea is that all human beings, regardless of gender, race, or social status, are created in the image of God. Moreover, the idea is that only they, among the created things on Earth, have this property. All species have the property of being created essentially, but only humans have the property of being created essentially in God's image. Being uniquely created in God's image implies that we have a higher moral status than other animals on Earth, but not that they lack moral standing. The doctrine of the *imago Dei* has multiple facets and can therefore be interpreted in various ways. Still, its core is that human beings reflect the divine reality in some crucial ways. Perhaps we could say that the image of God refers at least to all of humanity's abilities and relations that have an analogical parallel to God's nature. In my rational reconstruction, I will take the doctrine to include the idea that God has created us so that we (like God) are self-conscious, loving, and morally responsible agents who can know essential things about our world and ourselves and act with intention. Hence,

(7) Humans are unique because, unlike other beings on Earth, they are created in the image of God, which means at least that they are, as God is, thinking, acting, loving, and morally responsible self-conscious beings (*the imago Dei*).

To say that God created humans in God's image is also to say that personhood is not a temporary or accidental feature of the universe because, at the bottom, reality itself is personal (the mind-first view). To this idea, as expressed in statement (7), it is worth adding that theists maintain that God has created humanity with a specific goal: to relate to God. We are meant to exist in a relationship with the Creator. Part of this role is that we are called to be stewards of God's creation. We are not only the crown of creation (on Earth) but also God's responsible deputies, vicegerents, or co-creators on Earth. We could say that there are two purposes inherent in theistic anthropology:

(8) We exist for a reason because God intended creatures like us to emerge in the evolutionary process. God also had a particular purpose for us to fulfill: to love and obey God, to love each other, and to be God's deputies on Earth (*the telos thesis*).

Not only is meaning *of* life (or ultimate meaning) possible within a theistic universe, but there is also a specific meaning *in* life. We are meant to be here and to accomplish specific tasks.

A theistic conception of human nature includes the idea that the human condition is characterized by certain fundamental defects or deficiencies that we must seek to remedy. It also contains suggestions for effective remedies. One defect that theists believe we suffer from is that many people lack a relationship with God and intentionally or unintentionally turn their backs on God, which has consequences for their self-understanding, how they treat other people, and how they treat God's creation. This idea can be understood in various ways, but let me express it in a manner that links it to two theistic traditions, Christianity and Islam, while highlighting an essential difference between them.

A classical Christian view, developed in particular by Augustine (354–430) and emphasized by both Martin Luther (1483–1546) and John Calvin (1509–1564), is that the first humans, Adam and Eve, disobeyed

God. As a result of this event (symbolized by eating the forbidden fruit), all humans inherit the sin of Adam and Eve and are, therefore, indebted to God from birth and subject to death. The idea of original sin suggests that humanity has an inherent inclination toward sin and an inherent inability to do good. Augustine emphasized it strongly to show that humans are totally dependent on God's grace for their salvation. Humans cannot reestablish their relationship with God through their own efforts.

Other Christians maintain that the idea of original sin has no support in the Bible but want to hold on to the idea that salvation is a gift from God made possible by the death and resurrection of Jesus Christ and that all people need access to this gift from God in order to be saved from their precarious situation. In other words, no human being is sinless. The difference between this idea of *acquired sin* – that all human beings are sinners and are separated or alienated from God – and that of original sin can be explained if we think of sin (or alienation from God) as a kind of disease of a spiritual nature. According to the idea of original sin, this disease is passed on genetically from one person to another, so that every child born suffers from it. The idea of acquired sin merely says that everyone will get this disease. It is like a cold, which eventually affects us all. However, it differs from a cold in that we cannot heal ourselves. Once we have caught it, we cannot break out of its grip ourselves. Children are then born without sin but acquire it later in life and cannot free themselves from it. For this reason, humankind needs a *savior*. Jesus Christ enables us to be reconciled with God despite our shortcomings and guilt. A savior is the remedy to correct the fundamental flaw in our (inherited or acquired) nature.

These ideas have implications for developing a Christian view of human nature. The idea of innate or acquired sin implies that human nature is profoundly flawed. The question that remains is in what way it is corrupted: whether it is wholly corrupted so that this spiritual disease should be likened to Alzheimer's disease, whereby large parts of our personality are destroyed, or more analogous to color blindness, where the personality is intact, but some cognitive, emotional, or volitional capacity is destroyed? Either way, if all people have sinned against God, then it seems to follow that we have or develop during our life a tendency to be selfish, to be attracted by evil, desire for power, and would rather not have anything to do with God. Theists who have such a view have, we might say, a *pessimistic view of humanity*. This view of humankind can be more or less pessimistic, encompassing everything from a completely to a partially depraved human nature.

We can say that there are three theories about the presence of evil
and good in human nature. We have conceptions of the sole nature of
humanity, either that humans by nature are ultimately good but that certain factors threaten this goodness or that they by nature are ultimately
evil, and that we must either acknowledge this or try as best we can to
mitigate these adverse effects, or rely entirely on the grace of God. The
third theory posits the dual nature of humanity, suggesting that humans,
by nature, are essentially both good and evil. People have both good
and bad qualities, but they tend to show their good sides and hide their
darker ones. I suggest that we primarily interpret pessimistic and optimistic views of human nature as different versions of the idea of the dual
nature of human beings. Pessimists believe that the evil side is stronger, and optimists believe that the good side dominates. Genetic factors,
hereditary sin, social norms, and voluntary decisions can determine the
degree of goodness or evil an individual expresses at different times.
Thus, pessimists think we are working uphill, while optimists think it is
more a question of working downhill.

Muslims have this notion of the dual nature of human beings.
Muslims refer to the Qur'an, which states, among other things, that:
"We have indeed created man in the best of creations, but have made
him lower than the lowest except those who believe and live a righteous
life; indeed their reward will be without end!" (Sura 95:4–6). They share
this view with Christians and agree that we are at a crossroads; we can
turn to God or go our own way. However, Muslims lean more toward
optimism than pessimism and reject the idea of original sin, but also
indirectly reject the idea of acquired sin. Although the Qur'an confirms
that Adam (the first man) sinned, his sin has not been passed on to
future generations. While all people *can* sin, not everyone has done so.
Nor do Muslims expect people necessarily to fail to believe in God, submit to God's will, and live a righteous life. Muslims can expect to fulfill
what God requires of them during their lifetime on earth. Muslims think
that God also does not demand anything from us that we cannot fulfill.
Generally, sin does not play a central role in Islamic thought. Its equivalent, *najat*, is used only once in the Qur'an, and more central is *falah*,
which means success in life, especially in the Hereafter.[12]

Christians view themselves and others as sinners in need of God's
grace and reconciliation. Guilt and the need for forgiveness are central

[12] Harold Coward, *A Short Introduction to Sin and Salvation in the World Religions*.
Oneworld, 2003, pp. 59–88.

to their view of human beings. Muslims see themselves and people in general as essentially good but as beings who need God's guidance to believe in the true God, submit to God's will, and live a righteous life. According to Islam, humankind's fundamental problem is a lack of guidance. What we lack and desperately need to know is which path to follow, not salvation. What Muslims want and expect from God is clear guidance in various situations, preferably in all the situations they encounter in life. This is one of the reasons why *sharia* (laws or norms) and *fiqh* (jurisprudence) play such a central role in Islam. Therefore, the solution to humanity's fundamental problems lies in the guidance provided by God, through God's mercy, in God's numerous revelations, and above all, in the final revelation, the Qur'an.

Still, we could add one more core conviction of a theistic worldview:

(9) Humans find themselves alienated from God in need of God's guidance, mercy, or forgiveness (*the alienation thesis*).

Theists do not have to believe in an afterlife, but they typically do. If so, they maintain that we shall each exist in an afterlife as essentially the same person we were in our earthly life, and, in this life to come, we shall stand face-to-face with God. However, this belief has been given two main interpretations. The *immortality theory* is the idea that the soul of each human being, but not the body, survives death. The human soul is immortal. The *resurrection* or *re-embodiment theory* is the idea that the body will be resurrected at a given time, not merely the soul. After death, the body disintegrates, but at some point in the future, God will raise it together with the soul and create the human person anew. Theists can hold any of these views. Either way, a central theistic conviction is as follows:

(10) There is an afterlife where we shall stand face-to-face with God.

Whether theists embrace the immortality theory or the reembodiment theory has implications for their stance on dualistic or materialistic anthropology.

Mind–body dualists argue that the physical and the mental are so radically different that we cannot simply see consciousness as part of the material world. Consciousness is not just a collection of thoughts but *that which thinks*, an immaterial substance that exists beyond and independent of our bodies. We are made up of two elements or substances, not just one. However, we are essentially an immaterial substance and contingently a body. We are a self or soul that has a body.

This view is in philosophy called substance dualism. Some dualists have an essentially negative view of the body. They may see the body as evil or undesirable. However, theistic dualists typically see the body as something good, something created by God, for example, to enable our moral and spiritual development and maturity. The body is more like a temple we are in than a prison, but it is nevertheless something we will not need in the afterlife.

Mind–body materialists, on the other hand, think that we are essentially both a body and a soul. It can be expressed as a form of reductive materialism where consciousness is reduced to or seen as identical to our brain. Reductive materialists maintain that you and I are identical to the physical elements that make up our bodies. We not only have a body, but we are nothing but a material body. This is not the form of materialism that some theists embrace. Instead, they see the mental or consciousness as a property and not a substance we have that cannot be reduced to something material. We have a body, essentially, but we are more than our body. This view is called irreducible materialism and sometimes property dualism – in contrast to substance dualism.

Immortality theories presuppose substance dualism. When the body dies and decays, there is nevertheless something left of us (a soul or self) that persists and continues beyond this life. If we are nonphysical or immaterial souls or selves currently embodied, then even the complete destruction of our physical bodies cannot result in the annihilation of our self or personhood. Immortality theories assume that we can exist without our bodies. Resurrection or reembodiment theories, on the other hand, presuppose irreducible materialism because these theories imply that we cannot exist without a body. However, we can exist without the body we have now, and instead, our first-person perspective, or our self, can be joined with a new body in an afterlife. For example, Christian materialists such as Lynne Rudder Baker and Peter van Inwagen argue that an afterlife is only possible if God gives us a new body because they believe humans are essentially embodied beings.[13]

EPISTEMOLOGY AND GOD

How do theists think we can know that God exists and created the world, or at least be rationally entitled to believe these things and many

---

[13] Lynne Rudder Baker, "Death and the Afterlife." In *The Oxford Handbook of Philosophy of Religion*, edited by William J. Wainwright. Oxford University Press, 2005, pp. 366–391.

other core convictions that make up a theistic worldview? They, as I will understand their stance, think that there are, in fact, good arguments for theistic beliefs, arguments as good as any philosophical arguments get. Arguments that show why it is as rational or more rational for intelligent, honest, and well-informed people to embrace a theistic worldview rather than a naturalistic or any other worldview.[14] Still, the problem with these theistic arguments is twofold. First, they are not strong enough to confer knowledge on one who believes in God on their basis, and many theists maintain that they know that God exists, created the world, and loves us. (This is obviously not a problem for those theists who merely think that it is rational for them to believe in God's existence.) Second, they require that we be able to assess complicated arguments correctly. But if God exists and loves us all, why would God privilege highly intelligent or educated people and require the rest of us to submit to their authority on such important matters?

For these reasons, some theistic intellectuals have suggested that if God exists and cares about people, it is not unlikely that God has created us in such a way that we can know God's existence without relying on complicated arguments. Alvin Plantinga writes:

If theism is true, God would presumably want human beings to know of his presence (and in fact the vast majority of the human population believe in God or something very much like him); he would therefore arrange for human beings to be able to come to knowledge of him. But if knowledge of God is depended on the theistic argument, or other arguments from the deliverances of reason, then, as Aquinas says, only a few human beings would ever come to a knowledge of this truth, and then only after a long time, and with a substantial admixture of error.[15]

Experiences of God's presence in the world are of great importance from an egalitarian perspective because if God desires to have a relationship with people, we would not expect God to limit the knowledge of God's existence to those individuals who are capable of formulating and understanding, for example, the cosmological and the fine-tuning arguments we previously mentioned. Similarly, we would not expect God to limit knowledge of God's existence to a particular gender, race,

[14] Jerry L. Walls and Trent Dougherty, eds., Two Dozen (or so) Arguments for God. Oxford University Press, 2018.

[15] Alvin Plantinga (2013), "Religion and Science." In Stanford Encyclopedia of Philosophy, edited by Edward N. Zalta, https://stanford.library.sydney.edu.au/archives/sum2013/entries/religion-science/.

or nation, but rather to make God's presence known so that all people can establish a relationship with the ultimate source of existence, God. God should then be accessible to all people, regardless of their particular divine revelation, such as the Torah, the Bible, or the Qur'an, regardless of whether they can formulate and understand theistic arguments, their level of intelligence, or the time period in which they live.

Most theists do not rely on arguments for their belief in God. Presumably, most of them have barely heard of, for instance, the cosmological or the teleological argument. Why, then, do they believe? A theistic answer is that awareness of God is activated spontaneously and non-inferentially in many situations for many people because there is a kind of instinct, a natural human tendency or disposition to believe in God, and that is why so many people believe that God exists. Thomas Aquinas says, "To know in a general and confused way that God exists is implanted in us by nature."[16] Belief in God is formed in us under certain circumstances. It is not so that we consciously choose to have those beliefs; instead, we find ourselves with them, just like we find ourselves with perceptual and memory beliefs. I find myself believing that you just entered the room or that I had breakfast this morning. My belief that I had breakfast this morning is not based on any argument or inference to the best explanation; I simply remember it. Awareness of God is natural, widespread, and not easily ignored or destroyed. Still, it could be more or less confused, and theists maintain that we should accept it, provided that we do not encounter any good reason to think otherwise.

Theists believe that the disposition to believe in God is activated naturally within us in various situations. It could be when one sees the blazing glory of the heavens from a mountaintop. One finds oneself filled with awe, wonder, and a profound belief that God must be truly great to have created the heavens. It could be in prayer, singing, being overwhelmed by God's grace during liturgical meetings, or reading the Holy Scripture.[17] Faith in God spontaneously and irresistibly arises in many people's lives, which is what we would expect if we lived in a theistic universe. But that does not mean that everyone believes in God because natural and instinctive theistic belief could be overridden by, for instance, the influence of nontheistic parents, the hegemony of a secular society, or experiences of horrendous suffering and evil. Still, theists think that belief in God will naturally emerge in one's thoughts

---

[16] Thomas Aquinas, *Summa Theologiae* I, q. 2 a. 1, ad 1.
[17] Alvin Plantinga, *Knowledge and Christian Belief*. Oxford University Press, 2015, p. 35.

under the right circumstances. Similar ideas can be found in Islam's theory of *fitrah* (human natural knowledge and dispositions). God has created humans so that they have a strong inclination to believe in God. Abbas Yazdani writes that the theory implies that humans "have an innate disposition towards the transcendent reality, that is, God ..., because they have immediate knowledge of God naturally."[18]

Hence, theists believe that humans are naturally disposed to form immediate beliefs about God. God causes people to hold theistic beliefs by endowing humans with a disposition that generates those beliefs, provided a specific stimulus is present. Theists understand and develop the idea of natural, immediate knowledge of God or belief in a God instinct differently. Some think it is innate or a special cognitive faculty (a god faculty or *sensus divinitatis*). However, here, we will merely assume that the idea is that some collection of cognitive processes in our bodies generates non-inferential and unreasoned, but spontaneous and immediate, belief in God, and, if theists are correct, also human knowledge of God. Consequently, and according to this epistemology, theistic religion does not originate as a system of explanation or set of arguments in competition with or as a complement to science or philosophy. Belief in God is non-inferentially evoked in particular circumstances, so experiential evidence exists for theistic belief. For this reason, the theistic beliefs of ordinary people are mostly okay (or rationally permissible) as they are.

C. Stephen Evans argues that if we live in a theistic universe, we could thus expect a *wide accessibility principle* to apply; that is, belief in and knowledge of God would be widely available, not difficult to gain. On the other hand, he suggests that an *easy resistibility principle* should also apply if we live in a theistic universe. It must also be possible for people to reject God and a relationship with God. Knowledge of God can, therefore, not be imposed on people, but it must be relatively easy to reject the idea that there is a God. Evans writes, "To allow such people this option, it is necessary for God to make the evidence he provides for himself less than fully compelling. It might, for instance, be the kind of evidence that requires interpretation, and include enough ambiguity that it can be interpreted in more than one way."[19]

[18] Abbas Yazdani, *Evidentialism and the Rationality of Religious Belief.* Lambert Academic Publishing, 2010, p. 157.

[19] C. Stephen Evans, *Natural Signs and Knowledge of God.* Oxford University Press, 2012, p. 15.

Most theists believe that God has also revealed Godself in extraordinary ways, through instances of divine speaking or acting in history, disclosing something previously unknown or unrealized. We can say that a *revelation* (or special in contrast to general revelation) is a purported disclosure made directly or initially to a limited group of people at specific points in history where God reveals things about God's nature or intention that are not available through human reason alone. Hence, we can say that theists believe that we can know things about God through both the *deliverances of reason* and the *deliverances of faith*. They typically maintain that the latter gives additional and more reliable knowledge about God than the former. For instance, some Christian theists would say that they know God exists through the deliverances of reason, but through the deliverances of faith (revelation), they also know that God is a Trinity.

However, theists neither agree on what constitutes a special revelation nor which one is more reliable than the others (if there is more than one) nor on what it is that God reveals. Typically, Muslims believe that God has revealed Godself to "the people of the Book," such as Jews and Christians, but that the Qur'an is the supreme and final divine revelation. Christians would either deny that the Qur'an is a divine revelation or that it is much less accurate than the one documented in the Christian Bible. Moreover, theists disagree about what is revealed, that is, the content of the revelation. Christians and Muslims could agree that what is revealed is the truth about God, God's intentions, and guidelines for how we should live and worship God. Some theists think that what God reveals is not a body of truths expressed in propositional form, through prose, poetry, or historical narratives, but rather events or God's actions toward us. This latter alternative is perhaps especially emphasized by Christians because of the doctrine of the incarnation, which claims that God "became flesh and lived among us" (John 1:14). A combination of both *alethic revelation* (from the Greek term for truth) and *manifest revelation* is also possible. Minimally speaking, we can say that a core belief of theism is as follows:

(11) By experience, reason, or revelation, we can come (to some extent) to know God or at least to be rationally entitled to believe or have faith in God.

GOD, MORALITY, AND SUFFERING

Theists maintain that our moral beliefs make better sense if we live in a theistic universe than in any other universe that alternative worldviews presuppose is the actual world. There is nothing strange in such a universe with moral beliefs and our convictions that they can be truth-aimed. Morality, its reality, and objectivity can be better understood and explained in a godly, as opposed to a godless, world.

If we suppose that Adolf Hitler was depraved and evil, that wife beating, rape, and child molesting are vile, and agree that such moral beliefs are bedrock, the confidence in these or similar basic moral beliefs is only justified if we have reason to believe that the human faculties responsible for them are truth-aimed and not merely fitness-aimed. (Fitness is the capability of an organism to survive and reproduce.) As a theist, one can believe this is so because God has influenced or directed evolution toward the emergence of self-conscious, rational, and moral beings capable of discovering moral truths. Such an option is not available to secular people, since, in a naturalistic universe, one would expect the evolutionary process to select a propensity for moral judgments that track survival, rather than moral truths.[20] Theists maintain that such a skeptical conclusion about the likelihood of tracking moral truth and obtaining moral knowledge is unsurprising, as secular worldviews assume that our universe is indifferent to morality. Values and moral judgments are emergent features of nature. (We will return to this issue in the chapter on secular humanism.) In a theistic universe, neither the personal nor the valuable are emergent features of reality but are basic. Values and obligations are deep in such a world. They have a grip not merely upon surface phenomena, such as humankind. Instead, a moral order is at the heart of reality since it is God's creation. Theism can therefore explain why we know that Adolf Hitler was depraved and evil, that wife beating, rape, and child molesting are vile, and avoid moral skepticism (the view that no member of *Homo sapiens* has moral knowledge). If we live in a theistic universe, it makes sense that our moral faculties are truth-aimed, and we can discover some essential moral truths.

Similarly, theists think that humanism, or the belief that humans possess a special kind of intrinsic value, which we refer to as dignity (underpinning certain fundamental human rights), is best explained and justified if humans are created in the image of God. A good, personal God, who has created everything that exists, has endowed human beings

---

[20] For an argument along these lines, see Mark D. Linville, "The Moral Argument." In *The Blackwell Companion to Natural Theology*, edited by William Lane Craig and J. P. Moreland. Wiley-Blackwell, 2009, pp. 391–417.

with intrinsic value, a worth bestowed by God to all participants of the human race. The dignity of humans and human rights are grounded in the state of affairs that, as bearers of the *imago Dei*, they – in contrast to other living creatures on Earth – manifest a significant resemblance to God in their very personhood, and, crucially, as being loved in a unique way by God. God loves each and every creature who bears the image of God equally and permanently, and therefore, God holds us accountable for how we treat one another. Theists maintain that their worldview provides a way to ground human dignity and rights where other worldviews fail, especially in extending it to all human beings. Primarily, they contrast their view with secular alternatives: Why think that human beings have dignity, given a worldview in which the universe has come to exist by chance, not by design, but by purposeless, value-indifferent natural forces and processes – a universe ultimately indifferent to morality?

However, can we have equal and permanent dignity or rights simply because God bestowed us with worth by loving us in a unique way as a response to us being made in the image of God? Does that not make inherent worth dependent on what God declares as such (which could be an arbitrary divine decision) and not because it is indeed of inherent worth independently of God's will (so God has nothing to do with what is of inherent worth)? This is often referred to as the *Euthyphro dilemma*: Is something good because God wills it, or does God will it because it is good? Contemporary theists think they can avoid both alternatives because they maintain that the divine nature is inherently good. God cannot do anything but good because it is part of God's essential nature; therefore, there is no need for God to invent inherent worth or goodness, as it is already inherent in God. Therefore, the bestowed worth to humanity by God is not arbitrary, and the standards of what is of intrinsic value are not independent of God because it is grounded in God's essential nature.[21]

Since God loves us and being loved by God provides an essential part of the theistic grounding of human dignity, humanity's relationship to God is at the center of concern for theists. It says something about what we should value in our lives to flourish as human beings and what should be our ultimate concern. Hence, one more theistic core belief is the following:

---

[21] Paul Copan, "Theism, Naturalism, and the Foundations of Morality." In *The Future of Atheism*, edited by Robert B. Stewart. Fortress Press, 2008, pp. 157–160.

(12) The highest good, but not the only good, for humans or self-conscious beings is to be in the right relationship with God and live a life characterized by this relationship (the *summum bonum*).

Theists believe that living a life in a relationship with God provides them with unique resources to cope with hardship, anxiety, and suffering, to understand true love, and to harbor an attitude of existential optimism. Everything for everyone will eventually work out for the best, as God cares about human welfare. One day, God will finally defeat evil and suffering. Meanwhile, we should do everything in our power to love our neighbors, care for God's creation, minimize suffering and evil as much as possible, and strive to create a just and peaceful society. Moral evil exists in the world because God has given people significant freedom, and they have misused their freedom. Natural suffering (i.e., suffering that is not caused by humans, at least not directly, but by earthquakes, fires, floods, and the like) exists because it is necessary to create a stable natural order constituted by objects that behave according to physical laws. The possibility of suffering is inherent in such a natural order. The same water that quenches our thirst can also drown us; the same neurons that transmit great pleasure can also transmit intense, unbearable pain. Hence, God has good reasons for allowing some forms of evil and suffering.

Theists often make two assumptions to try to show why moral evil and natural suffering, even on a vast scale, such as the 1755 Lisbon Earthquake, the Nazi Holocaust, the great purge of Stalinism, or the Tsunami, can be reconciled with a good God creating the universe, including beings like you and me. Suppose God intended to create beings who were like God in the sense that they would be free to decide in a significant sense how they want to act. In that case, it follows that if these beings, humans, choose to perform evil acts such as killing or torturing others, God cannot simultaneously prevent these horrible things from happening and allow humans to be genuinely free. God can choose to create such beings or not, but once God has created them, God cannot decide how they should act. This means that these theists embrace *incompatibilism*. Unlike *compatibilists*, they believe that determinism and free will are not compatible with each other. People cannot have significant freedom or genuine choice and, at the same time, perform actions that are predetermined to occur because of past events in the history of the universe or because God wants them to act in a certain way. Theists need not be incompatibilists; they can believe that God, for example, guides the hearts of kings like streams of water (Proverbs 21:1), while still claiming that they have free will (*theistic compatibilism*). However, if they hold this view, the extent of evil in a theistic universe seems inexplicable. An additional thesis many theists embrace, therefore, consists of the following:

(13) God has created humans with significant freedom to choose between evil and good, so not all actions they perform are determined by the causal chain of past natural events or by God's will (*the idea of significant freedom*).

Even if claim (13) is not something that theists must embrace, it is not unexpected if theism is true because a free choice on their part to love God and their fellow humans, in accordance with the idea of *summum bonum* (claim 12), reasonably constitutes a higher good than an automatic or robotic form of love.

If so, much evil becomes less surprising in a theistic universe. But can the intrinsic goodness of beings with free will really outweigh the senseless evil some individuals experience in life, such as the torture and murder of young children? What about the lives of these children? It does not seem sufficient to refer to a general good, such as genuine freedom of choice, to make these events comprehensible and, not least, morally acceptable in a world supposedly created by a good God. The theistic thinker Marilyn Adams, therefore, argues that such a God must be able to guarantee that each person's life as a whole is good, and this, in turn, requires that there is a life after death in which evil is defeated or redeemed through the participation of all people in God's life.[22] Similarly, Linda Zagzebski maintains that overall, a life can only be good if "it were possible for the creature to know ahead of time what living through a life in need of redemption would earn it in the end, that creature would choose to live that life."[23] This then means – and here we come to the theist's second assumption – that there is a life that continues after our biological death, in which God ensures that each individual's life is something that can be said to constitute a good life.

Even if John Hick acknowledges the problem evil creates for theism, he emphasizes that the possibility of an afterlife with God inspires a hope that secular worldviews cannot provide. He writes,

[22] Marilyn Adams, *Horrendous Evil and the Goodness of God*. Cornell University Press, 1999.
[23] Linda Zagzebski, *Philosophy of Religion*. Blackwell, 2007, p. 188.

with the exception of tough-minded atheists, such as Bertrand Russell, they [naturalists] do not seem to be aware that they are announcing the worst possible news to humanity as a whole. They ought frankly to acknowledge that if they are right the human situation is irredeemably bleak and painful for vast number of people. For – if they are right – in the case of that innumerable multitude whose quality of life has been rendered predominantly negative by pain, anxiety, extreme deprivation, oppression, or whose lives have been cut off in childhood or youth, there is no chance of their ever participating in an eventual fulfillment of the human potential. There is no possibility of this vast century-upon-century tragedy being part of a much larger process which leads ultimately to limitless good.[24]

The critical question Hick wants us to ask is: *Who* has or has had this potential fulfilled? The answer is that the potential that human life has in these respects for many people throughout human history has never been realized because they died in early youth, suffered extreme hardship, were forced to go to war as youngsters and died, were bombed or raped and beaten to death, or were born with severe disabilities. There is no possibility in a naturalistic universe that this vast century-upon-century tragedy is part of a much larger process ultimately leading to limitless good. Therefore, naturalism is bad news for humanity at large, and we should, Hick believes, reject it unless there are strong reasons to believe it is true.

CHALLENGES FOR A THEISTIC WORLDVIEW

What challenges does theism face? What would seem to be problematic aspects of it? Let me highlight some of these challenges without suggesting that a theistic worldview lacks the resources to deal with them in a satisfying way.

Is it not so that evolutionary psychology (the study of the origin of our psychological and cognitive dispositions and faculties) and cognitive science (the study of how the mind is structured and processes information) jointly have offered a good and convincing explanation of why people believe in God, explanations that undermine the rationality of belief in God and natural knowledge of God? Many scientists or scholars have given an affirmative answer to that question.[25] The idea is that belief in God is an instance of a broader kind of belief common to almost

---

[24] John Hick, *The Fifth Dimension*. OneWorld, 1999, pp. 24–25.
[25] See, for instance, Jesse Bering, *The God Instinct*. Nicholas Brealey Publishing, 2013; Paul Bloom, "Is God an Accident?" *The Atlantic Monthly*, 2005, 296, pp. 105–112; Richard Dawkins, *The God Delusion*. Houghton Mifflin Company, 2006; and Daniel C. Dennett, *Breaking the Spell*. Allen Lane, 2006.

all forms of religion, namely, the belief that the world contains invisible agents that typically have an impact on human affairs: agents such as Yahweh, Allah, angels, demons, forest, mountain, and ancestor spirits. The most reasonable explanation of these beliefs in invisible agents is that they are a by-product of belief-forming processes that are fitness-aimed but not truth-aimed.

According to evolutionary psychology, human thinking and the belief-forming processes that generate our beliefs originated in the environment in which our gathered-hunter ancestors lived 10,000–15,000 years ago, and these are essentially the same as the ones we have today. In that environment, it was crucial for people's survival and reproduction that they could perceive danger, so a specific belief-forming process evolved to detect agents immediately. An "agent" in this field of study is any being that seems to move of its own volition, and for its own purposes, so nonhuman animals are agents too. Selection pressures produce an agency detection device (ADD) in the human mind, causing us to behave appropriately when confronted by a potential predator, enemy, prey, or friend. However, this evolved ADD produces a high percentage of false positives (mistakenly indicating the presence of an agent when, in fact, there is none) to avoid false negatives (mistakenly indicating the absence of an agent when, in fact, there is one). Such an outcome promotes human survival or fitness, as the cost of a false negative is extremely high. If our ancestors failed to detect just one lion approaching from the bushes, they would die. An ADD is, in fact, HADD, a hypersensitive agency detection device.

Now, belief in God and other invisible agents is most likely the accidental outcome of HADD. Hence, our ancestors' cognitive faculties detected God and supernatural beings where none existed. These beliefs are by-products of belief-forming processes gone awry. An evolutionary psychological explanation of the natural, non-divine origin of theistic belief shows that belief in God is irrational. Survival pressures, rather than God, caused theistic belief. More precisely, error-prone belief-forming processes lead to the formation of a belief in God. Once one becomes aware of this naturalistic explanation, it is not rational to believe in God anymore or to think that one knows that God exists. This explanation provides an undermining defeater for theistic belief. The connection between belief in God and truth is insufficient for rationality and knowledge. The cognitive processes that produce theistic beliefs are not functioning properly; they are not geared toward producing true beliefs. Let us refer to this as *the debunking argument against theism.*

What is tricky about the debunking argument is that it is unclear why theists should find it convincing. On the contrary, this research appears to offer empirical evidence for what many theists have believed for centuries to be true: A cognitive architecture in human minds often produces spontaneous, nonreflective, and non-inferential beliefs in God. Theists believe that God guided or directed the evolutionary process so that people – cognitively hardwired like us – would, in certain circumstances, naturally form a belief in God. But then God would be the ultimate cause of theistic belief. If so, people would, it seems, have natural knowledge of God.

On the other hand, if one is a secular person, then the debunking argument probably contains one of the best naturalistic explanations of belief in God. If one does not believe in God, one would expect an explanation along these lines, broadly conceived, to undermine the reliability of natural theistic belief formation. In fact, the advocates of the argument I have referred to are not merely scientists or scholars but also secular people, so it is perhaps not surprising that they find the debunking argument convincing. What seems like a scientific argument turns out to be a *worldview-immanent argument*, that is, an argument containing premises or reasons that depend, directly or indirectly, on accepting a secular worldview of one kind or another. However, that, of course, is also true for the theistic response to the debunking argument; it is a reasonable reply only if one already believes in God.

We have seen that theists believe that the existence of evil and suffering is not a surprising feature of reality if we live in a theistic universe and that theism can offer hope for everyone's redemption from these facets of human existence that secular worldviews cannot. Many critics would likely agree with the last part of that statement, which is that a grim implication of naturalism is that it is bad news for the unfortunate among us in life's lottery. Still, they would argue that a decisive problem with theism is that there is so much evil and suffering, or horrifying instances of them, in the world, such as the 1755 Lisbon Earthquake, the Nazi Holocaust, the Great Purge of Stalinism, the Tsunami, or the new wars that start time and time again. A good and powerful God would surely be able to significantly reduce the amount of evil and suffering in a world that God has created without losing something greater good. But this is not the state of affairs in the actual world. There have been, and there still are, instances of horrendous evil and suffering. Therefore, it is unlikely that God exists.

Many philosophers refer to the existence of evil and suffering, or rather the extent of them, as an important, even decisive, reason why they do not believe that God exists. (Many theists agree that this is the strongest argument against God's existence.) To take just one example, Michael Ruse says that he does not believe in God's existence for several reasons. These reasons, he says, have very little to do with science, the most important of which is that as an atheist, he is a "metaphysical naturalist primarily because of the problem of evil."[26] If there is a good God capable of creating an entire universe, it is hardly surprising that instances of suffering and evil exist in the world; however, what is surprising is the extent of suffering and evil that do exist. If God exists, we might reasonably expect a better creation in this respect. This is the "evidential argument from horrendous evil and suffering," or, abbreviated, *the argument from evil and suffering*.

A related challenge is the hiddenness of God. We saw that theists maintain that not only should we expect that belief in and knowledge of God would be widely available and not difficult to gain but also that it must be possible for people to reject God and a relationship with God. However, is God's hiddenness not a reason to think that God does not exist? The problem is not that if there is a God, we do not see or comprehend God fully in this life. That is not surprising. What is unexpected and might even indicate that God does not exist is that if God wants to be known and enter a relationship with us, God would reveal Godself to anyone who honestly seeks to find out the truth about God. However, that is not the case, so it is likely that God does not exist. This is the *argument from hiddenness*.

If God is unsurpassable in knowledge and power, then there is no risk that God does not know how to reveal Godself and no chance that God lacks the ability to do so. However, God has not provided sufficient evidence for all of us to believe that God exists and cares about us. This could be a problem for the theist, too. She believes that God has provided her with evidence that makes God's existence obvious enough, but she might be perplexed as to why her friends fail to form a belief in God. The critics, however, argue that if the *summun bonum*, the greatest good, is union with God, then people who honestly seek God but fail

---

[26] Michael Ruse, "Naturalism, Evil, and God." In *The Cambridge Companion to the Problem of Evil*, edited by Chad Meister and Paul K. Moser. Cambridge University Press, 2017, pp. 251–252.

to experience God's presence in their lives provide evidence against the existence of a perfectly loving God. Such people exist. Therefore, God does not exist or, alternatively, God probably does not exist.[27]

The *telos* thesis of theism (core belief 8) contains two parts. First, God intended for human beings, or self-conscious moral beings, to emerge in the evolutionary process. God planned for us (or beings like us) to come into existence. As a species, our existence is not a cosmic coincidence or a lucky outcome in the evolutionary lottery. Let us call this the meaning *of* (human) life. An analogy might be helpful: Some couples do not plan to have a child; it just happens. In such a situation, their intention was not to have a child. On the other hand, my wife and I (and many other couples) planned to have children, so there is a reason why Jacob and Beatrice exist. There is a "meaning of" their life in this sense. The second part of the *telos* thesis is that God intended us to fulfill specific tasks. God plans for us to be here for a particular reason: to love and obey God, love each other, and be God's deputies on Earth. God has purposes for us and formed us accordingly. When we do these things, we can flourish as humans. This is an example of what we can call meaning *in* life. If we live in a theistic universe, there is, in addition to a meaning of life, also a specific meaning in life.

Some critics have maintained that the theistic idea of a specific meaning in life is deeply problematic, even offensive. It is degrading for humans to be regarded as serving a purpose.[28] Secular thinkers such as Kurt Baier and Jean-Paul Sartre believe that God's existence undermines the meaning of human life. Sartre even believes that life can only have meaning if there is no God.[29] He argues that if there were a theistic God, such a God would constrain our ability of self-creative autonomy in ways that would evacuate our life of all meaning. A paper knife gets its meaning from its maker's purpose in creating it. We humans may give our lives meaning by choosing for ourselves which purpose to adopt. Sartre argues that we only have this freedom because we live in a godless world. If God exists, our essence precedes our existence; however, in a naturalistic universe, human existence precedes our essence.

---

[27] The most well-known advocate of the argument from hiddenness is the philosopher John L. Schellenberg. See, for instance, John L. Schellenberg, *The Hiddenness Argument.* Oxford University Press, 2015.

[28] Kurt Baier, "The Meaning of Life." In *The Meaning of Life*, edited by E. D. Klemke. Oxford University Press, 1981, pp. 102–115.

[29] Jean-Paul Sartre, *Existentialism and Humanism* (English translation). Methuen & Co, 2007, pp. 27–31.

We are living in a godless universe, free to choose our destiny, and our lives can, for this reason, have meaning. Contrary to what theists think, there is no meaning *in* life if God exists or, at the very least, God undermines such a meaning. This is the *meaning-erasing challenge to theism*. Just as Hick's argument that naturalism is bad news for humankind (see page 72), this is a pragmatic argument. Thus, unlike epistemic arguments, pragmatic arguments are benefit-oriented rather than truth-oriented. Hence, the idea behind the meaning-erasing challenge is that if theism is true, it is bad news for humankind because it erases or undermines the possibility of genuine meaning in life. It is not meant to establish that God does not exist but to point out a grim implication of believing that we live in a theistic universe.

4

A Buddhist Worldview

Like many of the world's other great religions, such as Christianity and Islam, Buddhism comprises numerous teachings and traditions across a wide range of cultures. I will reconstruct an interesting version that incorporates specific core beliefs and values, which Buddhists hopefully may recognize as part of their rich religious heritage, even if they do not hold all of these views themselves or accept them exactly as I explicate them. The aim is to identify a Buddhist worldview that differs from the others considered in this study and thus constitutes a genuine alternative to them. However, other rational reconstructions of Buddhism are undoubtedly possible than the one I offer in this study. It also provides a background for understanding the New Spirituality (the focus of Chapter 5), whose advocates often see their worldview as a form of Buddhist or Eastern mysticism. The chapter ends by outlining several challenges a Buddhist worldview encounters.

As Victoria Harrison underscores, studying the form worldviews have taken in Asia often involves getting to grips with ideas that are unlikely to be part of your natural way of thinking if you have grown up in a non-Asian part of the world. They are unduly unfamiliar ideas from a Western intellectual and philosophical perspective, which is my interpretative perspective in this book. (Thus, in all probability, you will gain an understanding of Buddhism from that particular viewpoint in this chapter.) For this reason, I have had to rely more on other experts than when writing most of Chapters 3 and 6–9. Still, as Harrison points out, many of the questions these worldviews address are remarkably similar wherever and whenever they are found. These are questions such as "What is the self?" "What is the best way to live?" "Where do we come from?"

and "What happens when we die?"[1] These questions arise directly from the human condition. Yet, Buddhism contains distinct ideas about the nature of reality, the self, knowledge, and ignorance, as well as the path to human fulfillment and how to live a morally good life.

The most obvious difference between the Western monotheisms (or what I have previously called a theistic worldview) and Buddhism is that the former's preoccupation with who God is, with God's relationship to us, and what it means that God created and sustains the world, is absent from a Buddhist worldview. Instead, we can sometimes find Buddhist arguments against God's existence. Other times, the gods are part of the natural order and subject to its laws. Gods are taken to be like other sentient beings, such as humans and animals, creatures who will die and be reborn as part of *samsara*, the cycle of birth, death, and rebirth. If gods exist, they are certainly not the creators of the world and thus cannot be held responsible for the suffering in the world.[2] For this reason, Buddhism is a prime example of a *nontheistic* religious worldview. It is a religious worldview in which God does not exist, and gods play no essential role.

Buddhism shares certain features with the Vedanta tradition of Hinduism, which eventually evolved into a distinctive alternative religious worldview. Harrison thinks that this bedrock of belief makes it possible to talk about these worldviews as part of the same family in a similar manner to how we can talk about Western monotheisms as part of the same family (theism).

A core element of this broad framework is the cyclical view of time (in contrast to theism's linear view of time) and the idea of an *eternal* and *oscillating universe*. This is the view that the world is never definitively created or destroyed; instead, through endless eons of time, the universe undergoes cycles of creation, destruction, and recreation. Something similar happens to each individual being. Humans and animals are trapped within a cycle of birth, death, and rebirth, known as samsara; karma holds individuals within this cycle of endless rebirths. *Karma* can be described as a principle of moral causality and cosmic justice, and rebirth enables karma to operate across many lifetimes. Karma also explains why bad things happen to good people and good things happen to bad people. Good people can experience bad things

---

[1] Victoria Harrison, *Eastern Philosophy*. Routledge, 2019, p. 6.
[2] Sebastian Gäb, "Why Do We Suffer? Buddhism and the Problem of Evil," *Philosophy Compass*, 2015, 10/5, p. 345.

in this life because of the evil actions they committed in previous lives. Bad people can experience good things in this life because of the good actions they performed in earlier lives. Eventually, cosmic justice will be achieved because people will reap what they sow in due time, thereby restoring the moral balance over many lifetimes. The basic idea is that everyone goes from one life to another without end unless liberation or enlightenment occurs.

Still, we need to find a way out of this circle of rebirth or reincarnation, and, indeed, such a way can be found. We need enlightenment or liberation; that is, we must find the means to overcome our entrapment in the cycle of rebirth. Within this broad common framework, *ignorance (avidya)* is widely regarded as a principal source of suffering because it gives rise to attachment, which in turn leads to rebirth. Harrison writes, "Humans were, by and large, thought to be ignorant of the correct answers to two important questions: 'What is the fundamental nature of reality?' and 'What is the true self?'."[3] Ignorance about our true nature is, in Buddhism in particular, taken to be the root problem of our predicament, and it is only by liberating us from this ignorance that we can be free from rebirth. This explains why arriving at a correct understanding of the self should be of such importance in our lives and something an adequate worldview must provide. We need to replace ignorance with knowledge, especially about our true nature and the true nature of reality.

Hence, three of the core beliefs of Buddhism, which it has in common with the Vedanta tradition of Hinduism, are as follows:

(1) The universe has always existed and, therefore, has no absolute beginning; instead, it goes through endless cycles of creation, destruction, and recreation (*the eternal and oscillating universe*).

(2) Humans and animals die but are reborn into and animate new sentient bodies in an endless circle of birth, death, and rebirth (*reincarnation*).

(3) Human actions have consequences in subsequent lives, which explains why bad or good things happen to people now or in future lives (*the law of karma*).

Core belief (3) suggests that these Eastern religions align with theistic religions in holding that the universe is essentially moral. As we will see in Chapters 7–9, naturalism and the secular worldviews that accept its ontology contain a rejection of this claim. Buddhists believe that the

---

[3] Harrison, *Eastern Philosophy*, p. 35.

universe does not operate with complete indifference to morality, unlike the movements of the planets or the law of gravitation. There is a moral law inherent in the very constitution of the universe, so there is not merely physical causation but also karmic causation of events.

Moreover, these Eastern religious worldviews all agree that rebirth is not a good thing, nothing we should consider attractive. But of course, that is a possibility for us. We can think of karma as a moral law that enables you and me to transition from one life to another. If we live sufficiently good lives, our next life will contain enough positive consequences to make it desirable. We can improve as we go along, and the variety of situations in which we are reborn will make sure that we never get bored. Within the new spirituality, we can find a positive evaluation of reincarnation (see Chapter 5). Hence, we should add a fourth core Buddhist belief, which expresses a negative stance toward reincarnation. The goal is not an improvement of our human life through the process of reincarnation but a liberation (*moksha*) from it:

(4) Rebirth or reincarnation is not a desirable state of affairs, and we ought to strive to be released from the bondage of the cycle of birth, death, and rebirth (*the liberation from reincarnation*).

THE NO-SELF VIEW OR THE SELFLESS WORLD

It is crucial to take into account not merely that the Buddhist worldview contains a negative evaluation of the cycle of rebirth but that Buddhists also reject the idea of the self (*atman*) that such a positive view presupposes, namely, that there is something of you and me – of our personalities – that remains in the new forms we take in these future lives. Buddhists reject the view of the self found in many Hindu traditions, although these religious worldviews share similar ideas, including karma, rebirth, and the importance of liberation. Let us call the latter view "the enduring-self view" and the former one "the no-self view." Hinduism is far from the only religious worldview that embraces the enduring-self view. Many worldviews assume that each person is a real individual being with an essence or a self. It is also true of many secular worldviews since they contain the beliefs (a) that the self is real and comes into existence with the body, but (b) it ceases to exist when the body ceases to exist. A significant secular exception to (a) is scientism. Roughly, the idea is that science cannot discover the self, and since science sets the limits for what we can know, we should not believe that the self is a real entity. A significant exception to (b) is transhumanism, which maintains that it will be possible for the self to survive the body's death in the near future. (Both a scientist and a transhumanist world-view will be discussed in Chapters 7 and 9.) According to Buddhists, this widely held view of an enduring self, which exists in this life only or beyond it, is false. There is no self who continues to exist for a span of eighty years or so.

Within Hindu traditions, as they develop, we can find the idea that the self is unborn, eternal, and everlasting. The idea is that the physical body is mortal, but the immaterial self is immortal. The same human mind or soul (*jiva*) can successively animate different bodies in future lives. After death, our bodies permanently disintegrate, but our individual immaterial selves will be reborn in other bodies. After that reincarnation, they will be reborn again many times as long as we are trapped in the cycle of endless rebirths. The true self, the transcendent *atman*, is not dependent on the physical body. For this reason, the immaterial self could be related to more than one body over a connected sequence of lives. This is a Hindu understanding of the *unified* or *enduring-self view*. The law of karma ensures that the enduring self reaps the rewards or punishments it deserves in its subsequent lives.

While the Buddha accepted the idea of the cycle of endless rebirths, he did not accept the existence of an enduring self, which could be reincarnated and retain its identity as the same self throughout subsequent lives. He taught that contrary to what seems to us to be the case, the self is actually a concatenation of transient events. There are no enduring selves. This is the doctrine of *anattā* (no self). Hence, there are no persons, in any sense of the word "person," that have affinities to common usage. A person is merely a useful conceptual fiction. No particular mental state is the subject and unity of consciousness. Instead, the self is nothing more than the combination of various states temporarily clustered together in what we (falsely) believe to be a person. There is no self that is the subject of all our mental states and has an identity that transcends the various, specific, and fleeting mental states experienced. The unified and enduring self is an illusion. Our sense of being a self or having a first-person perspective is mistaken. Instead, the self is a complex conglomeration of causally connected impermanent events. This is the core of the *no-enduring-self view* or the *no-self view*. However, the idea is that the karmic consequences of our actions can occur in future lives that are causally connected to our present lives, even though no enduring selves are reincarnated. Rebirth occurs without an enduring self that is reborn. It can be seen, metaphorically, as one candle lighting another in an endless series of events.

Anattā (no self) is often referred to within Buddhism as one of the "three marks of existence." We have already seen that Buddhists maintain that there are other fundamental features of reality (such as core beliefs 1, 2, and 3), so the idea here is that these three marks are distinctive characteristics of a Buddhist worldview. We will come back to the other two, but let us, for now, add one more core belief to Buddhism:

(5) There is no self that is the subject of our mental states, which has an individual identity over and above the particular fleeting mental states (*the no-self view*).

"We" live in a selfless world. As David Burton points out, many Buddhists acknowledge that the false belief in an enduring self is exceptionally hard to give up. This is the case whether we think our enduring self ends with our physical death, continues in one afterlife, or is subject to rebirths. He writes that this is because "One feels, subconsciously or consciously, that one has an autonomous self which directs and coordinates one's thoughts, emotions, feelings and perceptions and that this self remains the same while one's thoughts, emotions, feelings and perceptions change."[4] However, we must understand that this is not our true nature because our realization that personality and individuality are illusions provides the key to our liberation. Liberation from suffering, which Buddhists view as the most fundamental existential problem we must seek to solve, requires, first and foremost, liberation from the desire to attain permanence – in this life or the circle of rebirths – for oneself.

ULTIMATE REALITY AND A BUDDHIST THEORY OF TRUTH

Not merely do we lack permanency and unity, but all things that constitute the world are impermanent and lack independent existence. No thing in the world can retain its identity from moment to moment, and since we are a thing in the world, it is true of us as well. Hence, the impermanence thesis entails the no-self view. The Buddha teaches that everything is characterized by impermanence (*aniccā*). Buddhists then reject the view that many defenders of theistic and secular worldviews hold that material particles exist for vast periods of time. However,

---

[4] David Burton, *Buddhism: A Contemporary Philosophical Investigation*. Routledge, 2017, p. 10.

unenlightened people do not understand that impermanence and insubstantiality are the way things are because it seems as if all change involves something that changes and something that remains the same. So, our misconception of reality is not merely about our view of human nature but also about the nature of the world. We misread our experience of being an enduring subject of experience and take the external world to be made up of enduring objects. Still, there are neither enduring subjects nor enduring objects. This is the second mark of existence (*anicca*), so we have one more core Buddhist belief:

(6) Everything is in constant flux so that all things lack individuality or enduring existence; that is, nothing can continue to exist while changing some properties over time and entering into new relations over its lifetime (*the impermanence thesis*).

The key to the impermanence thesis is the Buddhist understanding of the causal relations that underlie our experience of ourselves and our world. This *theory of dependent origination (pratītyasamutpāda)* posits that all things lack enduring existence because they rely on causes to bring them into being and sustain their existence. Everything is constituted by a vast number of events (*dharmas*). They exist in complex patterns of dependency, and only the momentary causally connected events ultimately exist. Composite things such as human beings, cars, and dogs are nothing more than the sum of their component parts, which enjoy only momentary existence. Wholes such as these do not really exist. Everything that exists comes into existence due to conditions causally connected with everything else. All things are interrelated, so everything is empty of its own independent existence. There are no things that can continue to exist while changing some properties over time and entering into new relations over their lifetime. Everything is in constant flux, an unending process of entering and passing out of existence. Things arise and pass away; while they exist, they constantly change. As Matthieu Ricard states, "One of Buddhism's essential ideas states that because things have no independent reality, they can't really 'begin' or 'end' as distinct entities."[5] Things do not possess an underlying stability and unity.

Even the gods – if Buddhists believe they exist – come into being and pass out of existence; although they live very long lives, they are

---

[5] Matthieu Ricard and Trinh Xuan Thuan, *The Quantum and the Lotus: A Journey to the Frontiers Where Science and Buddhism Meet*. Three Rivers, 2001, p. 31.

bound to the cycle of rebirth. The theory of dependent origination also provides a clue as to why Buddhists reject that **God** exists and can be identified as atheists. (It cannot be the belief in karma and the cycle of rebirth since, according to Hindu monotheism, God administrates the law of karma, and God has the power to release persons from the cycle of rebirth.) Theists believe that God is the ground of being, the creator and sustainer of everything that exists, and thus the reason why the universe exists at all, and God, moreover, has always existed. However, this cannot be true if nothing has an autonomous existence, and everything that exists depends on the totality of other things. The idea of God as the first cause of the universe is incompatible with the idea of dependent origination. However, the theory of dependent origination is a nonnegotiable part of the Buddhist worldview, as it provides the rationale for the no-self view. Hence, if Buddhists were to begin believing in God, as opposed to gods, they would adopt a different worldview.

A second reason for this incompatibility with theism is that Buddhists believe the world is never definitively created or destroyed, but instead undergoes cycles of creation, destruction, and recreation. If the universe exists eternally, with no beginning or end, then there is no need for a creator to account for its existence. The Fourteenth Dalai Lama of Tibet writes:

At the heart of Buddhist cosmology is, therefore, not only the idea that there are multiple world systems – infinitely more than the grains of sand in the River Ganges, according to some texts – but also the idea that they are in a constant state of coming into being and passing away. This means that the universe has no absolute beginning. ... From the Buddhist perspective, the idea that there is a single definite beginning is highly problematic. If there were such an absolute beginning, logically speaking, this leaves only two options. One is theism, which proposes that the universe is created by an intelligence that is totally transcendent, and therefore outside the laws of cause and effect. The second option [or naturalism] is that the universe came into being from no cause at all. Buddhism rejects both these options.[6]

Although many theists today hold the view that the Dalai Lama describes, it is still possible for them to believe that the world is God's creation but simultaneously hold that it has always existed. It is what some Hindu monotheists maintain is the truth, and what important medieval Muslim, Jewish, and Christian philosophers and theologians,

---

[6] Dalai Lama, *The Universe in a Single Atom*. Abacus, 2006, pp. 86–87.

such as al-Ghazali (1058–1111), Maimonides (1135–1204), and Thomas Aquinas (1225–1274), believed. However, the Dalai Lama is correct in saying that Buddhism, for this reason, is incompatible with the theistic worldview described in Chapter 3. One of its core beliefs is the idea of creation *ex nihilo*: God created the universe out of nothing, meaning that before God created the universe, there was nothing distinct from God or something that was part of God used as raw material for the formation of this world. The problem for Buddhists (and Hindu monotheists) is that the Big Bang theory raises questions about the universe's eternal existence and suggests that its existence had a beginning.

One way to resolve this apparent conflict with science is to introduce yet another element in a Buddhist worldview, namely, what has sometimes been referred to as the *two-level theory of truth*. According to this theory, we must distinguish between what is conventionally or relatively true and what is ultimately true.[7] Buddhists do not agree on how to understand and apply this distinction precisely (and some Buddhists reject the theory). However, Matthieu Ricard uses it to resolve the apparent conflict between the Buddhist view of an eternal and oscillating universe and the Big Bang. The Big Bang theory is the cosmological theory that the universe began to exist in the finite past. The universe is the totality of physical reality, space-time, matter, and energy, and it began to exist some 13.8 billion years ago. Ricard maintains that the idea of "the universe beginning and ending belongs to relative truth. In terms of absolute truth, it's meaningless. When you consider a castle seen in a dream, for instance, you don't need to worry about who actually built it. … Buddhism [eliminates] the very idea of a beginning."[8] This statement arguably implies that the natural world, as experienced by us in everyday life and through the instruments of science, is, in some sense, unreal or illusory. Sense experience (what we can see, hear, touch, and feel) is a reliable source of knowledge and rational belief when it comes to conventional truth, but not when it comes to ultimate truth.

A second example of an application of the two-level theory of truth is Charles Goodman's account of the Buddhist idea of the impermanent self. He writes, "Ultimately, I am not the same person I was yesterday, because ultimately, I don't exist. Conventionally, I am the same person I was yesterday only because so many of the characteristics I have now

[7] Mark Siderits (2019) "Buddha." In *The Stanford Encyclopedia of Philosophy*, edited by Edward N. Zalta, https://plato.stanford.edu/archives/spr2019/entries/buddha/.
[8] Ricard and Thuan, *The Quantum and the Lotus*, p. 31.

are causally explained by the characteristics I had yesterday."[9] It is sometimes a helpful fiction to talk as if the self and persons exist and endure
for more than one lifetime, but past a certain point, namely when we
take it too seriously and fail to see it as merely conventionally true, it –
as Mark Siderits explains – "results in existential suffering. The cessation
of suffering is attained by extirpating all sense of an 'I' that serves as
agent and owner."[10]

The *conventional truth* is how things, properties, and relations
appear when we employ our ordinary cognitive faculties, such as perception and reason. However, Ricard maintains that the "intellect has
its limitations, and we can't grasp the true nature of reality just by
means of ordinary conceptual processes."[11] Due to these limitations, we
also require access to the ultimate truth. The *ultimate truth* is the truth
of how reality really is, which is not available to our ordinary reasoning abilities, scientific methods, and empirical observations. Instead, we
gain access to it through meditative techniques and focused attention.
By using meditative techniques, such as yoga or mindfulness, we can
transcend our everyday experience of ourselves and ultimately come
to understand the impermanence of the self and reality. Through these
means, the enlightened consciousness – in contrast to the reasoning
consciousness used in everyday life and the sciences – can have a direct
or unmediated perception of emptiness, or that things (including ourselves) lack permanency, unity, or intrinsic nature (*sabhāva*). Buddhists
maintain that these insights about what the fundamental nature of reality is and what the true self is have powerful transformative effects
on the enlightened person's character because they undermine, even
eradicate, the attachment to things that are merely concatenations of
transient events without individuality or permanence and which are
the source of our suffering. The deeper reality behind the world of our
experience is thus not accessible to common sense, the humanities, or
the social or natural sciences. They merely give us conventional truth
when successfully performed, but we need access to the ultimate truth
so that our lives can be transformed and we can escape the law of
karma and the cycle of reincarnation. Hence, I will take a core element
in Buddhist epistemology to be as follows:

[9] Charles Goodman, "Buddhism, Naturalism, and the Pursuit of Happiness," *Zygon*,
2014, 49/1, p. 222.
[10] Siderits, "Buddha," p. 10.
[11] Ricard and Thuan, *The Quantum and the Lotus*, p. 32.

(7) We can only gain genuine knowledge of what the constituents of reality are, rather than how they seem (conventional truths), through meditative techniques, such as yoga or mindfulness (*meditative cognition*).

KARMA AND REBIRTH

A core Buddhist belief is that the karmic consequences of one's actions can occur in future lives, causally connected to the present life, even though no permanent soul or self transmigrates. This means, of course, that besides belief in dependent origination (which we could say includes the no-self view and the view of impermanency), belief in karma and rebirth are central elements in a Buddhist worldview. Without an assumption that rebirth happens and that our actions have consequences in subsequent lives, the idea that suffering is the most pressing problem we face loses its plausibility. If we, instead of this kind of reincarnation theory, embrace a death-end-all theory, then, of course, we should try to reduce much of the suffering we experience. Still, we should also strive to enjoy the goods and pleasures of this life for the limited time that we exist, given that we do not cause unjustified harm to others. If all we have is this life and no other, then why should we be so wholly preoccupied with overcoming suffering and the desires that fuel it? Why not strive to live as happy lives as possible for as long (or short) as they last? The preoccupation with suffering makes no sense. However, if suffering is the essential problem we must solve *to escape the cycle of endless rebirths*, focusing on its causes and how to dismantle the desires or cravings that cause suffering makes eminent sense. What pleasure seekers fail to recognize is that their intentional actions will have proportional consequences in subsequent lives, and their actions will ultimately lead to future suffering.[12]

Within a Buddhist worldview, rebirth is intrinsically linked to karma, as karma explains our suffering and why our actions have consequences in subsequent lives. Karma provides the link between one existence and another, and rebirth allows the law of karma to operate across many lifetimes. Karma can be described as a principle of moral causality and cosmic justice, explaining why bad things happen to good people and good things happen to bad people. An obvious objection to this idea is that good things do not always happen to good people; at least in

---

[12] Burton, *Buddhism*, p. 11.

this life, bad people often seem rewarded. A Buddhist response is that the consequences of an action need not be experienced in the same lifetime in which the action is performed; instead, the consequences may manifest in the next life or subsequent lives. Eventually, cosmic justice will be done because people will, in due time, reap what they sow so that the moral balance will be set right over the course of many lifetimes.

If so, it is crucial that we, as Harrison points out, understand that the moral law of karma is significantly different from the physical laws of nature that science has discovered.[13] Natural laws have temporal immediacy. So, when I throw a stone at the window, it shatters immediately, not next week or in a future lifetime. Because karmic consequences lack temporal immediacy, it is hard to track the connection between karmic cause (good or bad actions in $life_1$) and karmic effect (good or bad consequences in $life_1$, in reincarnated $life_2$, or reincarnated $life_3$, and so on). Another difference between physical causation and karmic causation is that the latter applies only to the particular impermanent self who acted. That is not the case with physical causation. For example, if I intentionally set fire to a forest, it will kill whoever happens to be trapped in that fire. There is yet another dissimilarity between the law of karma and natural laws. Suppose I set fire to the forest because I intended to kill all bark beetles that have massively attacked and threatened all the big trees on my property, but I happen to kill non-intentionally many other animals, including some deer. Although my intentions are irrelevant to physical consequences, the theory of karma implies that only my intentional acts have karmic consequences. This implies, as Harrison writes, that "the same action can have two independent streams of consequences: one physical and one karmic. While all physical actions will have physical consequences, not all of them need to have karmic consequences (whether they do or not depends on the agent's intention)."[14] Given this, we might want to modify core belief (3) somewhat. We could rephrase it as follows:

(3*) Intended human actions and only such actions have consequences in subsequent lives, which explains why bad or good things happen to people now or in future lives (*the law of karma*).

---

[13] Harrison, *Eastern Philosophy*, p. 99.
[14] Ibid., p. 101.

Understanding the Buddhist worldview in this way implies that not everything that happens to us is the result of karma. It is a significant cause, but it cannot be the only one. This means that both good and bad things can happen to us sometimes due to karma and sometimes due to other causes. For example, a tsunami is the result of physical causation. Still, if this tsunami seriously harms us, it may result from previous bad karma, or it could be merely an unfortunate coincidence, or a combination of both. Either way, it follows that if the law of karma is restricted in this manner (as stated in core belief 3 *), some suffering is undeserved.

Consequently, an action's karmic quality depends on its intention. Therefore, one can perhaps say that within the Buddhist worldview, karma is ethicized because it is moral and immoral actions that have karmic consequences.[15] Furthermore, it is universalized, so that the same ethical values and standards apply to everyone, regardless of social class, nationality, or gender.

At least from a Western intellectual perspective, what is hard to understand is how moral justice and rebirth can occur in subsequent lives when there is no enduring self to reap the rewards or punishments in those subsequent lives. How could the causal link between the past, present, and future self be sufficiently strong if no enduring self is reincarnated? Goodman explains how this is possible:

> if there is some kind of causal process that transfers large amounts of information from a dying sentient being into a sentient being that is coming into existence. It would then have to be the case that many aspects of that new sentient being's life are causally explained by the actions and characteristics of the sentient being who died. In saying "many aspects," I mean, for example, that even though my actions and characteristics have many consequences for how my daughter turns out, nevertheless, the causal links between me and my postulated future self in another life are tighter than those between me now and how my daughter turns out. But these links don't have to consist in similarities. It would be enough, for example, if the fact that I am aggressive and brutal now causally explains the fact that my reborn future self is timid and fearful.[16]

In this way, Goodman argues that reincarnation can happen in a selfless world. The connection between my present impermanent self and "my" future impermanent self in the next life or life thereafter would then be causally strong enough to transfer the relevant type of karmic consequences.

---

[15] Burton, *Buddhism*, p. 34.
[16] Goodman, "Buddhism, Naturalism, and the Pursuit of Happiness," p. 222.

SUFFERING AND LIBERATION

Buddhists believe that we are ignorant about the true nature of ourselves and reality as a whole. In particular, we are ignorant that suffering is the most pressing problem we face and how it can be overcome. A third mark of existence is suffering or dissatisfaction (*dukkha*). Every experience is marked by some quality of suffering, whether extreme pain or a sense of unease. Suffering is the fundamental feature of reality that we must overcome to achieve enlightenment. The desire to be an enduring self is the source of suffering and many of the desires that result in various misguided attempts to establish permanence by attaching to oneself other things, such as material possessions, fame, family, and friends, which are falsely believed to provide stability and security for oneself. The Buddhist solution to the problem of suffering is to remove the ignorance and craving that cause suffering and fuel the cycle of rebirth. We can see suffering as akin to a disease, with Buddhism providing the diagnosis and the cure.[17]

The Four Noble Truths provide us with an identification of the disease we have, the diagnosis of it (its cause), and its cure. The first noble truth is that there is suffering (*dukkha*). More precisely, since hardly anyone would question that there is suffering, the belief is that all of existence is characterized by suffering, or that suffering is found in every aspect of existence. Still, the most important part is that the primary negative characteristic of human existence is suffering, which we must overcome to obtain liberation. The basic idea is that suffering or craving is our core existential problem and the problem we must solve to escape the cycle of endless reincarnations. The obvious instances of suffering are old age, sickness, and death, but Buddhists maintain that the problem of suffering goes much deeper. We are unsatisfied even when not suffering from causes like illness, grief, or death. We are subject to desires and cravings, but even when we can satisfy these desires, the satisfaction is only temporary. Pleasures do not last; if some do, they become monotonous. In fact, suffering permeates reality in that everything is of the nature of suffering. This is the ultimate truth of suffering. Hence, another essential Buddhist belief is as follows:

(8) Suffering is a fundamental feature of all reality, and it is a problem or disease that we must overcome to escape karma and the cycle of rebirths and obtain enlightenment and nirvana (*the problem of suffering*).

---

[17] Keith Yandell, *Philosophy of Religion*. Routledge, 2016, pp. 20f.

The "disease" or "disorder" is the state of affairs that a worldview considers the fundamental existential problem (if any) facing human beings. To summarize, a key to escaping reincarnation is realizing the essential truth about our existence, namely, that it is characterized by suffering, impermanence, and nonself.

The second noble truth expresses the belief that desire or craving is the root cause of suffering. Suffering results from craving for and attachment to things that lack permanence, which are all things in life. The things one thinks matter so much are not worthy of being unhappy or happy about, and one fails to see that such attitudes will bring future suffering. I will understand this to mean that the idea is not to promote the ending of all desire (which is a possible Buddhist stance), merely those manifestations of selfish cravings, such as the desire to attain permanence for oneself and others. The desire to compassionately help others who suffer is an aspiration that is not a result of craving if we do not attach ourselves to their pain and suffering by fully acknowledging that we, as well as they, have no enduring selves and that all things in the world are impermanent and lack independent existence.

This view might be difficult to comprehend from a Western intellectual perspective because, from that perspective, it is typically taken for granted that we should focus as much if not more, on happiness than on suffering and that attachments can enrich life so that having a family and friends are of great value and actually essential parts of what makes life worth living. A Buddhist response is that we should not trust this inclination since the habitual cravings that contribute to suffering are deep-rooted in all of us. However, we need to dispel this innate misconception because this craving is the fundamental cause of our suffering, and, more importantly, the cause of our entrapment in the cycle of reincarnation. We overlook the painful consequences of our cravings and attachments because we want our desires for these things – a good job, a lovely house, a family, friends, and so on – to be a source of happiness. The consequence is that the law of karma will keep us (or rather the concatenation of transient events we happen to consist of at the time) spinning in the wheel of samsara forever. If craving or desire is the cause of rebirth, ceasing desire will prevent rebirth by removing its cause, leading to *nirvana*. Still, happiness is not necessarily beyond us, because, on some accounts, nirvana can be construed as a higher, unconditional happiness that far exceeds any temporary pleasure our sensory experiences may bring.

However, as I previously said, I do not think we should rationally reconstruct this idea of the cessation of craving or desire so that the

Buddhist worldview necessarily rubs us of all enjoyment of life, because if we do so, it makes the view seem less reasonable. If, as Burton points out, "Buddhists claim that the cause of suffering is that we overvalue worldly things because of craving and ignorance, this implies that such things may still have some value if the inappropriate motivations are removed. It might be the case that these things could be valued through a non-acquisitive appreciation, where they are enjoyed without being the object of craving."[18]

Buddhists acknowledge the deep-rooted nature of ignorance and craving in human life and that they are very difficult to remove. However, the third noble truth is the claim that suffering can cease and that our spiritual disease is curable. It is curable neither by (a) the complete and permanent satisfaction of desire nor by (b) accepting vulnerability to loss as part of one's account of human flourishing, but (c) in its cessation. More precisely, it means eliminating the selfish craving and attachment to what is wrongly thought will bring lasting satisfaction. Nirvana is achievable for us, implying that we can be liberated from karma and its associated perceptual suffering through the process of reincarnation. There are numerous examples in Buddhist literature of individuals who are said to have achieved the ultimate goal of complete and irreversible awakening. They have reached nirvana. However, it is simultaneously acknowledged that achieving the goal of liberation is highly challenging and requires considerable effort. The awakening typically results from numerous lifetimes of striving and effort. Nevertheless, Buddhists believe that it can be achieved through our own effort, although the assistance of a powerful and wise Buddha or Bodhisattva may be required for many. A Buddha or Bodhisattva is an enlightened, impermanent self that stays within the rebirth cycle instead of achieving nirvana for herself to help others achieve the same goal. Hence, one core Buddhist belief is that:

(9) Desire and craving for enduring things, individuals, and relations are the cause of suffering, but we can escape from karma and the cycle of rebirth by eliminating our cravings for things and the desire to attain permanence to oneself and others (*the diagnosis of the problem of suffering*).

The "diagnosis" is what a worldview considers the cause of the illness or disorder identified (if any) as the fundamental problem we face.

---

[18] Burton, *Buddhism*, pp. 27–28.

The fourth noble truth describes the path to end suffering, the Buddhist way to awakening or enlightenment, the cure for our spiritual disease. The result of the cure could perhaps be expressed as a deep religious experience in which we clearly comprehend the absence of our enduring self and everyone else's, and indeed of the impermanency of all things, and are released from all attachments. We can reach this enlightened state of mind if we learn how to remove or dismantle the desires or cravings that cause suffering. That is to say, if we successfully learn to master the techniques that Buddhists think are effective in the cessation of suffering.

Notice, however, that the talk about "we," "you," or "I" obtaining enlightenment or awakening is misleading because it might suggest that there is an individual who becomes enlightened, who was the same individual who was unenlightened before he or she became awakened. However, if enlightenment entails no longer clinging to the belief in a permanent self, then there cannot be the same unenlightened self who becomes an enlightened self, which is still identical (or at least partially so) to the self who was formerly unenlightened.

ETHICS, MEDITATION, AND WISDOM

The Noble Eightfold Path is a common formulation of the Buddhist path to enlightenment or liberation from the cycle of rebirth, comprising right views, right intentions, right speech, right action, right livelihood, right effort, right mindfulness, and right concentration. It can be divided into three basic sets of practices that jointly reinforce each other, which are as follows:

(A) The *practice of ethics* leads to the right action, makes the mind less distracted by cravings, and facilitates the concentration required for meditation. If that is the goal of the practice of ethics, how should we act? We should act with compassion (*karunā*) for all sentient beings without excessive concern for ourselves or, for that matter, without excessive concern for others. An essential means toward the goal of awakening is to refrain from destructive actions that cause harm to ourselves, other humans, and animals.

Like several other Eastern traditions, Buddhism does not perceive a crucial gap between humans and animals, unlike theistic religions such as Judaism, Christianity, and Islam. Humans are in a theistic worldview taken to be the only living things on earth created in the image of God.

One reason for this Buddhist stance is the conviction that through the cycle of reincarnation, the impermanent self that is a human in this life could have been an animal in the past or could become one in the future. In fact, any animal you meet is likely to have been a human at one time and may even have been your mother or father in a previous life, since every living being has undergone a beginningless series of lifetimes. Still, within a Buddhist worldview, humans are understood to have greater value than animals, simply because only in a human body can one attain enlightenment. Becoming a Buddha is not possible in an animal body. For this reason, killing a human is worse than killing an animal. Ideally, which is not always possible, we should – in accordance with the principle of the sanctity of life – refrain from killing animals, adopt a vegetarian diet, and renounce all forms of violence.

The Five Precepts should guide lay Buddhists; that is, they ought to refrain from killing, stealing, engaging in sexual misconduct, lying, and drunkenness. (Monks and nuns have stricter rules to attend to.) Following the Five Precepts is essential for enlightenment because it leads to rebirth as a human and prevents rebirth as an animal or in one of the lower realms of suffering.[19] Right actions are necessary deeds on the path to enlightenment, but we should still avoid emotional and evaluative attachments to things, individuals, and relationships that lack permanence, which are all things in life.

The Buddhist ethical ideal of selflessness (not unselfishness) and compassion has distinctive features because Buddhists maintain that we live in a selfless world, which is easily overlooked from a Western intellectual perspective. The no-self view entails that, without exception, no suffering belongs to anyone because there is (contrary to appearance) no one – there are no selves or distinctive individual persons. This idea can be developed into an argument against moral egoism. Goodman tells us that such a strategy to justify altruism is sometimes called the "ownerless suffering argument" by philosophers. So, if "you are not a real thing, there is no reason to place any greater intrinsic importance on preventing your own future suffering than on preventing the future suffering of others."[20] Since no suffering belongs to "you" or "me" – because there are no distinct individuals who experience suffering – yet

[19] Charles Goodman (2021), "Ethics in Indian and Tibetan Buddhism." In *The Stanford Encyclopedia of Philosophy*, edited by Edward N. Zalta, https://plato.stanford.edu/entries/ethics-indian-buddhism/.

[20] Goodman, "Ethics in Indian and Tibetan Buddhism."

all suffering is bad. We should try to eliminate it wherever we find it. Hence, we should practice compassion toward all sentient beings. There is no one to whom suffering belongs, just as there is no one who has pleasure, makes choices, or has basic human rights.

Strictly speaking, we should strive towards not overcoming selfishness – to put our interests above those of others unjustifiably – but the desire to be a self. Hence, a certain ambiguity is present on this moral issue in a Buddhist worldview. The ethical message is, on the one hand, that everyone ought to be cared for as if they were one's mother or one's child because they probably have been that in a previous life. On the other hand, and as an implication of the no-self view and the belief in no attachment, the message, as Mikel Burley points out, could just as readily be "understood to mean that one's ties to others, including immediate family, should be loosened to the point where one is capable of abandoning those relationships with ease."[21] Compassion is prized as a means of cultivating detachment from everything. Hence, I suggest that we add this core belief to our rational reconstruction of Buddhism:

(10) Ideally, we should show equal compassion or kindness to all sentient beings and, in particular, to all human beings, but without any (non-acquisitive) attachment or affliction to them, since attachment prevents enlightenment (the *ethics of non-attached compassion*).

We can also find an interesting form of *moral realism* within the Buddhist worldview. What is morally right and wrong is not up to us. Ethics is not a social construction of one kind or another (moral constructivism). Regardless of our perceptions of what is right or wrong, a moral order exists in the universe, as manifested in the law of karma, which governs how our actions impact us and other sentient beings in our present and future lives. Living according to this moral order and understanding its karmic consequences is vital to our lives, even if it is ultimately an order we leave behind when reaching enlightenment and nirvana.

To summarize, ethically virtuous attitudes such as moderation, kindness, and compassion that lead to the right actions play a positive role in the pursuit of awakening. Overall, we could perhaps say that a Buddhist worldview encourages actions that relieve suffering, produce good karma, overcome the character traits of craving and ignorance, and – which is of fundamental importance – move us closer to enlightenment. Hence, the practice of ethics is the first of the three basic sets of practices

[21] Mikel Burley, *A Radical Pluralist Philosophy of Religion*. Bloomsbury, 2020, p. 104.

that jointly reinforce each other and constitute the noble eightfold path. Let us now, more briefly, turn to the other two:

(B) *Meditative practices* calm and concentrate the mind, make one aware of the afflictions of craving and ignorance, and focus the mind on the truth that liberates it from suffering. The meditative techniques of yoga or mindfulness help us recognize the impermanence of all feelings, and we learn to respond to them with neither greed nor aversion, neither hate nor love, hence averting the consequent suffering. Stilling the mind is vital because the activities of the mind entrap us in a seriously mistaken view of the self and the world. Obtaining inner harmony, which includes the cessation of discursive thought, is believed to be a necessary means to final liberation.

(C) The *practice of wisdom* achieved by reading and listening to Buddha texts, contemplating these truths, and attentively reflecting on the teachings, such as those on the cycle of rebirth, suffering, the impermanence of reality, no attachment, and no self, until these truths become self-evident to us. These activities are what we can call "scriptural practices."

As I have already emphasized, Buddhists maintain that these practices aim to enable us to develop the power of mindfulness and the mental and moral discipline required to liberate the impermanent self from craving and ignorance, thereby ending suffering. The result of these practices, when performed correctly, is spiritual awakening or enlightenment. They provide the means by which we can learn to free ourselves from desire or craving and thereby avoid rebirth. If each element of the path is pursued, we will develop all of the qualities necessary to achieve enlightenment.

Hence, let us end this survey of some key elements of a Buddhist worldview by adding one more core belief:

(11) Through the exercise of the right ethical, meditative, and scriptural practices, we can reach the stage when we experience the absence of suffering, an enduring self, and any enduring things at all, and be released from all attachments and cravings that cause suffering, and thus obtain enlightenment (*the cure of the problem of suffering*).

The "cure" is the account a worldview offers of the permanent solution or remedy to the fundamental problem (if any) facing human beings. The goal of Buddhism is to help people escape the cycle of reincarnation, find a cure for suffering, and attain enlightenment. As a Buddhist, one believes that such a state is real and attainable.

When our craving ceases, its effect, suffering, ceases, resulting in nirvana. But what is nirvana? From a Western perspective, it is easy to assume that it resembles the idea of paradise or heaven found in Christianity. However, we cannot enter nirvana since it is no place, and there are no enduring selves or persons who could enter it if it were a place. Still, nirvana is not annihilation, the absence of existence, or nothingness. It is rather what is most real and thus unchanging. It represents a state of liberation from suffering and impermanence now and forever, but with the twist that no one is there to experience this state.

CHALLENGES FOR BUDDHISM

What challenges does a Buddhist worldview like the one I have identified face? What would be its problematic aspects, at least from a Western intellectual perspective? Let me highlight some challenges without suggesting that Buddhism has no resources to deal with them satisfactorily.

Arguably, there are three alternatives about the universe's existence: (a) The universe has always existed. It has no beginning, so it has an infinite past. (b) The universe was caused to exist by something outside it; for instance, theists maintain that a God is the creator of the universe. (c) The universe came into existence from nothing without a cause. Secular worldviews are committed to this third option if secular individuals accept the Big Bang theory, as they typically do today. The Buddhist understanding of the first alternative is that this eternal universe is an oscillating universe. This view posits that the world is never definitively created or destroyed, but instead, the universe, through endless eons of time, undergoes cycles of creation, destruction, and recreation. However, the problem is that the Big Bang theory raises questions about the universe's eternal existence, suggesting that it had a beginning. The universe began to exist in the finite past. The Dalai Lama writes that he is told by the scientists with whom he has consulted that the "jury is still out as to whether the Big Bang is the absolute beginning of everything."[22] This might be true. If so, it is possible that what began to exist 13.8 billion years ago is only one part of a much larger multiverse. It is possible that our universe is just one member of a much grander and more immense multitude of universes: a multiverse. However, critics argue that it does not appear to resolve the conflict

---

[22] Dalai Lama, *The Universe in a Single Atom*, p. 90.

with science, as there is still an absolute beginning to any expanding multiverse at some point in the finite past.

Three challenges to a Buddhist understanding of karma related to the one we addressed previously – about how the causal link between the past, present, and future self could be sufficiently strong if no enduring self is reincarnated – are the following: The first problem is how to explain coherently the interaction between physical and karmic causation and due to this difficulty find any confirmation or indication that this kind of moral law exists. If the moral law of karma, in contrast to the natural laws that science has discovered, lacks temporary immediacy and depends for its karmic causation on whether the actions performed were intentional (see the previous discussion in Section "Suffering and Liberation"), then we cannot know which good and bad fortune is explained by karma. This makes it difficult to find any evidence or indications in this life or future lives that the law of karma exists, because it is then, as Burton points out, so flexible and imprecise that whatever happens can be made consistent with the theory of karma.[23]

The second problem is ethical. Karma is a principle of moral causality and cosmic justice, and rebirth enables karma to operate across multiple lifetimes. Those born into fortunate circumstances do so due to good deeds in prior lives, while unpleasant births result from past evil deeds. Good people can also experience bad things in this life because of the evil actions they committed in previous lives. Similarly, bad people can experience good things in this life due to their good actions in previous lives. Eventually, cosmic justice will be achieved because people will reap what they sow in time, and the moral balance will be set right over the course of their lifetimes. But the critics ask, how could such a system be fair and just? Is it not necessary that the recipient of pleasant or unpleasant karmic fruit is the same reincarnated person as the agent of the good or evil action? The no-self view blocks this possibility. In this regard, a Hindu understanding of karma and rebirth seems compatible with this moral intuition because it contains the belief that the same human mind or soul can successively animate different bodies in future lives.

The third difficulty has been referred to as "the karma management problem" by Robin Collins. William Hasker and Charles Taliaferro reference Collins and state the challenge in this way. Although they are radically different, the laws of nature and the law of karma must be

---

[23] Burton, *Buddhism*, p. 47.

closely related, for it is the former laws and the physical processes they guide that are to be disposed of in accordance with people's karma. But they maintain that it is "wholly implausible that two diverse systems of cosmic order such as this should arise from unrelated sources and come together accidentally; they must, then, have a common source."[24] So, there needs to be a "program" for coordinating physical and karmic causation, but where did it come from, or what is its source? This seems to be less of a problem for Hindu monotheism because these Hindus can understand the "program" as the intentional work of God. In such a worldview, there is a personal source of both the natural and the moral order. It is assumed that a God exists who desires that there be enduring selves and wishes to provide a stable physical and karmic order within which they could live and be reincarnated so that they, over many lifetimes, reap what they sow.

Let me end this section by formulating a further challenge for a Buddhist worldview but one that raises a more general issue about (a) what we, in the formation and regulation of our religious or secular worldview, should take to be reliable sources of knowledge and rational belief and (b) how we should handle a situation when these sources seem to contradict each other. Most people, presumably, believe that they have a self. They take for granted that they have an autonomous self that directs and coordinates their thoughts, emotions, feelings, and perceptions and that this self remains the same while their thoughts, emotions, feelings, and perceptions change. Why make such a presumption? Arguably, by introspection – reflection on one's own mental life – we come to believe that we have a self and a personal identity that makes us (as selves) different from people besides us. It is about looking within oneself, getting to know what it is like to be Mikael Stenmark, and being that particular self. That is to say, to see and identify oneself from a first-person perspective, not a third-person perspective. I can learn that I am angry by seeing my facial expression in the mirror (sensory knowledge), but I can also become aware that I am angry because I feel angry (introspective knowledge). Hence, introspection is a cognitive process that generates knowledge and rational beliefs about one's own mind and its mental states and not about affairs outside one's mind. Many philosophers in the West have even maintained that introspective knowledge is

[24] William Hasker and Charles Taliaferro (2023) "Afterlife." In *The Stanford Encyclopedia of Philosophy*, edited by Edward N. Zalta and Uri Nodelman, https://plato.stanford.edu/archives/spr2023/entries/afterlife/.

a more secure and immediate form of knowledge than sensory knowledge or knowledge obtained through perception.

Buddhists maintain that meditation is a reliable means of gaining knowledge and forming rational beliefs about reality and oneself. Suppose we develop meditative cognition through advanced yogic or other meditation techniques. In that case, we can come to know that karma and rebirth exist and that human beings are merely a causal series of impermanent, impersonal psychophysical elements. Meditation gives us access to dimensions of reality and ourselves that we cannot reach through any other source of knowledge, such as introspection, perception, reason, memory, and testimony. By perfecting our meditative cognitive abilities, we can learn that we do not have a self, even though introspection may suggest otherwise. The problem is that even if we think that meditation can generate knowledge and rational belief about reality or ourselves, why should we think that the beliefs that meditation generates are more reliable than those we obtain by employing introspection? Moreover, it appears that Hindu monotheists and other theists' use of meditative techniques does not yield the same results as Buddhist meditative techniques regarding the (non-)existence of the self. Hence, the situation is not such that we usually obtain the same beliefs through meditative cognition.

The problem of which source of knowledge should have priority over others is not merely one that religious people face. In his attempt to develop a secular alternative to what he conceives to be the dominant secular worldview of today among Western intellectuals, scientific naturalism (or what I, in Chapter 7, call "scientism" and "a scientistic worldview"), Thomas Nagel maintains that our understanding of the world must include not merely data about the physical world that science delivers but also, for instance, data about conscious minds who have access to evident truth in ethics. However, the problem for Nagel is not merely that some people deny that we should accept other reliable sources of knowledge and rational belief besides science but that moral realism (the natural conviction that our moral judgments are true or false independent of our beliefs) is undermined by science, more exactly, by evolutionary biology. He agrees with Sharon Street that there is, on this point, a conflict between his moral intuition and science. However, instead of following Street and treating science as the source of knowledge that has priority over the moral sense, thus replacing moral realism with moral constructivism (the view that it is we as a society of rational people who decide what is morally right or wrong), he draws the opposite conclusion. "Since moral realism is true, [Nagel maintains that] a Darwinian account of the motives underlying moral judgment must be false, in spite of the scientific consensus in its favor."[25]

In both cases, we face two epistemic problems. One problem is determining which sources of knowledge and reasonable belief we should consider reliable (i.e., those that generate more true than false beliefs). The second is that if these sources generate conflicting beliefs, we also face the difficulty of determining which sources are the most reliable. We face profound philosophical issues in our attempt to develop and maintain an intellectually deliberated worldview, issues that science cannot solve.

[25] Thomas Nagel, *Mind and Cosmos*. Oxford University Press, 2012, p. 105.

5

A Spiritual Worldview

The religious worldview I will try to rationally reconstruct in the chapter lacks a generally accepted label. Specialists have referred to it as "Western esotericism," "New Age," or "New Age spirituality."[1] However, we rarely find people today who identify as New Agers. The label "New Age," so common during the 1980s to 1990s, signals a vision of an imminent transformation of a broken society into a united, enlightened new society, the Aquarian Age (a new astrological age). This conviction is deemphasized today, giving way to a vision of personal spiritual transformation, which may or may not lead to a new spiritual awakening that permeates the entire human population in the future.

Today, many practitioners of this outlook on life and reality would rather describe themselves as "spiritual but not religious" and view themselves as embracing a spiritual, rather than a religious, worldview. The increasing popularity of this phrase has even given rise to the acronym SBNR. The SBNRs would maintain these things, although they tend to believe in the divine or our inner divinity and that we have an inborn capacity to know the divine or the deeper spiritual realities of the cosmos. I will, for this reason, often use the term "spirituality" when referring to this worldview, but also add, now and then, the qualifier "new" to spirituality to remind the reader that in the "old" view, spirituality was (and still is) seen as an essential part of traditional religions. However, most of the time, I will talk about the spiritual worldview and use the acronym to refer to its practitioners.

---

[1] Wouter J. Hanegraaff, *Western Esotericism*. Bloomsbury, 2013, pp. 1–3.

As I have already indicated, the common tendency to avoid "religion" in favor of "spirituality" reflects and facilitates many who hold this worldview. The assumption is that religion is narrow-minded or dogmatic, expressing a deep-rooted faith in authority and tradition, and requiring its practitioners to belong to an organized community. In contrast, the new spirituality is none of these things. The basic idea is that people are free to search for the spiritual within themselves, and there is no particular group to which one has to belong and swear allegiance. Individuals are at liberty to follow their convictions in choosing what works for them to combine elements of belief and practice taken from different spiritual sources without committing themselves to any single community to the exclusion of others.

The SBNRs are "not religious" in the sense that they want to disassociate themselves from the authoritative expressions of organized religion. However, the way I have defined a religious worldview and the examples we have studied so far, nothing intrinsic to them makes them dogmatic, exclusivist, or necessarily institutionalized entities. Moreover, we would find people who, for instance, believe in God or, more precisely, embrace the theistic worldview, but rarely attend religious services and perhaps are merely formal members of religious institutions. For this reason, I will *not* include in my SBNR category people who no longer see organized religion as the best space for spiritual life but who still affirm a theistic conception of God, for instance, those Christians who say that they "love Jesus but not the church."[2] This is of great importance because, in a recent survey in the US, more than 90 percent of SBNRs affirm a belief in some form of God,[3] although it is unclear how many of them embrace the pantheistic conception of God that I will associate with the new spirituality (more on this topic in Section "The Divine Self and Pantheism"). The numbers may differ in Europe, but it is essential to keep in mind that I employ a restricted use of the category SBNR. Moreover, I will classify the new spirituality as a religious worldview since it affirms the existence of a transcendent, divine, or spiritual dimension of reality and its importance for how we understand and live our lives (see Chapter 2).

The SBNRs are "spiritual" in the sense that they, in the words of George D. Chryssides, believe:

---

[2] J. Aaron Simmons, "Religious, but Not Spiritual: A Constructive Proposal," *Religions*, 2021, 12/6, p. 433.

[3] The Pew Religious Forum, "Religious Landscape Study: The Spiritual but Not Religious," www.pewresearch.org/religion/religious-landscape-study/religious-denomination/spiritual-but-not-religious/#beliefs-and-practices.

that there is something (or maybe Someone) that exists beyond the empirical realm – whether it is God, Brahman, buddhas and bodhisattvas, or some kinds of spiritual beings such as Ascended Masters or devas. Additionally, spirituality requires more than simple belief in the existence of such beings: in some sense they are capable of being experienced, and interact with human beings, whether by being "channelled," or through the practitioner's personal experience.[4]

This spirituality manifests itself in various ritual acts, including prayers, meditations, spell-castings, and Tarot readings. Moreover, it is, as one of its advocates, Marilyn Ferguson, claims, meant to be a new spirituality in the sense that it relies on direct knowledge, experience, and human wholeness, a spirituality that emphasizes meditation, healing, and recognition of one's inner divine nature, and not like the old spirituality stresses tradition, authority, faith, ritual, and, we should add, belief in an external God.[5]

Hence, this new form of spirituality does not reject the existence of divine reality as secular worldviews do. Instead, the spiritual worldview is deliberately set up as an alternative to various kinds of naturalism, rather than merely as an alternative to traditional religions. The last point is essential because the practitioners of the new spirituality are critical of naturalism, although they seldom use that terminology themselves. Most of the time, the opposed secular worldview is called atheism, materialism, or reductionism. Deepak Chopra rejects the "rude atheism," whose proponents deride religion as superstition and, in particular, reject the inner spiritual world, which he believes is the deeper source of religion. The physical world is all that exists for scientific atheists. But, he asks, what is reality? "Is it the results of natural laws rigorously operating through cause and effect, or is it something else? ... Either reality is bounded by the visible universe, or it isn't."[6] Chopra takes the spiritual worldview to entail a rejection of the idea that the physical world is all that exists, affirming instead that there is an unseen spiritual reality that is the source of all visible things. The "superstition of materialism" is a danger we face today, and the new spirituality provides an alternative. Hence, the spiritual worldview entails as much a rejection of secular worldviews as of the worldviews of traditional, institutionalized religions.

---

[4] George D. Chryssides, "Defining the New Age." In *Handbook of New Age*, edited by James Lewis and Daren Kemp. Brill, 2007, p. 14.
[5] Marilyn Ferguson, *The Aquarian Conspiracy*. Penguin, 2009.
[6] Deepak Chopra and Leonard Mlodinow, *War of the Worldviews*. Three Rivers Press, 2012, pp. 9–10.

What then are the central beliefs of the new spirituality? Philosophers have largely neglected this emerging worldview; therefore, in identifying some of the core elements of the new spirituality, I will draw on the work of scholars of religion who are anthropologists, historians, and sociologists. Identifying core or central beliefs is also challenging for the reason (I gave earlier) that individuals are much at liberty to follow their convictions in choosing what they like on the spiritual "smorgasbord," so they can combine elements of belief and practice taken from different sources. If it is possible to rationally reconstruct the other worldviews in a manner different from how I do in this study, it is certainly so regarding the new spirituality. Still, I think certain themes or features are frequently present in the new spirituality literature or the writings found on the mind–body–spirit shelves of bookshops. If we focus on these, we can develop an interesting worldview that differs significantly from the others surveyed in this book.

INDIVIDUALISM, SELF-TRANSFORMATION, AND TRANS-LIFE PROGRESSION

I will take individualism to be a central feature of the new spirituality. We can say that *individualism* is an outlook on life that stresses human independence or freedom and the importance of individual self-reliance, self-fulfillment, and liberty. You, yourself, make the decisions and have to find your life satisfying. It is not a group, a community, an organization, or an institution that should decide on your behalf. Instead, our personal choice should be at the center of concern. A core value is self-actualization. In this sense, the spiritual worldview contains a typically contemporary Western conception of human life and individual freedom. The strong commitment to individualism, to some extent, explains why there is no emphasis in this worldview on belonging to an organized religious group or community. Advocates of the new spirituality tend to be "religious nones" (see Chapter 2), rejecting institutional religion, even though many meet in small, special-interest groups or participate in mind–body–spirit fairs and festivals. That is not to say that the other worldviews cannot embrace individualism; they can, and often do, certainly in the West. However, it is not one of their defining features in the way it is for the spiritual worldview. In my terminology, individualism constitutes a core claim of the spiritual worldview, whereas it is an extension claim of, for instance, a theistic worldview.

Collectivism, as I will understand it in this context, is an outlook on life that emphasizes the desirability of living life in accordance with external expectations, roles, and duties. We should think of ourselves as primarily belonging to an established or a given – divine, natural, or social – order, and we are essentially members of that order (system, tradition, community, or family). Individualism entails the rejection of such an emphasis on the given order or the group above the individual. Instead of living life primarily according to external expectations, we should live it essentially in accordance with our individual goals and desires. Central to Charles Taylor's account of modernity, in which divinely guaranteed truth gives way to the personal and human, is what he calls "the massive subjective turn of modern culture, a new form of inwardness, in which we come to think of ourselves as beings with inner depths."[7] The good life will then not be lived according to external expectations but consists of living one's life in the way one finds fulfilling. The aim is not primarily to become what others want one to be but to become who I truly am.[8] Whether we refer to this feature of modern Western culture as the subjective turn or individualism does not matter for my purpose in this study.

Within the spiritual worldview, there is thus a strong emphasis on the individual spiritual development and the spiritual authority of the self. We are encouraged to pursue our own chosen spiritual path or explore a plurality of spiritual paths to become aware of our inner divinity, and there is an unseen spiritual reality that is the source of all visible things. This does not mean we are equally adept at discovering spiritual truths, practicing spiritual techniques correctly, and achieving human wholeness. Some people have come further on the path to enlightenment and human fulfillment than others, and it would be wise for us to listen and learn from them. However, the idea is that religious authority is not given *ex officio* but must be earned in practice and thus granted by other SBNRs, rather than being conferred by some traditional or divine authority.

Individualism presupposes, of course, that persons really exist and are unique and intrinsically valuable features of the world. There is only one of me and one of you. Hence, I will argue that the spiritual worldview entails a denial of one essential feature of Buddhism: that no self is

---

[7] Charles Taylor, *The Ethics of Authenticity*. Harvard University Press, 1991, p. 26.
[8] See also Paul Heelas and Linda Woodhead, *The Spiritual Revolution: Why Religion Is Giving Way to Spirituality*. Blackwell, 2005, pp. 2–5.

the subject of our mental states, which have an individual identity over and above the particular, fleeting mental states. That is to say, the new spirituality rejects the no-self view and embraces the *enduring self-view*. There is something of you and me – our personalities – that provides our continued identity in this life and remains in the new forms we take in future reincarnated lives. The self or our personality is real. As Wouter J. Hanegraaff points out, the individualism of the new spirituality, with its values of autonomy and self-determinacy, is "hardly congenial to ideas of spiritual self-annihilation which suggest that the soul is like a drop of water that should aspire to be 'swallowed up' in the ocean of the One."[9]

A matter of great concern in this worldview is the shortcomings in our lives. The central idea is that we are living well below our optimal potential, but there are ways to fulfill our true potential and overcome the obstacles in our lives. *Self-improvement, self-transformation*, or *individual empowerment* is central to the new spirituality. Physical and spiritual healing, or "balancing one's energies," is considered a more immediate concern than understanding the structures of reality that make these forms of healing and well-being possible. The idea is that trapped or blocked energies will manifest in mental and bodily illness and spiritual disorder. The aim is to unblock energy, allowing it to flow more freely and thereby promoting human well-being and wholeness. Various means have been developed to achieve this goal, including meditation, yoga, Reiki, mindfulness, channeling spirits, crystals, prayers, spell-casting, Tarot readings, and alternative medicine.

For example, *Reiki* is an energy healing technique that promotes relaxation and reduces stress and anxiety through gentle touch. Reiki practitioners use their hands to channel energy into the body, enhancing the flow and balance of energy to support healing. It derives its meaning from the Japanese words *rei*, meaning "universal," and *ki*, which refers to the vital life force energy that flows through all living things. The idea is that an unseen life force flows through us, causing us to be alive. If one's life force energy is low, we are more likely to get sick or feel stressed; if it is high, one is more capable of being happy and healthy.

Channeling is the idea that we, or at least some of us, can enter a meditative or trance-like state to convey messages from sources other than our usual selves – from higher realms, from spirits, disincarnated higher selves, or the divine consciousness that infuses everything in the cosmos. According to Sanaya Roman and Duane Packer:

---

[9] Hanegraaff, *Western Esotericism*, p. 115.

channeling is a powerful means of spiritual unfoldment and conscious trans-formation. As you channel you build a bridge to the higher realms – a loving, caring, purposeful collective higher consciousness that has been called God, the All-That-Is, or the Universal Mind .... Channeling involves consciously shifting your mind and mental space in order to achieve an expanded state of conscious-ness that is called a "trance."[10]

Channeling is intertwined with the belief in reincarnation. As Hanegraaff and Hammer have pointed out, *reincarnation* has become one of the most widely held and prevalent beliefs in New Age milieus and is profoundly important for self-improvement.[11] The conviction is that each of us is on a journey of spiritual development, in which our true, inner self evolves as we reincarnate repeatedly over the course of many lives. It is part of our spiritual progression toward realizing our divinity.

Just like in the Buddhist worldview, the belief is that reincarnation ensures cosmic justice, and karma is the law of cause and effect that assures cosmic balance. Buddhists, however, maintain that rebirth is not a good thing and that our aim should be to escape the endless cycle of rebirth and the suffering it generates. In contrast, the new spirituality views karma and reincarnation as something attractive. Karma is a spiri-tual or moral law that allows us to progress from one life to the next and improve ourselves to fulfill our true potential. If we live sufficiently good lives, our next life will contain enough positive consequences to make it desirable. If we recognize that we evolve over many lifetimes, we can continually improve as we progress. There can be steady progress of our true, higher self through successive lives.

In Buddhism (and Hinduism), reincarnation is an automatic process. The law of karma connects a karmic cause to a karmic effect, and "you" and "I," as impermanent selves, have no say in what will happen once we are dead. The law of karma determines what our embodiment will be in subsequent lives. We can also find this understanding of rebirth in the new spirituality, but what is reincarnated is our enduring or higher self, since SBNRs reject the no-self view of Buddhism. According to this view, channeling opens a window for us to understand why we are reborn in the way we are.

---

[10] Sanaya Roman and Duane Packer, *Opening to Channel: How to Connect with Your Guide.* Kramer Inc, 1987, p. 13.

[11] Hanegraaff, *Western Esotericism*, p. 135, and Olav Hammer, "The New Age." In *The Cambridge Handbook of Western Mysticism and Esoterism*, edited by Glen Alexander Magee. Cambridge University Press, 2016, p. 35.

However, we can also find those who see the process of reincarnation as a voluntary rather than automatic process. They believe the higher self can choose the body and circumstances into which it will be born. In this way, reincarnation can be used as a process through which we can learn new lessons and thus advance our spiritual transformation and growth.[12] One expression of this idea can be found in the writing of Louise L. Hay. She writes: "Each one of us decides to incarnate upon this planet at a particular point in time and space. We have chosen to come here to learn a particular lesson that will advance us upon our spiritual, evolutionary pathway."[13] The idea is that in the period between death and the next rebirth, our higher self evaluates what we have achieved in our previous life and what kinds of experiences we need to further our spiritual growth and development.

Hammer identifies three other ideas of how reincarnation is understood as a way to fulfill our true potential as persons. He writes, "Firstly, we all are said to have a prehistory that is normally hidden to us, but which can be unveiled by psychically gifted individuals. Secondly, this hidden prehistory gives coherence and meaning to facts about our present life histories. A third, latent element … [is that] knowledge of our past lives is not reserved for an elite of psychics, but can potentially be accessed by us all."[14]

Past life therapy, also known as past life regression, is a frequently used and accepted practice in the new spirituality. It is a technique that attempts to use hypnosis to recover memories typically hidden from us from previous lives. This hidden prehistory can help us understand who we are in this life and to overcome mental illness and spiritual disorders. Through hypnosis, the spiritual therapist can take us back in time (regression) to our infancy and, in particular, to periods before we were born with our current body, but when our higher selves were embodied in other bodies in past lives. The belief is that various mental and spiritual disorders can be treated by addressing the events we went through before we were born in this life. The third idea is that even if some people might be more gifted in these spiritual matters than others, we can all have past life experiences. We can be taught the techniques to access the prehistory usually hidden from us. Ted Andrews, for instance,

[12] Wouter J. Hanegraaff, *New Age Religion and Western Culture*. SUNY Press, 1996, p. 266.
[13] Louise L. Hay, *You Can Heal Your Life*. Hay House, 2005, p. 4.
[14] Olav Hammer, *Claiming Knowledge*. Brill, 2003, pp. 482–483.

offers a do-it-yourself manual describing ways to access past life memories without relying on regression therapists.[15]

We can summarize these aspects of the spiritual worldview in terms of several core beliefs. The first two are as follows:

(1) Our individual preferences and needs should be at the center of concern in developing what we find to be an adequate spiritual worldview (*spiritual individualism*).

(2) We are living well below our optimal potential, but we can improve and transform ourselves to fulfill the potential of our true inner self and experience unity with the cosmos if we learn to master certain spiritual techniques, such as meditation, yoga, Reiki, and mindfulness (*self-transformation*).

It is perhaps possible to hold only the spiritual-individualist thesis and the self-transformation thesis and still be an SBNR or adherent to a spiritual worldview of some sort. However, one of its crucial elements in my rational reconstruction is missing: Our spiritual journey and time for progress are not restricted to this life only but must be seen within a large cosmic framework. The conviction is that we can improve ourselves over many lifetimes. Our spiritual progress is neither limited to nor starts with our present physical embodiment. Hence, another core belief is as follows:

(3) Our selves are engaged in subsequent spiritual development in this life and many afterlives, and throughout this process, we can learn from past lives, allowing for steady progress of our true, higher self (*trans-life progression*).

These ideas of spiritual individualism, self-transformation, and trans-life progression are interconnected with a particular understanding of who we are and our relationship to the cosmos or the divine.

THE DIVINE SELF AND PANTHEISM

Even if practitioners of the spiritual worldview embrace individualism as a core idea, they also believe that we are part of the divine; we can find the divine within ourselves. Not just we, but everything is infused with the divine. In much of the new spiritual thought, there is a belief

---

[15] Ted Andrews, *How to Uncover Your Past Lives*. Llewellyn, 2006.

in something greater than the individual self, which is of a spiritual nature. Shirley MacLaine, for example, speaks of the "Divine spark" we can find in us as a part of God, a part of the "universal energy of which the Higher Self is a part [that] has always existed".[16] She takes the basic message of the new spirituality to be as follows: "Begin with self; recognize the God within, and the result will be the recognition, with tolerance and love, that everyone else possesses God within as well. In other words, we are each part of God experiencing the adventure of life."[17] The divine imbues the whole universe, including human beings themselves.

Our self is, of course, a small part of God, but since it is also God, it provides us with direct access to the divine. Therefore, the self becomes of great importance because:

self-realization is God-realization. Knowing more of your Higher Self really means knowing more of God. That inner knowledge is radiant with life, light and love ... When I go within I look for communication and guidance ... I like to ask questions, check my perceptions as to my opinions, my progress ... So when we go within and come into alignment with our spiritual power, we come into connection with that spark of Divinity ... which I call the Higher Self. Some call it the Divine Oversoul, the Divine Center, the God within, the personal interface with God ... whatever one calls it, it is the personalization of the God Source within us. When I first made contact with my Higher Self I was aware that I could, from then on, better touch my purpose on Earth and have it fit in with everyone else's.[18]

Although I will mainly use the terms "God" or the "divine" to describe this feature of the spiritual worldview, it is important to realize – as MacLaine acknowledges – that some SBNRs instead talks about "Infinite Spirit," "Ultimate Reality," "Mind," "Consciousness," "a Higher Self," "the Source," "Gaia," "Spiritual Energy," or "the Life Force."

Hence, according to the spiritual worldview, the divine is located within the self – as one's higher self – but the divine is more than the self since everything that exists (or the universe) is infused with the divine. Therefore, we, as well as all nature around us, are part of the divine. This understanding of God is called *pantheism*. Typically, it is defined as the view that God is identical to the world/nature/universe. *Theists* believe that God created the universe and, therefore, is separate from it

---

[16] Shirley MacLaine, *Going Within*. Bantam Books, 1990, p. 82.
[17] MacLaine, *Going Within*, p. 108.
[18] Ibid., pp. 82–83.

in the sense that God's existence does not in any way depend on the universe's existence. *Panentheists* believe that the universe is a part of God, so God is more than the universe, but whose existence still, in a significant way, depends on the universe's fate. *Pantheists*, however, believe that God is the universe and nothing beyond the universe, so God's fate is entirely intertwined with the universe's fate. Both panentheists and pantheists agree that everything is a part of God, but the latter (but not the former) deny that God is more than the universe.

We can find advocates of the new spirituality that would embrace panentheism, but I will take pantheism as the default position because pantheistic themes are predominant in the new spirituality. In fact, I would argue that they often hold a narrower form of pantheism than the one I have described earlier. People like MacLaine seem to be suggesting that everything is part of God, but not thereby implying that God is identical to everything that exists. Instead, God is akin to the world's soul, a spiritual energy, or a life force that we can find within ourselves and in everything else. It is like a stream of water that runs through everything, but there are more things in the world than this stream. So, the higher self is the divine part of us, but our selves include more than that part. When we fail to connect with our higher self, we fail to find the divine within, but we can still be in contact with other parts of the self. Perhaps we can say that the divine resides in the deeper layers of the self and, consequently, not in the shallow layers of the self. We as selves are composed of both divine and non-divine parts or properties, and so is the rest of nature or the universe as a whole. The universe consists of more things than the divine, but this stream of consciousness is still present in all these things. Everything is infused with but not identical to the divine. According to this restricted form of pantheism, God is less than the totality of the universe, but still, the universe is infused with divine consciousness. From now on, this specific understanding will be what I have in mind when I speak about pantheism.

Hence, two other core beliefs of the new spirituality are as follows:

(4) God is the world soul we find in us and everything else, so the world is infused with divine consciousness, but nothing of God exists beyond or outside this world (*pantheism*).

(5) We are divine, or the higher self is the divine part of us (*the divine self-view*).

It also follows from this cosmology that the universe is not ultimately a vast collection of physical particles without inherent meaning or value, as in naturalistic worldviews. Instead, the universe is a great, interconnected web of not merely matter but also meaning and purpose. We could say that the cosmos exhibits both a natural and teleological–axiological order. This is so since the underlying substance of the cosmos is not (merely or primarily) matter but something identifiable as consciousness or spiritual energy. For example, Chopra believes that "Spirituality holds that consciousness is basic to creation. It has always existed, and the visible universe unfolds as a display of what consciousness wants to explore. ... To arrive at DNA, life on Earth, and the human mind, the universe was self-aware and could understand what it was doing."[19] According to the spiritual worldview, there is an invisible and inner spiritual or divine dimension that pervades all life, nature, and the cosmos.

Chopra embraces a personal conception of pantheism, as do many other SBNRs; that is to say, they believe it is appropriate to understand the divine as some kind of immanent self-awareness. We could say that they embrace *personal pantheism* in the sense that they believe that God or the divine is conscious or mind-like, or personal or person-like, or at least has properties similar to a person. A self-conscious being or spirit is someone aware of themselves *as themselves*. It is manifest to them that they are the object of awareness. They have a first-person perspective on life. The idea is that the unseen spiritual reality possesses certain important qualities that we associate with ourselves as persons, or qualities that are at least similar to those.

However, not all SBNRs are prepared to go that far. They are content to say that the divine is a part of the cosmos and us, is conscious (i.e., it experiences things or is a stream of experiences), but not self-conscious (i.e., being aware that it has a self that is the subject of these experiences). We could say that the latter group embraces *impersonal pantheism*. They maintain that God or the divine is not personal but a teleological, beneficial, and conscious force, power, or energy infused in everyone and everything. Therefore, it cannot be said to be self-aware other than in a metaphorical sense. In sociological terminology, they believe in "higher powers" rather than in a personal divine reality. These higher powers can be referred to as "divine" due to their creative, beneficial, and teleological properties. In other words, besides physical powers

---

[19] Chopra and Mlodinow, *War of the Worldviews*, pp. 35–36.

and laws (which science can discover), there are also spiritual powers and laws in the universe (which we can access through the deep layers of the self). The self or our consciousness provides a window into aspects of reality that science cannot discover.

On either of the two construals of pantheism, it remains true that we contain a spark of this divine consciousness within us, a resource that we can tap into to understand who we truly are and what ultimately exists. The human being is thus not only a material body with a mind (or a self-conscious material being) but also contains a spiritual element. Humans are mind–body–spirit creatures. The spirit is the divine part of us, which we all have, whether or not we are aware of it. This contrasts with the theistic worldview in which nothing in us or nature is divine, but all of nature, including us, is taken to be the creation of the divine and to be creatures who depend on God for their continued existence.

Some SBNRs have expressed this pantheistic idea in terms of the biochemist James Lovelock's Gaia hypothesis, which posits that the Earth acts like a single living organism.[20] The Earth, taken as a whole, is assumed to be a complex system that functions according to the same principles of self-organization found in lower levels of complexity in living things in nature.[21] If so, it is not essentially different from an organism. The proponents of the spiritual worldview expand Lovelock's Gaia hypothesis to include the idea that the Earth has consciousness and intelligence, and even possesses some form of self-awareness. However, the idea of the Earth as a conscious, living organism raises the question of whether certain other planets in our solar system or beyond also consist of centers of consciousness and intelligence. If the idea is to be understood as a spiritual expansion of the Gaia hypothesis, the answer must be that it is possible. However, a requirement is the previous development of life on these planets because consciousness is a novel property that emerges from the lower levels of biological organisms. In the extended Gaia hypothesis, consciousness is assumed to reach beyond human organisms to the planet itself. However, this will result in *emergent pantheism*. Cosmos, particularly in locations such as Earth, is slowly awakening and becoming conscious of itself. One day, far in the future, the universe as a whole will evolve some kind of consciousness, even self-awareness.

[20] Hanegraaff, *New Age Religion and Western Culture*, pp. 155–158.
[21] James Lovelock, *Gaia: A New Look at Life on Earth*. Oxford University Press, 1987.

The problem with this rational reconstruction of the spiritual world-view is that it will not be true (yet) that everything that exists or the cosmos is infused with the divine. Hence, it is better to interpret this idea that everything is infused with the divine and the belief that divine consciousness is fundamental to creation within the framework of a panpsychistic ontology. *Panpsychism* is the philosophical theory that consciousness did not evolve to meet the survival needs of the organism, nor did it emerge when brains became sufficiently complex. Instead, since the beginning of the universe, consciousness has been inherent in everything that exists, but in various degrees.[22] All natural objects have *parts* with both physical and mental properties, or we could say that everything in nature has both physical and mental poles. Mind or consciousness is, in this view, a basic building block of nature or the universe. Is *animism*, the oldest perhaps of all forms of religion, also a part of panpsychistic spirituality? It is not because animists typically reject the claim that all things are living and that the universe as a whole is a living being. Instead, the animists take particular features of the natural world as endowed with personhood or some form of interiority, often having their own social lives and communities akin to those of human beings.[23] We must also take into account that panpsychism as such is not an expression of a religious view of the world; secular people can also embrace it. However, all of its adherents believe that there is much more consciousness or some kind of experience, no matter how basic, in the world than most Westerners and contemporary philosophers today tend to think there is. It is attractive to some secular thinkers (and some religious thinkers as well) because, if true, it can offer a way out of the reductionism of scientific naturalism while simultaneously avoiding dualism.

However, if one adds to panpsychism the idea that Chopra expressed – that the universe was self-aware from the beginning, understands, and causes the development of life and can provide people with a way to spiritual well-being – it becomes a religious worldview. In the new spirituality, an immanent spiritual reality is the source of all visible things. Alternatively, as in impersonal pantheism, the belief is that this spiritual energy or life force, literally speaking, cannot be considered personal or

---

[22] Philip Goff, William Seager, and Sean Allen-Hermanson (2022) "Panpsychism." In *The Stanford Encyclopedia of Philosophy*, edited by Edward N. Zalta, https://plato.stanford.edu/archives/sum2022/entries/panpsychism/.

[23] Tiddy Smith, "Animism." In *Internet Encyclopedia of Philosophy*, https://iep.utm.edu/animism/.

possess self-awareness. Still, it pervades all lives and can be harnessed to heal, protect, and repair relationships and help people realize their true potential. The divine life force provides us with the means for spiritual transformation and enlightenment. Moreover, this spiritual energy or life force was a decisive mental cause that, together with the physical causes, formed the natural world as we find it today. Hence, SBNRs can see the world as a (self-)creation if they believe the universe was already self-aware from the beginning. The present form of the universe is an intentional but purely immanent or internal outcome of the divine, and it is not, as theists take it to be, an intentional but transcendental or external outcome of the divine. But nor is the world as we find it, as advocates of secular worldviews typically believe, an immanent but unintentional outcome of purely physical stuff – and thus no creation. Instead, the SBNRs maintain that consciousness underlies everything in our world. It is the unseen (personal or impersonal) force that directs evolution on Earth and at other places in the universe where life has evolved. As Chopra points out, "Consciousness-directed evolution isn't the same as invoking a creator God. Instead, it introduces a property inherent in the cosmos: self-awareness."[24] Hence, another core belief in the spiritual worldview is as follows:

(6) Consciousness infuses everything in our world; it is the immaterial, good, and purely immanent force – whether personal or impersonal – that directs evolution on Earth and elsewhere in the universe where life has evolved; so, it is not surprising that life and self-conscious beings emerge in the cosmos (*divine-immanent teleological evolution*).

Belief in beings who inhabit the realm between the divine and the mundane is also significant for large groups of advocates of the new spirituality. These entities are known by various names, including gods and goddesses, angels, spirits, or ascended masters. For instance, the ascended masters once lived as normal human beings but have learned their karmic lessons and raised their consciousness to the point where they now live permanently in a higher dimension. Examples of ascended masters include Buddha, Vishnu, Jesus, Mother Mary, and Muhammad. Each ascended master has completed many lifetimes of experience and has undergone a series of spiritual transformations or rebirths. These masters can assist us in our ascension and increase our awareness of the spiritual forces that permeate the universe. (In this

[24] Chopra, *War of the Worldviews*, p. 55.

way, they resemble the Bodhisattvas' role within a Buddhist world-view.) The ascended masters are not the only inhabitants of this super-natural realm; there are also gods, goddesses, angels, and spirits that populate this realm of reality. We can interact with all these beings through channeling and meditation.

Now, a challenge we face when rationally reconstructing the new spirituality is that many SBNRs do not at all speak about gods, god-desses, angels, spirits, and Ascended Masters, but merely about the God within, the world soul, the divine spark in everything, the divine life force, or the divine consciousness inherent in the cosmos. There seem to be two viable options for us here. First, we can say that belief in super-natural beings in the universe is not a core claim of the spiritual world-view but a frequently made extension claim. If so, one could still count as an adherent to the new spirituality even if one disbelieves in the exis-tence of these supernatural beings. The other alternative is that we could understand these personal supernatural beings in terms of the account of pantheism that I previously developed. Both are fine, but I will suggest how the second alternative could be stated coherently.

If (a) a divine stream of consciousness is present in all things, (b) we contain a spark of this divine consciousness within us, and (c) the higher self of us reincarnates, then (d) there will always be possible for us to encounter other higher selves that are parts of the larger divine stream of consciousness. This ontology could also be compatible with impersonal pantheism since, in this life or in lives to come, we are local streams of self-consciousness within the larger stream of (impersonal) divine con-sciousness. Hence, these higher selves have come much further in their spiritual transformation than we have, whom some practitioners of the new spirituality choose to call gods/goddesses, angels, spirits, or ascended masters. Other advocates of the spiritual worldview avoid such personal identifications of supernatural beings in the universe, but both groups can accept the same basic ontological structure of reality.

THE EPISTEMOLOGY OF THE NEW SPIRITUALITY

As we have seen earlier, a core conviction in the new spirituality is that whether we know it or not, the divine power of the cosmos is not just available to us; it is in us. Such anthropology has important implications for epistemology. The divine-self view opens up new possibilities for us to access the deeper spiritual dimension of reality. Chopra maintains that "beyond the reach of the five senses lies an invisible realm of infinite possibility, and the key to unfolding its potential is consciousness. Go within, the sages and seers declared, and you will find the true source of everything."[25] We should not begin our spiritual quest by considering external states of affairs and physical experiences, but rather with inner wisdom and access to unbounded awareness. The higher self can be the uninterrupted link between the encompassing cosmic consciousness and us. The very nature of our souls, our divinity, allows us direct access to the divine stream of consciousness, which is infused with everything.

Hence, we need neither the testimony of others (provided by prophets, sages, seers, or official religious authorities) nor divine revelations (like the Bible or the Quran) to know that there is an unseen spiritual reality that is the source of all visible things. That is not to say that SBNRs reject that people can have spiritual experiences, revelations, and visions from which we can all benefit. Nor do they deny that some prophets, sages, and seers have come much further on the path to self-transformation than we have, so it would be wise to listen to what they say. Rather, religious testimony and revelation are unnecessary for obtaining religious belief or knowledge. What is crucial is that we understand that we can go within and find the essential spiritual truths about reality by connecting with the divine spark within. Knowing more of one's higher self really means knowing more of God. A core belief in the new spirituality is that humans have an inborn capacity to know the divine. Let us call this epistemic capacity or process "higher consciousness." Hence,

(7) Since the higher self is the divine part of us, it provides a resource we can tap into or a cognitive capacity to activate to understand who we truly are and what ultimately exists (*higher conscious cognition*).

The self is the point of entry to the deeper spiritual world that secular people often fail to see, or whose nature traditional religious individuals (to varying degrees) have misunderstood. For this reason, the new spirituality emphasizes the human mind and its latent potential.

So, what is the difference between introspection and higher conscious cognition? Both seem to be processes that happen exclusively in our minds. *Introspection* is the mind-internal mental process by which an individual forms beliefs and obtains knowledge about their own mental state. For example, I can learn that I am angry by seeing my facial expression in the mirror, but I can also become aware that I am angry

---

[25] Ibid., p. 4.

because I feel angry. Similarly, we might form a belief that a group of people is sad or happy by perceiving their behavior. However, we typically do not have to observe our behavior to determine whether we are sad or happy. Instead, we make this determination by introspecting. Through introspection, I also know that I am now thinking about some of the key features of the new spirituality. Perception and introspection are two different sources of belief and knowledge. The term "introspection" literally means "looking within," so what is the difference between this form of looking within and the one advocated within the new spirituality? Perhaps we can define *higher conscious cognition* as the mind-internal process by which someone can form beliefs and obtain knowledge about the spiritual world, or understand who they truly are and what ultimately exists.

One difference between it and introspection is that we cannot fail (other than through dysfunction or illness, such as dementia) to obtain beliefs and, if successful, even knowledge through introspection. In contrast, the cognitive process of higher consciousness remains a hidden potential within us, yet many of us are unaware of and unable to access it. In this regard, our higher consciousness is akin to our unconsciousness, comprising those thoughts and feelings (typically of past events and memories) that exist in the mind, influencing our behavior, although we are often unaware of them. Humans cannot examine these processes and their outcomes because they occur underneath our conscious awareness. Therefore, the unconscious is not available for introspection. However, researchers have hypothesized that the unconscious exists and affects human thought and behavior. Sigmund Freud famously claimed that we could access it through psychoanalytic therapy. Someone else, the psychoanalyst, can use various techniques (dream interpretation, free association, and so on) to gain insight into these processes that occur underneath our conscious awareness and affect our behavior. The SBNRs maintain that spiritual therapists can access our unconsciousness and help us become aware of hidden meanings or patterns in what we do or say that may contribute to our problems.[26] Moreover, in past-life therapy, these therapists can use hypnosis to recover memories typically hidden from us from previous lives. This hidden prehistory can help us understand who we are in this life and to overcome mental illness and spiritual disorders.

---

[26] They frequently talk about the subconscious instead. However, within psychology, as far as I understand, the subconscious is the part of the mind that is not currently of focal awareness.

However, the core idea in the epistemology of the new spirituality is that, if we learn how to do so, we – all of us – can access the deeper layers of reality by going within or connecting with our higher self. MacLaine explains that when she meditates, she allows her higher self to reveal itself to her. Since it is our personalized reflection of the divine spark, higher self-realization becomes God realization: "Knowing more of your Higher Self really means knowing more of God."[27]

Hence, another significant difference between introspection and higher conscious cognition is that the former can merely reveal something about what is going on in our inner world, which occurs exclusively in our minds. The second, however, can also reveal something about what is happening in the external world; it is similar to perception in this way. Because our higher self is a part of the divine, it is like a microcosmos that mirrors the macrocosmos, or, more precisely, mirrors parts of it. Higher conscious cognition would not replace our everyday use of perception, the humanities, or the sciences when it comes to discovering the natural and social world around us, but it gives us access to the deeper spiritual dimension of reality that exists inside and outside our individual selves. Within ourselves, we possess a hidden potential that holds the key to understanding who we truly are, what ultimately exists, and what we must do to fulfill our true potential and overcome the obstacles in our lives.

Perhaps the closest resemblance to this kind of epistemology is found within the Buddhist worldview. Buddhists maintain that meditation gives us access to dimensions of reality and ourselves that we cannot reach through other sources of knowledge, such as introspection, perception, reason, memory, and testimony. The difference lies in the Buddhist worldview, where there are no selves and thus no higher selves, as human beings are merely a causal series of impermanent, impersonal psychophysical elements. If we learn to master meditational techniques adequately, we can discover that this is the case by, phenomenologically speaking, "going within," even though, ultimately, Buddhists believe that there is no within or without since there are no selves, no centers of consciousness.

HOLISTIC ETHICS

It seems that SBNRs are preoccupied with their inner transformation or personal development, so one might wonder what view of ethics

---

[27] MacLaine, *Going Within*, p. 82.

(if any) is not merely compatible with the spiritual worldview but is actually affirmed or even implied by its core beliefs.

Indeed, the inner transformation and hidden potential of the mind are the starting points of the new spirituality, but it does not have to stop there. As MacLaine writes, "the transformation of the world we see begins with the transformation of how we see ourselves."[28] The idea is that doing good will naturally follow from such an inner transformation. What doing good amounts to is less articulated, partially because we must stop blaming and judging other people or ourselves. We are not to be seen as fundamentally flawed by evil, sin, or guilt, which makes salvation possible only by grace, or as oppressed and living in false consciousness because we are born into an unfair capitalistic society with liberation being possible merely through social revolution. Instead, these beliefs produce the problem in the first place. They turn our attention away from the root problem, our spiritual ignorance. In the process of inner transformation, we realize and experience that we and everything else are infused with the divine. Everything is, in this profound sense, interconnected, rather than in the "shallow" sense that everything is composed of physical particles and governed by natural laws. Within the new spirituality, this holism has evolved into an ethical outlook in two distinct ways.

The first is to take holism to entail the rejection that there really is something evil or good. We ought to avoid or transcend the duality of good versus evil. All forms of dualism ought to be avoided in a spiritual worldview. Hanegraaff suggests that such a view of good and evil explains the striking absence of moral indignation and the presence of an educational or therapeutic reaction to what people generally understand as evil. He writes that the idea is that "If people behave aggressively towards others, it is only because their consciousness is so limited that they do not realize how their actions hinder their own evolution."[29] Hanegraaff then exemplifies this stance with what Kevin Ryerson asserts in his discussion with Shirley MacLaine and her lover, that there is no such thing as evil:

"I think," said Kevin, "that what you are calling evil is really only the lack of consciousness of God. The question is lack of spiritual knowledge, not whether or not there is evil." ...

---

[28] Ibid., p. xi.
[29] Hanegraaff, *New Age Religion and Western Culture*, p. 281.

"But where is the place of evil in this scheme then?"

"It doesn't exist. That's the point. Everything in life is the result of either illumination or ignorance. These are the two polarities. Not good and evil."[30]

The second possibility is to understand the emphasis within the new spirituality on holism as opposed not to dualism but to atomism and anthropocentrism. Essentially, *holism* is the idea that the whole is greater than the sum of its parts, whereas atomism entails rejecting this idea. As Fritjof Capra writes, "It can be called a holistic worldview seeing the world as an integrated whole rather than a dissociated collection of parts."[31] Transformed into an ethical outlook, it suggests that for anything to be healthy, the whole person – encompassing body, mind, and spirit – should be taken into account, and the entire environment in which we live should be our concern, rather than merely the present and future needs of human beings.[32] Not only do humans have intrinsic value but nature does too since the same life force pervades all lives. In accordance with this interpretation, Gordon Lynch takes one of the key tasks of SBNRs to be the development of a spirituality that reflects an "understanding of the relationship of humanity to the wider natural order and which motivates constructive action to prevent ecological catastrophe."[33] Moreover, recall that Roman and Packer maintained that the higher realms we build a bridge to when channeling is "a loving, caring, purposeful collective higher consciousness that has been called God, the All-That-Is, or the Universal Mind."[34] Likewise, MacLaine says that "inner knowledge is radiant with life, light and love" and that we should treat everyone with tolerance and love because they all possess God within.[35] Hence, goodness exists, and at least some things that oppose the unseen spiritual reality are evil because the divine consciousness that imbues everything that exists is a loving and caring force.

On this issue, it appears that advocates of the new spirituality have radically different understandings: One group affirms the existence of good and evil, whereas the other denies that good and evil are real.

---

[30] The quotation of Ryerson is taken from Hanegraaff, *New Age Religion and Western Culture*, p. 281.

[31] Fritjof Capra, *The Tao of Physics*. Shambhala, 2000 (25th ed.), p. 326.

[32] This is the way Daren Kemp understands the ethics of the New Age, as presented in Daren Kemp, *New Age*. Edinburgh University Press, 2004, pp. 53–54.

[33] Gordon Lynch, *The New Spirituality*. I. B. Tauris, 2007, p. 35.

[34] Roman and Packer, *Opening to Channel*, p. 13.

[35] MacLaine, *Going Within*, pp. 82.

They differ in a similar way that some SBNRs embrace personal pantheism and others impersonal pantheism. However, I believe there is a way to reconcile them. Ryerson might, after all, have misunderstood his own view. If everything humans do is the result of either illumination or ignorance, then we have an *explanation* of evil and good deeds, not a replacement for them. People often do evil things or behave aggressively because their consciousness is so limited that they fail to realize how their actions hinder their spiritual progress. It also explains why they should not be condemned because no intrinsically evil or good people exist. However, their actions could be evil or good, discriminating or just, and unfair or fair. If so, there is, after all, evil and goodness in the world.

Still, we also need to understand how good and evil, if such states of affairs exist, relate to the ideas of reincarnation and karma. Would the belief in trans-life progression change our interpretation of whether evil or goodness exists and whether certain courses of action are morally praiseworthy or blameworthy? A central idea, if not the most important one, in the spiritual worldview is that each of us is on a journey of spiritual development, in which our true, inner self evolves as we repeatedly incarnate over a series of many lives. This trans-life progress of the individual takes place in an interconnected world with an inherent disposition toward moral balance and cosmic justice (the law of karma), even cosmic evolution, presumably due to the divine stream of consciousness that permeates everything. What complicates the picture is that many SBNRs frequently maintain that this inbuilt disposition toward moral balance and cosmic justice does not involve punishment; there is no retribution for moral transgression. As Roberts/Seth phrase it: "Karma does not involve punishment. Karma presents the opportunity for development. It enables the individual to enlarge understanding through experience, to fill in gaps in ignorance, to do what should be done. Free will is always involved."[36]

Suppose we ignore the last sentence for a moment. In that case, we can interpret this as the claim that, given personal pantheism, the divine higher consciousness does not cause our new reincarnation to punish but instead educates us and provides an opportunity for self-improvement and transformation. Hence, karma is not merely a process of retribution but also a process of training. However, given impersonal pantheism, there is no punisher, since there is no cosmic

---

[36] Jane Roberts, *The Seth Material*. Bantam Books, 1970, p. 151.

divine self-awareness, but neither is there any educator or teacher. There is only an automatic karmic process that reincarnates us according to what we have done and what we have not done. The possibility for improvement that remains is that we can, in this life, access our higher self and recall past life memories that may assist our spiritual growth and transformation. In this way and through channeling that puts us in contact with other higher selves (and also angels, gods, and other supernatural beings, depending on how rich the SBNR's ontology is), we can embark on a journey of spiritual development in which our true, inner self evolves as we incarnate again and again over a series of many lives.

Suppose now we do not disregard the last sentence in the quotation above ("Free will is always involved"). In that case, we can develop an alternative account in our rational reconstruction of the spiritual worldview. As I pointed out in my previous discussion of reincarnation in this chapter, we can also find many SBNRs who see the process of reincarnation as voluntary rather than automatic. They believe the higher self can choose the body and circumstances into which it will be born. For this reason, free will is involved, and Roberts/Seth can say that karma does not involve punishment. On the contrary, karma presents the opportunity for development. Whatever happens to us can be seen as a moment of education offered by our own higher self, *if* we react to the lesson positively and constructively. Meaningless suffering or pointless evil is nonexistent, and nothing ever happens to anybody without reason. So, there is an educator but no punisher simply because there is no reason why the higher self would want to punish its normal self. This view, however, is also compatible with the idea that good and evil exist; it merely denies that there is any pointless evil or meaningless suffering.

We can perhaps say that the holistic ethic of the spiritual worldview amounts to at least the embrace of the following core belief:

(8) Ethics must begin with an inner personal transformation, since our bad or evil actions are often caused by spiritual ignorance, and once enlightened, we will see that the good consists in taking the unity and integral wholeness of ourselves and the cosmos into account in our actions.

It is worth pointing out that the holistic ethic of the new spirituality, even if it is not explicitly stated in (8), differs in a crucial way from what is typically taken to be a holistic ethic within environmental philosophy or environmentalism[37] – and not just in that SBNRs take any sustainable ethics to start with an inner personal transformation. They share the idea that both forms of holistic ethics emphasize the unity and integral wholeness of everything. However, environmental holistic ethics (the land ethics or ecocentric ethics) also emphasize the moral significance of the whole *and* assert that the whole has ethical priority over its parts. It has a collectivistic rather than individualistic twist, in contrast to the new spirituality. Rather than beginning with individual organisms or individual selves, holistic environmental ethics starts with species, ecosystems, or the land. Individual organisms or selves are parts of this whole. As part of a whole, they are relatively insignificant. Their worth lies in what they contribute to the whole (their ecological function) rather than in whether they are moral, rational, or sentient individuals. The ecological system, not the individual, is of primary value.

THE ROLE OF SCIENCE

Today, any worldview that aspires to intellectual credibility must take into account the theories and discoveries of science. Of the religious worldviews considered in this study, only two emerge as prominent in a culture as dominated by science (as we understand its key features today) as ours. New spirituality is one of those. In Chapter 6, we will examine the other one, religious naturalism. Both theistic and Buddhist worldviews predate the development of modern science; neither of these religious worldviews was initially formulated in a scientifically infused culture. If the prestige of science could somehow be transferred to a particular worldview, many think its credibility would increase significantly. In the book's second half, we will see that advocates of one of the secular worldviews, scientism, employ this argumentative strategy to enhance its intellectual standing.

One unique feature of the spiritual worldview is that many of its adherents consciously chose a scientifically inspired vocabulary to express their religious views. Hence, the language of the new spirituality frequently contains terms such as "energy," "frequency," "vibration," "dimension," and "quantum," and its practitioners sometimes talk about yoga, Reiki healing as a science, or occult sciences. Moreover, the worldview of the new spirituality is often expressed in educational terms and assumed

[37] See, for instance, Baird J. Callicott, *In Defense of the Land Ethic*. ASUNY Press, 1989; and Mikael Stenmark, *Environmental Ethics and Policy Making*. Ashgate, 2002.

to resemble science; thus, gatherings or meetings are sometimes described as workshops, lectures, or classes.[38] Lastly, there appears to be a near consensus among SBNRs regarding the need for science and spirituality to come together in some higher, holistic unity, even if they may have different understandings of how to achieve this unity.

How could we then think about the relationship between the new spirituality and science or, more fundamentally, between our worldview and science? I suggest that we have essentially five options to choose from when expressing our view on the relationship between our worldview and science today, and six options if we include how some individuals consider others' worldviews. The relationship concerns the compatibility, coherence, and relevance of science for the particular beliefs, values, and attitudes that, taken together, constitute our worldview. I suggest that we can embrace one of the following options:

(1) Our worldview is entailed by science; it starts from and stops with science (*the scientistic view*).

(2) Our worldview privileges science but nevertheless goes beyond science (*the extension view*).

(3) Our worldview goes beyond science, but science can support or enhance its credibility (*the contact view*).

(4) Our worldview is compatible with science, but that is all we can ask for since science and worldviews do different and unrelated jobs in our lives (*the independence view*).

(5) Our worldview is incompatible with contemporary science, but as science progresses, it will become clear that our worldview is compatible with, and perhaps even supported by, science (*the tension view*).

(6) Other individuals' worldview are incompatible with science, but that is what we should expect because these commitments go against reason, including scientific reason (*the irreconcilability view*).[39]

Notice that the way these six alternatives are expressed here is a shorthand version for a more precise statement, which also contains the denial of a central claim of the previous option. So, alternative (2) should be understood in the following way: Our worldview is not entailed by science, as

---

[38] James R. Lewis, "Science and the New Age." In *Handbook of New Age*, edited by James Lewis and Daren Kemp. Brill, 2007, p. 211.

[39] I first developed these ideas in Mikael Stenmark, "Worldviews and Science," *Zygon: Journal of Religion and Science*, 2025, 59/4, pp. 925–948.

in alternative (1). It merely privileges science or is grounded in science but still goes beyond what science can tell us about reality. According to alternative (3), our worldview is neither entailed nor guided by science because its central motives or grounds are obtained from or provided by other sources. Still, there is contact between our worldview and science, so science can support or add to its credibility. Advocates of alternative (4) do not think that science supports or adds to the credibility of their worldview. However, they see nothing problematic about this because science and worldviews do different and unrelated jobs in our lives; they occupy separate domains at a safe distance from each other. Still, they take their worldview to be compatible with and not in conflict with what science teaches us – and this is all we can ask for. The difference between these alternatives will become more evident as our study of worldviews proceeds.

As the worldviews are rationally reconstructed in this book, there are neither examples of (5) nor (6). There are presumably not many who actually say they embrace the latter view, the irreconcilability view. However, we need to include this view in the typology primarily because some claim that *other* people's worldviews are incompatible with science. Perhaps the most obvious example of alternative (5), the tension view, would be those adherents of a theistic worldview who embrace creationism or intelligent design. They are often referred to as fundamentalists. The fundamentalists acknowledge that evolutionary theory, as it is stated today, conflicts with their belief in, for instance, a young Earth or that humans lack genealogical kinship with the rest of the animals and plants on Earth. However, they would still maintain that science will eventually progress, so that these apparent conflicts will be resolved.

The SBNRs may hold different views on which of these alternatives best applies to the relationship between the new spirituality and science. Still, I think the most reasonable interpretation of the views surveyed in this study is to take it as expressing option (3), namely, that science supports or adds to the credibility of the spiritual worldview. The idea is not, as it is in alternative (4), that the new spirituality is merely compatible with science, so SBNRs would be satisfied if science does not contradict their core commitments. Instead, as I pointed out, there is a near consensus among them about the need for science and spirituality to come together in some higher, holistic unity.

Nor would the adherents of the new spirituality start with science and then develop a worldview by incorporating spiritual insights that go beyond science. Rather, they would first go within and discover, through practices such as meditation, channeling, and spiritual guidance, that they possess a spark of the divine within themselves and a higher self, which is connected to the divine consciousness that permeates everything. Therefore, SBNRs believe that there is a higher or deeper unity and integral wholeness to reality than what the naked eye (or science) perceives. Our consciousness is a part of the cosmic stream of consciousness, and together, they profoundly shape the world and how it has emerged, making trans-life progression possible. Hence, option (1) would also be a no-go. The new spirituality neither begins with nor ends with science.

Capra's *The Tao of Physics* (first published in 1975) is perhaps the most well-known attempt to develop a higher synthesis of science (or, more precisely, quantum physics) and the new spirituality, or what he calls Eastern mysticism. Could we plausibly understand his project as a version of the contact view? The first thing to notice is that he has been criticized for misunderstanding Eastern mysticism and failing to acknowledge the significant differences between Hinduism, Buddhism, and Taoism, as well as the diverse internal variations within these religions. This is true, but it does not matter for our purposes because we have described the new spirituality as a distinct worldview, which differs from, for instance, a Hindu or Buddhist worldview. Henceforth, I will interpret "Eastern mysticism" as the new spirituality described in this chapter.

Second, Capra states that he seeks to identify parallels between quantum physics and the new spirituality. His central claim is that a "view of the world is beginning to emerge from modern physics which is harmonious with ancient Eastern wisdom."[40] He thinks that physicists and other readers "will find that Eastern mysticism provides a consistent and beautiful philosophical framework which can accommodate our most advanced theories of the physical world."[41] For instance, he maintains that the awareness of unity and mutual interrelation of all things and events, the experience of all phenomena as manifestations of a fundamental oneness, that there ultimately are no parts at all, is something discovered in quantum physics, and it is the same realization that the mystics have reached by other means.

This sounds straightforward as an example of alternative (3). Capra argues that the spiritual worldview is not only compatible with modern science, but science also supports its credibility because they have both, by following different roads, come to the same conclusion. One problem with this rational reconstruction is that he also writes that the theories

---

[40] Capra, *The Tao of Physics*, p. 12.
[41] Ibid.

of quantum physics "all involve philosophical conceptions which are in striking agreement with those of Eastern mysticism."[42] However, these theories are expressed in a highly abstract mathematical formalism. They contain no philosophical conceptions, even though some physicists and philosophers have attempted to express them in linguistic rather than mathematical terms, often leading to quite paradoxical pictures of the subatomic world. (These theories of physics are not like the theory of evolution that could be expressed in ordinary, nontechnical language without too much misrepresentation.) Some of these philosophical interpretations, of course, fit quite nicely with the worldview of the new spirituality, but others do not. However, these interpretations are not part of science, but rather philosophical add-ons to quantum physics.

Hence, in Capra's account, philosophy sometimes becomes a part of quantum physics, whereas alternative (3) presupposes – something we have just seen that he maintains in other places – that we can interpret the findings of science within a larger philosophical framework. Of course, such a framework could also be proposed by advocates of other religious or secular worldviews. It is merely that the new spirituality, in Capra's view, provides the best one. There is nothing *un*scientific about these interpretations, but they are still *non*scientific, or, more exactly, not part of quantum physics. Whether or not the case Capra is making for the superiority of the new spirituality over other worldviews is convincing is beyond the scope of this study to evaluate. Many skeptics do not think so, but some of their arguments presuppose the (explicit or implicit) embrace of a rival worldview.

CHALLENGES FOR THE NEW SPIRITUALITY

What challenges does a spiritual worldview face, such as the one I have identified? What would seem to be problematic aspects of it? Let me highlight some of these challenges without suggesting that there are no resources within the new spirituality to deal with them in a satisfying way.

One challenge frequently made against pantheism is that if God includes everything and God is good or loving, then everything that exists ought to be good or loving.[43] Alternatively, since the universe is

---

[42] Ibid., p. 205.

[43] See, for instance, William Mander (2022) "Pantheism." In *The Stanford Encyclopedia of Philosophy*, edited by Edward N. Zalta and Uri Nodelman, https://plato.stanford .edu/archives/win2022/entries/pantheism/.

God insofar as there is good in the universe, there must be good in God. But consequently, insofar as there is evil in the universe, there must be evil in God. However, if the pantheistic conception of the divine in the new spirituality is understood in the restricted sense I have proposed, it seems possible to overcome this challenge. If everything in the universe is infused with but not identical to the divine, then evil does not have to be a part of God, even if it is present in the universe. What is more problematic is the idea some SBNRs have that the distinction between good and evil is nothing but a remnant of dualistic thinking, so there is nothing in the world that is good or evil. Why then think of starvation, torture, and rape as things we should oppose or try to overcome? Saying that these states of affairs result from ignorance and not illumination presupposes that once we are spiritually transformed, we would not be engaged in actions that lead to starvation, torture, and rape. But why? The conceivable reason must be that these states of affairs are evil. If they are not, why think that the illumination we get by going within and connecting to our higher self and the divine stream of consciousness would guide our action in that direction rather than in the opposite direction?

As I have previously pointed out, many SBNRs see the process of reincarnation as voluntary rather than automatic. They believe the higher self can choose the body and circumstances into which it will be born. This belief in pre-incarnational choice is taken to entail that there is no pointless evil or meaningless suffering. We are where we are meant to be because our higher self has consciously chosen these circumstances as the most suitable for our individual progress. But suppose this is true for all people. In that case, we all get exactly what we need to get, even if our incarnation in a particular life means we become victims of a holocaust, torture, or any other form of extreme suffering. These individuals' higher selves have intentionally chosen to experience severe suffering for reasons that are not clear or obvious to their normal selves but are transparent to their higher selves. We choose for educational purposes what suffering, depression, and illness (if any) we should face in each incarnated life.

Let me point out two problems with this scenario of higher selves' pre-incarnational choices of what will happen to us in this and the next life. The first issue is one of coordination. There is more than one higher self, since each of us has one. In fact, there are at least as many as there are people on Earth. Suppose my higher self thinks that to grow as a spiritual person in my next life, I will need to experience certain things and encounter a particular set of challenges. However, whether I will experience them depends on the people who surround me in my next life and the spiritual lessons their higher self wants to teach them in that particular life. Therefore, what I will experience in my next life is not within the power of my higher self to determine. Far from it; it depends heavily on what other higher selves decide is appropriate for their reincarnated human life. So, who or what could coordinate this voluntary process of reincarnation? It is hard to say. For this reason, the idea that reincarnation is an automatic process makes more sense.

The second problem is that if everyone receives exactly what they need in this life due to the free decision of their higher self in an interim or transitional stage, there appears to be no good reason why we should try to relieve others from suffering and injustice. As an adherent to the spiritual worldview, one could bite the bullet and maintain that we can only (if we want to be consistent in our thinking) respond with compassion to what these people have to go through.[44] We should respond this way, not for their sake, but for our own, so that these actions promote our spiritual progress in this life and subsequent lives. Also, for this reason, the idea of an automatic reincarnation process seems preferable. After all, many of us firmly believe that it is morally right and even our duty to fight injustices and reduce the amount of evil and human suffering, not for our sake but for the sake of those who are wronged.

The next challenge is a problem for the spiritual worldview only if it is essential to overcome or reject dualisms of different kinds, because dualism seems to be present in one of the central beliefs of the new spirituality. The view of the self at the core of the new spirituality is dualistic, at least if we interpret it in terms of the categories and theories of contemporary philosophy.[45] The spiritual worldview entails the rejection of both cosmological and anthropological materialism or physicalism. According to the former, everything real is material or physical in nature and nothing more. According to the latter, humans consist of nothing other than material or physical things or properties. Our consciousness is identical to our brain. We not just have a body, but we are nothing other than the (physical) body. However, it is possible to reject materialism and maintain that everything real is mental, spiritual, or nonphysical and that human beings, consequently, are mental or spiritual in nature and nothing more. This is a form of cosmological and anthropological

[44] Such a stance is expressed in Harmon Hartzell Bro, *Edgar Cayce: A Seer Out of Season*, Aquarian Press, 1989, p. 43.
[45] Mikael Stenmark, "Theories of Human Nature: Key Issues," *Philosophy Compass*, 2012, 7/8, pp. 543–558.

idealism or mentalism. The new spirituality affirms a third possibility that there are two kinds of fundamental properties in the world,[46] the physical and the mental or consciousness (panpsychism), and this is also true of the constitution of human beings. People have both a material body and self-consciousness; the latter cannot be reduced to the former. Moreover, our consciousness (as well as the divine consciousness) has the causal power to change things.

The new spirituality is non-dualistic in that SBNRs emphasize that the whole person, comprising body, mind, and spirit, should be considered a healthy entity. We must develop holistic and integrative thinking about ourselves and the cosmos surrounding us. Still, a core belief is that our spiritual progress is neither limited to nor starts with our present physical embodiment. There is something of you and me – our higher self – that provides our continued identity in this life and remains in the new forms we take in future reincarnated lives. Some SBNRs even believe that the higher self can choose the body and circumstances into which it will be born or reincarnated again. In all these cases, the human personality we identify with during life on earth is only a part of a spiritual individuality or higher self. At death, if not before, one regains awareness of one's higher self; the normal self is typically believed to perish together with the physical body. Hence, our body is not essential for our continued existence because our spirit or self-consciousness can exist independently, although reembodiment will eventually or automatically occur. This view is, by all means, a form of dualism. Trans-life progression presupposes a dualistic anthropology. Again, this is merely a problem for the new spirituality if its adherents claim we should reject all kinds of dualism.

The SBNRs maintain that (what I have called) higher conscious cognition is a reliable source of true belief and knowledge. If we go within and get in contact with our higher self, we can come to know that we are a part of the divine, that everything is infused with the divine consciousness, and that we are on a journey of spiritual development, in which our true, inner self evolves as we incarnate again and again over a series of many lives. It is a private cognitive process, but unless we reject introspection (as we will see that advocates of a scientistic worldview do), we already possess one such cognitive faculty that we consider

---

[46] However, notice that some of its advocates, instead, seem to embrace cosmological idealism. See Deepak Chopra and Menas Kafatos, *You Are the Universe*. Rider, 2017, pp. 224–234.

reasonably reliable. Indeed, without the deliverances of introspection, our self-knowledge would be severely limited. From a third-person perspective, we would only know who we are by observing our behavior and listening to what others have perceived when scrutinizing us.

The problem is that Buddhists also encourage us to go within and alter our state of consciousness, but the beliefs that their meditational techniques generate are pretty different from those of SBNRs. By going within, Buddhists come to believe not merely in karma and reincarnation but also in the impermanence of all things, including the self; that attachment and cravings cause suffering; and that their cessation is the key to enlightenment and escape from the cycle of rebirth. Regarding belief in the self and the higher self, the spiritual worldviews concur more with a Hindu worldview; furthermore, these beliefs do not conflict with introspection. It also seems more reasonable to believe in reincarnation if there is a self that can confirm, to some extent, that it has existed in many lives. Still, if "going within," in both the spiritual and Buddhist worldviews, refers to the same cognitive mechanism or process in our minds. Its reliability could be questioned, as it appears to generate quite conflicting beliefs about the unseen, deeper spiritual reality that exists beyond the natural and social world.

Perhaps channeling could provide additional support to suggest that the SBNRs' understanding of the unseen spiritual things aligns more closely with what really exists than what Buddhists believe. While most of them channel to seek inner wisdom and guidance on how to live in this reincarnated life, nothing stops spiritual guides, or one's higher self, from providing insights into previous states of affairs that have taken place on earth, which we can also access by employing other cognitive faculties, such as perception. If it were to happen, it would not merely confirm the reliability of higher conscious cognition to some significant degree but also provide those of us who are not yet convinced with a good reason to embrace the spiritual worldview. So, for instance, many people have gone missing, and some clues from the channelers about what has happened to some of them would not merely help us find their bodies but give us an independent reason to trust the channelers and their other messages of a more spiritual nature. It would also help the missing person's family to go on living normal lives. Unfortunately, none of these things have happened, or at least I have not read or heard any independent reports about them. Therefore, no additional help confirming the reliability of higher conscious cognition appears to be forthcoming from this direction.

6

A Religious–Naturalist Worldview

In Chapters 1 and 2, I claimed that there are paradigmatic examples of religious worldviews and secular worldviews, but that there is also a gray zone in between where it is unclear, perhaps not even possible to say whether one particular worldview is religious or secular. We can say that these worldviews are semireligious or semi-secular in nature.[1] Given my tentative definition of a religious worldview, it is fairly evident that Buddhism, Christianity, Hinduism, Islam, and Judaism belong to this group of religious worldviews.

However, when we studied the new spirituality, we discovered a group of people who identify themselves as "not religious but spiritual" individuals. The SBNRs are not religious in the sense that they want to disassociate themselves from the authoritative expressions of organized religion. However, the way I defined a religious worldview (see Chapter 2) and in the examples I gave – a theistic worldview and a Buddhist worldview – nothing intrinsic to them makes them dogmatic, exclusivist, or necessarily institutionalized entities. We can find people who, for instance, believe in God, embrace a theistic worldview, and live a life in the sight of God but rarely go to religious services and, perhaps, are merely formal members of religious institutions. Hence, given my stipulation that a religious worldview affirms or assumes the existence of a transcendent, divine, or spiritual dimension of reality and upholds its importance for how we understand and live our lives, the new spirituality is classified as a religious worldview. The worldview we

---

[1] Carl-Johan Palmqvist and Francis Jonbäck, *Semi-Secular Worldviews and the Belief in Something Beyond*. Cambridge University Press, 2025.

will study in this chapter, *religious naturalism*, is claimed by its practitioners to be religious. However, it still affirms that the physical world is all that exists and denies that there is an unseen spiritual reality that is the source of all visible things. But, on my account, is it then a religious worldview? I do not think there is sufficient precision in my stipulation of a religious worldview to give a defined answer. Still, we will consider some possible answers. What I want to stress, however, is that a lesson to be learned from the chapter is that there is indeed a gray zone; it is genuinely unclear (and sometimes irrelevant) where the borderline is between religious and secular worldviews.

Like other worldviews, religious naturalism is not a unified view but rather encompasses a range of ideas, beliefs, and practices. Still, my idea is to identify and distinguish features that many religious naturalists agree on or at least recognize as central to their outlook on life, even if they do not hold all these views themselves or accept them in precisely the way I understand them. The aim is to identify a religious–naturalist worldview that differs from the others considered in this study and thus constitutes a genuine alternative to them. But there are undoubtedly other possible rational reconstructions of religious naturalism than the one I offer.

Like some of those who embrace the secular worldviews we will encounter in Chapters 7–9, religious naturalists are not as well-institutionalized as the other religious worldviews. However, there is the *Religious Naturalist Association*, a worldwide community of people interested in exploring or expressing support for the religious naturalist orientation.[2] Ursula Goodenough, the president of the association, writes on their webpage, "*If religious sensibilities can be elicited by natural reality* – and I believe that they can – then the story of Nature has the potential to serve as the context for the global ethos that we need to articulate."[3] Wildman believes that a significant portion of Unitarian Universalist members are religious naturalists, and he also mentions the Sunday Assembly movement.[4] However, one can also assume that a fair number of religious people who belong to traditional religious

---

[2] Ursula Goodenough, Michael Cavanaugh, and Todd Macalister, "Bringing Religious Naturalists Together Online." In *The Routledge Handbook of Religious Naturalism*, edited by Donald A. Crosby and Jerome A. Stone. Routledge, 2018, pp. 310–316.

[3] For more on this, see https://religiousnaturalism.org/anotherhome/.

[4] Wesley J. Wildman, "Religious Naturalism: Oxymoronic Muddle or Future Spiritual Juggernaut?" In *A 21st Century Debate on Science and Religion*, edited by Shiva Khalili, Fraser Watts, and Harris Wiseman. Cambridge Scholars Publishing, 2017, p. 59.

organizations, such as Christian churches, would rather express their religiosity in terms of a religious – naturalist worldview than the theistic worldview we examined in Chapter 3 (more on this in Section "Challenges for Religious Naturalism").

THE NATURALISTIC UNIVERSE

The core idea of religious naturalism is the conviction that science and reason have undermined traditional religious views of the world; however, something of truly religious significance can be retained after religion undergoes a process of naturalization. Donald A. Crosby suggests that what characterizes religious naturalists is that they:

find religious meaning, values, and importance solely in nature or in some aspect of the natural order. The antithesis of religious naturalism is any kind of supernaturalism, i.e., belief in supernatural beings, principles, or powers thought to reside in a supernatural realm. Nature and its ongoing changes are metaphysically ultimate for religious naturalists. Nothing exists beyond nature, and a supernatural ground of nature is unnecessary. Nature in some shape or form is all there is now, ever has been, and ever shall be.[5]

Religious naturalists differ from nonreligious or secular naturalists in that the former, but not the latter, maintain that religious meaning, value, or significance can be found in nature or some aspect of the natural order. It is possible to embrace both naturalism and religion – if religion is purified from its supernaturalism. Such a religious worldview is to be preferred over secular worldviews. Religious naturalism is thus best conceived as a reaction against both theists and other supernaturalists who are religious, as well as against naturalists who are secular. The best option is to be a naturalist who is religious.

Religious naturalists embrace two core beliefs they have in common with secular naturalists, namely:

(1) There is nothing beyond or besides nature, and, consequently, everything that exists is part of nature (*the naturalistic thesis*).

(2) There is no God, no gods, no beings such as spirits, angels, or demons, no processes like karma, reincarnation, and channeling, and no entities such as immaterial human or animal souls (*anti-supernaturalism*).

---

[5] Donald A. Crosby, "Religious Naturalism." In *The Routledge Companion to Philosophy of Religion*, edited by Chad Meister and Paul Copan. Routledge, 2007, p. 672.

Nature is all there is and ever will be. But what is nature, or what constitutes the natural world? That is not an easy question to answer, and we have yet to discover many aspects of nature. However, the received philosophical naturalist answer is that nature consists of the entities that science can discover and nothing more. Still, some naturalists, as we shall see in Chapters 7 and 8, are not happy to reduce what nature contains to merely those things that science can discover. Therefore, the second thesis is essential for naturalists: the rejection of what they call supernaturalism or supernatural beings, powers, or processes. Nature can contain many things, perhaps many things that science cannot discover, but it does not contain supernatural things and properties.

It is, of course, claim (2), the anti-supernaturalist thesis, that has the most significant implications for the religions of the world. To start with, it implies that naturalists reject the monotheism of Judaism, Christianity, and Islam. These theists typically believe that God is the creator of nature or the ground of being. But nature is all there is, so naturalists have to be atheists. Moreover, they cannot adopt agnosticism. An agnostic neither affirms nor denies the existence of God. Moreover, polytheistic religions are also precluded. So, for instance, those understandings of Hinduism, which are polytheistic, focusing on the great pantheon of Hindu gods and not seeing those gods as manifestations of one supreme God, are also incompatible with naturalism. Thus, the gods – those divine beings who exist in the natural order – and not merely God, the creator of the natural order, do not exist in a naturalistic universe. For similar reasons, the moral law of nature that makes rebirth and karma possible is not a part of nature; nor are there any spiritual energies, such as Reiki, auras, or the life force; nor is there a higher self or higher consciousness. Hence, central elements in Buddhism and the new spirituality are incompatible with a naturalistic ontology.

While none of the major world religions are animistic (though they might contain animistic elements), most other religions are. Animism is, roughly, the idea that life and will pervade nature: a belief that natural objects, other than humans, have souls. Animists believe many things in nature is material and spiritual, but they do not necessarily believe in God or gods. Ethnic or indigenous religions would be the world's sixth largest religious tradition if considered collectively. Religious naturalists reject ethnic or indigenous religions because of their animistic elements. They reject the notion of nature that views these spirits or certain spiritual properties of living things as natural, rather than supernatural, phenomena. Accordingly, Crosby writes, "religious naturalism makes no reference to any type of nature-pervading, nature-enveloping, or nature-personifying spirit or spirits, in contrast to pantheistic, panentheistic, mystical, polytheistic, or animistic traditions."[6] Therefore, it would not be appropriate to say that ethnic or indigenous religions are "naturalistic" because naturalism's second core claim prohibits these elements from being a genuine part of nature. In the naturalists' terminology, these entities should be classified as supernatural.

Religious naturalists take the methods and findings of the natural sciences seriously, viewing them as paradigmatic examples of knowledge and rationality. They seek to develop a worldview informed by the natural sciences. A significant number of participants (typically scientists, philosophers, and theologians) in the so-called science-religion dialogue embrace this worldview in one form or another.[7] Still, religious naturalists typically do not want to reduce what exists or what is a part of nature to what the natural sciences can discover, nor reduce our knowledge to what we can find out about reality by applying the methods of the natural sciences. Culture or human society is then a part of nature, but to detect some of its key or unique features, we need the resources of the social sciences. The social world is a nonreducible subset of the natural world. For this reason, religious naturalists reject the idea that regards, as ultimately insignificant and unreal, anything other than what is captured in the descriptions and explanations of the natural sciences. What the social sciences discover is real, so these sciences can also provide us with knowledge about reality. Knowledge that is inaccessible and not reducible to the knowledge that the natural sciences provide. So, religious naturalists are typically not scientific naturalists, but rather liberal naturalists (a fuller account of these different kinds of naturalists will be provided in our discussion of secular worldviews).

But what about the beliefs and knowledge claims of the humanities and those of everyday life? Crosby identifies divergent views on this matter.[8] Some religious naturalists argue that science, particularly as exemplified in the natural sciences, is capable of providing objective and reliable descriptions of both the natural and social worlds. Others maintain that the humanities, the arts, and the experiences of daily life should be called upon to complement the sciences and do justice to the

---

[6] Donald A. Crosby, *A Religion of Nature*. SUNY Press, 2002, p. 12.
[7] See, for example, the articles published in *Zygon: Journal of Religion and Science*, 2008, 38/1, pp. 85–120, and 2021, 56/4, pp. 950–1086.
[8] Crosby, "Religious Naturalism," p. 673.

fullness of our world. Hence, we need to add an epistemic thesis to the ontological theses. I suggest we give it the following content:

(3) The natural sciences provide the most reliable form of knowledge we can have about reality, but the social sciences also provide us with knowledge, and presumably, there are some less reliable instances of knowledge or at least rational beliefs to be found in the humanities and everyday life.

In this chapter, let us refer to the conjunction of the natural and social sciences as "science." Religious naturalists maintain that science, understood in this way, has not discovered anything beyond or behind nature, nor has it provided any compelling reason to believe that God, gods, or any other kinds of spiritual beings or processes, such as karma, reincarnation, and channeling, exist. For this reason, we should assume that the supernaturalism of the traditional religions of the world is mistaken.

If one accepts claims (1) and (2), it is assumed in contemporary philosophy, although not always stated, that one cannot be religious. It is taken more or less for granted that the point of being religious is gone once one embraces both of these theses. Thus, since there is no God, gods, or any other form of supernatural reality, there is no point in being religious; religious beliefs and attitudes are just unnecessary add-ons. This is so since no religious meaning, value, or significance can be found in a naturalistic universe, a universe in which claims (1) and (2) are true. What characterizes religious naturalists more than anything else is that they *deny* this secular entailment. A genuinely significant religious life can be lived within the boundaries of a naturalistic universe. Hence, the core thesis of religious naturalism is as follows:

(4) Religious meaning, value, or significance can be found in nature or some aspect of the natural order.

As Jerome A. Stone highlights, a religious naturalist "seeks to explore and encourage religious ways of responding to the world on a completely naturalistic basis without a supreme being or ground of being."[9] As he writes elsewhere, the use of the term "religious" is justified because "attitudes and beliefs among religious naturalists are sufficiently analogous to attitudes and beliefs among the paradigm cases of religion that they may be called religious."[10]

---

[9] Jerome A. Stone, *Religious Naturalism Today*. SUNY Press, 2008, p. xi.
[10] Jerome A. Stone, "Defining and Defending Religious Naturalism." In *The Routledge Handbook of Religious Naturalism*, edited by Donald A. Crosby and Jerome A. Stone. Routledge, 2018, p. 7.

Let us now try to understand what the fourth core claim means more exactly, because it is the most crucial one for religious naturalists. It must, of necessity, be given content that nonreligious or secular naturalists deny – otherwise, the two worldviews would collapse into one and the same. What is it, then, that makes religious naturalists religious? We will explore some answers to that question. I will distinguish between two forms of religious naturalism, one with and one without a traditional religious vocabulary, but both will be taken to accept the claims of (1), (2), (3), and (4). So, I will take their disagreement to be one about an extension claim or about one or another way of explicating the conviction that religious meaning, value, or significance can be found in nature or some aspect of the natural order.

THE SIGNIFICANCE OF TRADITIONAL RELIGIOUS MYTHS AND SYMBOLS

What characterizes the first form of religious naturalism is that its advocates (a) reject a literal interpretation of traditional religious concepts and instead maintain that they are metaphors or symbols that express the sacredness of nature. However, these religious naturalists still maintain that (b) traditional religious myths and symbols are indispensable because of their central role in human history or because they provide concrete objects of consciousness that stand in for abstract ideas, such as Nature or the Universe, and, therefore, can better motivate our actions.

We will explore this stance more precisely, but let me begin the inquiry with something Philip Kitcher writes about what a certain religious orientation looks like from his atheistic perspective. He has no problem identifying a theistic worldview even though he thinks it is an instance of supernaturalism and rejects it for that reason. However, he has noticed that another kind of religiosity is present in contemporary Western society, which is not obviously a form of supernaturalism. It is found in those people who "utter doctrinal sentences and to participate in the professions and ceremonies in which those statements find their home, but who clearly disavow any interpretation of the statements that implies substantive doctrine about transcendent entities."[11] He continues, "Many of them are inclined to take refuge in language that is resonant and opaque, metaphorical and poetic, and to deny that they can do any better at explaining

---

[11] Philip Kitcher, "Militant Modern Atheism," *Journal of Applied Philosophy*, 2011, 28/1, p. 5.

the beliefs they profess."[12] Kitcher would like to see these individuals state what this kind of religious conviction implies for retention, or at least what they no longer believe, and then stick to that confession.

Although Kitcher does not seem aware of it, some religious people, namely religious naturalists, do so. They claim to share the same core naturalistic beliefs as Kitcher, but also acknowledge that religious meaning, value, or significance can still be found in nature. Therefore, if we wish to continue using traditional religious language, we must understand these statements as myths and metaphors for the sacredness of nature. Wesley J. Wildman takes one of the central ideas of religious naturalism to be: "Religions encode wisdom about sacred nature but it is often expressed in myths and legends that harden into literal descriptions of reality. Therefore, religious naturalism can affirm traditional religions in some respects and must criticize them in other respects."[13]

For example, Gordon D. Kaufman maintains that the symbol "God" and certain other religious concepts must be retained because we have no better way of expressing the religious attitude that we humans should take toward the cosmos now that theism is no longer intellectually and morally defensible, but neither can we be satisfied with atheism or more substantive forms of nonreligious naturalism. God is the best symbol in our language for the creative power that exists in nature and, therefore, gives us a direction for life, even though God does not exist, and nature is all that exists.[14] Kaufman is also quite explicit about the importance of science in these religious matters. He writes, "As far as we know, personal agential beings did not exist, *and could not have existed*, before billions of years of cosmic evolution of a very specific sort and then further billions of years of biological evolution also of a very specific sort had transpired."[15] How, then, he asks rhetorically, can we today think of a person-like creator-God as existing before and apart from any such evolutionary developments? The answer is that it seems to Kaufman impossible to make sense of such an idea of God as the creator of the heavens and the earth.

Instead, we should think of God as the creativity of the universe. God is to be thought of as the "serendipitous creativity" of the evolutionary processes that brought us and many other living things into being. In

[12] Kitcher, "Militant Modern Atheism," p. 6.
[13] Wildman, "Religious Naturalism: Oxymoronic Muddle or Future Spiritual Juggernaut?" p. 55.
[14] Gordon D. Kaufman, *In Face of Mystery*. Harvard University Press, 1993, pp. 4–8.
[15] Gordon D. Kaufman, "On Thinking of God as Serendipitous Creativity," *Journal of the American Academy of Religion*, 2001, 69/2, p. 409.

Kaufman's religious naturalism, it appears that the unexpected creative power manifest throughout the cosmos captures an essential aspect of the sacredness of nature. Wildman expresses a similar idea when he says that the "sacredness of nature expresses the self-transcendent potential of nature" – even if he does not use the notion of God to refer to this serendipitous creativity of the natural processes.[16] Kaufman thinks that God is a significant religious symbol because – even when we reject a literal interpretation of it – it sums up, unifies, and represents what are taken to be the highest and most indispensable human ideals and values. It presents itself as the most powerful and significant symbol in Western tradition, and it can provide concrete objects of consciousness that stand in for abstract ideas. The kind of reality God has is then the reality of an ideal or ultimate symbol.

However, religious naturalists might find the myths, metaphors, or symbols of other religious traditions, rather than theistic ones (or, in Kaufman's case, Christianity), more effective or fruitful in expressing the religious meaning, value, or significance of nature. Hence, we should not think that religious naturalists must aim at naturalizing theism and thinking that God is the most important religious symbol.

Jay N. Forrest, for example, maintains that a religious naturalist cannot accept traditional Buddhism. Therefore, concepts such as karma, rebirth, and nirvana must be reinterpreted to make them compatible with naturalism. He proposes that a Buddhist religious naturalist can understand karma as "a psychological mechanism, not a cosmological law"; it is "something that has lasting psychological consequences."[17] Nirvana could be understood as "inner peace." Since rebirth serves the purpose of showing that our actions have consequences even after we die, Forrest suggests that a modern equivalent might be our "'legacy,' the positive or negative influence of our lives that is passed down from one generation to the next."[18]

Hence, we can add one more thesis to religious naturalism, namely:

(5) Some central traditional religious concepts are important or even essential metaphors or symbols to express the sacredness of nature, the highest and most indispensable human ideals and values, and central features of what human flourishing is all about.

---

[16] Wildman, "Religious Naturalism: Oxymoronic Muddle or Future Spiritual Juggernaut?" p. 54.

[17] Jay N. Forrest, "Buddhism and Religious Naturalism." In *The Routledge Handbook of Religious Naturalism*, edited by Donald A. Crosby and Jerome A. Stone. Routledge, 2018, p. 202.

[18] Forrest, "Buddhism and Religious Naturalism," p. 202.

These traditional religious concepts are important because they provide concrete objects of consciousness to replace abstract ideas such as Nature or the Universe and, therefore, better motivate actions.

For one group of religious naturalists, claim (5) is an essential feature of their worldview. In contrast, for another group, as we will see, this is not the case, even if the latter group acknowledges that the former group also holds a religious–naturalist worldview. Thus, for some religious naturalists, it is vital to emphasize that they are Buddhist, Christian, or Jewish religious naturalists; for others, it is not.

RELIGIOUS SYMBOLISM AND ALTERITY THEISM

Although religious naturalists such as Kaufman and Forrest believe that religious symbols and metaphors are essential in today's modern society, they nevertheless fulfill Kitcher's desire for clarity by being aware of the assumptions implied by their religious stance. Other religious people, however, do not make confessions of the kind Kitcher would like to see but feel fully justified in resorting to metaphorical and poetic formulations of their religious beliefs. In contrast to religious naturalism, there is no established name for this religious worldview. I will call it *religious symbolism*. Religious naturalism and religious symbolism are easily confused because they share one crucial element: their understanding of religious statements, doctrines, stories, or narratives as metaphors or symbols.

The core claim of religious symbolism is that religion provides stories and metaphors that cannot be translated into propositions about the nature of existence that can be true or false. There is no fixed interpretation of religious doctrines or beliefs; all we have are metaphors, images, and stories that convey meaning. A variant of this religious orientation is described by Anthony Kenny as follows:

If there is any truth in any religious revelation it is more likely that each of them is a metaphor for a single underlying truth that is incapable of being expressed in literal terms without contradiction. In this way religion would resemble poetry rather than science …. Disbelieving in religious narratives, however, does not necessarily mean discarding them. It means removing them from the history section of one's mind into the poetry section.[19]

---

[19] Anthony Kenny, "Knowledge, Belief and Faith," *Philosophy*, 2007, 82/32, pp. 395 and 396.

Peter Lipton suggests an alternative way to express this religious world-view. He thinks that we can see it as a particular form of bilingualism, where you have the ability to understand two different languages but lack the ability to translate statements in one into statements in the other.[20] We can say that religious symbolists are convinced that there is a profound truth to be found in religion. Still, they do not know how to express it in a language that is not purely poetic or metaphorical, or they cannot translate religious claims into mundane or nonreligious language. Thus, it becomes impossible for us to compare the claims that are part of these religious people's perception of reality with those that secular people hold to be true or with those beliefs that religious people who embrace the theistic, Buddhist, or spiritual worldview embrace.

Note, however, that virtually all religious people believe that metaphors and stories have a central and irreplaceable role in their religious practice. Jews and Christians obviously do not mean that when they say "God is their rock and fortress," that God is a rock and a fortress, but that it is a metaphor to express that God is faithful. Characteristic of the Jews and Christians who embrace religious symbolism, however, is the idea that *all* talk about God or *all* central religious ideas and attitudes can only be expressed in metaphorical or poetic language. They can never be expressed in direct, nonmetaphorical, or nonpoetic language. Not only is the speech about God as a rock and fortress to be understood as a metaphor but also the speech about God as faithful and loving. Or, the basic idea is that nothing in the Hebrew Bible's accounts of the creation of the world, the Christian Bible's accounts of the life, death, and resurrection of Jesus, or the Qur'anic accounts of God's revelations to Mohammad can be formulated as nonmetaphorical statements or assertions about the true nature of existence. They convey a mystery that we can only sense and, according to religious symbolists, access only through religious, poetic expression, participation in religious rites and rituals, or living a religious life. For this reason, religious symbolists cannot, like religious naturalists, embrace naturalism and believe that we live in a naturalistic universe. Perhaps the best we can say is that they are agnostic about the ontological assumptions implied by their religious stance.

One reason why some religious thinkers are, as Kitcher puts it, inclined to take refuge in language that is resonant and opaque, metaphorical and

---

[20] Peter Lipton, "Science and Religion: The Immersion Solution." In *Philosophers and God*, edited by John Cornwell and Michael McGhee. Continuum, 2009, p. 10.

poetic, and to deny that they can do any better at explaining the beliefs they profess is provided by their conception of God. They maintain that God is so radically different that we can never describe God or God's relationship to the world other than through poetry and imagery. Some of the things Kaufman says, at least in his earlier publications, point in this direction. He writes, "To regard God as some kind of describable or knowable object over against us would be at once a degradation of God and a serious category error."[21]

John Hick is a more explicit advocate of this kind of worldview. He thinks that there is a transcendent reality to which religion is a response, but it – God or "the Real," as Hick calls it – is something that is beyond human conceiving. We cannot say that God is personal or impersonal, good or evil, substance or process, one or many, because God is beyond human categories and conceptions. Here, we can identify the category mistake that Kaufman talks about. People can be selfish or unselfish; trees or genes cannot be because they are not the sort of things that could be either: "And nor is the Real. Indeed it is not a *kind* of thing at all. It is, using inevitably metaphorical language, the ground of everything. So human language can describe the various forms taken by the 'impact' of the Real upon us, but not the Real as it is in itself."[22]

Maybe there is no difference between religious naturalism and religious symbolism after all. But suppose you believe that God is not a being of some sort and is beyond human categories and conceptions; why also believe that there is nothing beyond or besides nature and that everything that exists is a part of nature? Is it not instead the case that you then believe that there is something beyond nature, namely, God? The idea is merely that we cannot say anything substantial about God, the Real, or Being-itself, or whatever we call it. It is for this reason, and that we can experience its presence in our lives, that Hick rejects both (secular) naturalism and religious naturalism.[23]

The God of religious symbolists is not a metaphor for the sacredness of nature or the highest and most indispensable human ideals and values but for something utterly nonhuman and nonnatural; it refers to the God beyond the God of theism, to the ground of being, or something of that sort. We could perhaps say that the theology of religious symbolism

[21] Gordon D. Kaufman, *The Theological Imagination*. The Westminster Press, 1981, p. 244.
[22] John Hick, *The Fifth Dimension*. OneWorld, 1999, p. 10.
[23] Hick, *The Fifth Dimension*, p. 21.

of the theistic kind (what I elsewhere called alterity theism)[24] is much thinner than the theology of the theistic worldview we have studied in Chapter 2. It is because of God's *radical otherness* or *alterity* – God is beyond our categories and conceptions – that religious symbolists utter doctrinal sentences and participate in professions and ceremonies in which those statements find their home but clearly disavow any interpretation of the statements that imply substantive beliefs about transcendent beings or processes.

However, there are other ways of stating religious symbolism. Therefore, this religious orientation should not automatically be equated with its proponents embracing an understanding of God as being beyond conceptualization. Religious symbolism can occur even in religions where God plays a minor or no role at all. Those who embrace religious symbolism would, despite Kitcher's urge, take themselves to be fully justified in resorting to metaphorical and poetic formulations of their religious beliefs and deny that they can do any better at explaining the beliefs they profess.

More importantly, religious naturalism and religious symbolism should not be confused, even if these religious worldviews share one crucial element in common: their understanding of religious doctrines, stories, or narratives, as, so to speak, metaphors or symbols that extend "all the way down." The previous affirms, and the latter denies or at least remains agnostic about whether there is nothing beyond or besides nature. Consequently, religious naturalists believe that everything that exists is a part of nature. Not, for that matter, should we think that religious symbolism is a form of positivism. A logical positivist would argue that since the theist's assertion that God exists is cognitively meaningless, so is the atheist's assertion that God does not exist; it is equally meaningless. It is not, however, a particular principle of meaning and verification that motivates why these religious symbolists reject both theism and atheism, but God's otherness.

I have not given a religious–symbolist worldview its own chapter because it lacks substantial beliefs that make it possible to critically compare it to the core claims of the other worldviews discussed. It should not be seen as a criticism of religious symbolism but rather as an illustration of the limitations of employing this study's philosophical method (see again Chapter 1).

---

[24] Mikael Stenmark, "Competing Conceptions of God: The Personal God versus the God beyond Being," *Religious Studies*, 2015, 51/2, pp. 205–220.

THE SACREDNESS OF NATURE

A second group of religious naturalists does not believe that we can reconceive or naturalize the idea of God or other traditional religious concepts
within a naturalistic framework, or at the very least, they do not think
it is desirable. Crosby writes that for this group of religious naturalists,
"the admittedly powerful symbol of God points in the wrong direction. It
should be given up because it stubbornly connotes – despite all efforts at
revision – a supernatural being that created the world out of nothing and
is required to sustain its existence. This symbol is therefore radically misleading and runs counter to the central claims of religious naturalism."[25]
Others, such as Stone, are not quite so negative. In circumstances where
religious language is called for, he simply uses his "translation device:
'God is the traditional term for the sum of the constructive and challenging aspects of the universe.'"[26] So, we should either reject God-talk or,
more generally speaking, traditional religious concepts altogether, or at
least urge caution in using them.

Instead, this group of religious naturalists thinks that *nature itself* will
suffice. We no longer need traditional religions. That is to say, a scientific
description of nature combined with the right attitudes toward nature
will do. Crosby believes that we should "grant to nature the kind of reverence, awe, love, and devotion we in the West have formerly reserved
for God."[27] Nature is religiously ultimate, and we do not need any God-
talk to express the core beliefs and commitments of a religious–naturalist
worldview. Nature can be of religious significance if it is, for us, something sacred, an object of awe and reverence. Crosby thinks that people
have this religious attitude when nature is primary in the sense that "it is
more important to them than anything else ... [It is] the ultimate loyalty
to which all of their other loyalties are subordinate."[28]

Similarly to Crosby, Loyal Rue states that the central core of religious
naturalism is this: "Nature is the sacred object of humanity's ultimate
concern," and what characterizes religious naturalists is their reverence
and awe before nature and their love of nature.[29] There is a way to live

---

[25] Crosby, "Religious Naturalism," p. 674.
[26] Stone, *Religious Naturalism Today*, p. 209.
[27] Crosby, *A Religion of Nature*, p. xi.
[28] Ibid., p. 127.
[29] Loyal Rue, *Religion Is Not about God*. Rutgers University Press, 2005, p. 366. Notice,
    though, that Rue is much more positive toward the future use of traditional religious
    myths than Crosby and Stone.

in harmony with the universe or nature rather than merely in it, and this is obtained if we let nature become our ultimate concern. So, certain religious attitudes are added to naturalism. This extra element justifies the qualifier "religious" before the word "naturalism," even when God and other traditional religious concepts are rejected. On this account, one is a religious naturalist if one's naturalism is life-orienting and appropriately connected with religious attitudes, such as love, awe, or reverence for nature, because one believes that nature is sacred. If that is not the case, one is simply a nonreligious or secular naturalist. Religious naturalists sense and appreciate nature's essence, grandeur, and magnificence, which they take great joy in, and this makes them believe in the sacredness of nature. Thus, religious naturalists also find certain values in nature and develop emotional responses or ethical attitudes toward it. We can say that religious meaning, value, or significance can be found in nature because:

(6) Nature is sacred and is, therefore, worthy of our reverence, awe, and devotion.

Religious naturalists believe nature is the proper object of these attitudes, but it is unsuitable for worship since there is nobody there who can be a proper object for worship. In my reconstruction of the religious–naturalist worldview, all of its adherents embrace claim (6), whereas, as we have just seen, some do not accept claim (5). The latter group maintains that we should leave traditional religious concepts or symbols such as God, spirits, dharma, karma, or higher consciousness behind and use the notion of nature instead. But one vital exception is "sacred" (and its associated notions like reverence, awe, and devotion). It is at the center of their worldview. It reflects the appropriate attitude that religious naturalists believe we should have toward nature.

In traditional religions, there are sacred spaces, times, and objects. A sacred space or ground is typically a special place set aside for religious worship or ritual. It could be a temple or a church, a mountain, or a holy land. Sacred objects can include holy scriptures, such as the Bible or the Qur'an, as well as artifacts like icons or relics. Sacred times are usually the days and times set aside for religious prayer or ritual. Religious people use sacred places and objects to contact a deeper or higher part of reality that most humans do not encounter in the ordinary course of their lives. Sacred spaces and objects should not be treated like ordinary spaces or objects. They require special care and reverence. For instance, in Exodus 3:5, we can read that God told Moses to remove his sandals when standing on holy ground. Because sacred things are associated with God's holy presence, they must be treated with solemn respect and utmost care. More generally, respect, care, reverence, and devotion are appropriate attitudes toward the sacred.

The understanding of the sacred by religious naturalists differs from the traditional one in at least two ways. First, they deny that sacred objects and places offer special avenues to a deeper or higher part of reality. In their eyes, this is an expression of supernaturalism and is thus rejected because they, according to core claims (1) and (2), maintain that we live in a naturalistic universe. Second, they do not think that only some objects and places are sacred. Instead, nature is sacred. Nature, as a whole system of things and relations, is worthy of our reverence and devotion. However, religious naturalists agree with traditional religions that what is sacred requires special care and reverence. Acknowledging something as sacred implies that one cannot treat it in any way one wants; it is to be treated with respect, care, awe, reverence, and devotion.

ENVIRONMENTAL ETHICS

We have seen that Rue and other religious naturalists maintain that nature is the sacred object of humanity's ultimate concern. He continues by asserting, "ecocentric values are justified by the claim that Nature is sacred."[30] As the highest object of human reverence, nature grounds an ethics of respect for nature and all its inhabitants. Wildman also considers this a core conviction of religious naturalism: the "sacredness of nature imposes moral obligations upon us."[31] Crosby maintains we "must learn to *reverence and hold in awe the sacredness of the earth as our beloved community and household.*"[32]

As we have seen earlier, Crosby even goes so far as to interpret this ethics of respect for nature and all its inhabitants to mean that the ultimate loyalty of religious naturalists is not to God, one's family, kin, country, or one's species (humanity) but to nature.[33] Conscientious care for all of nature, because of its sacredness, should take precedence over

[30] Rue, *Religion Is Not about God*, p. 366.
[31] Wildman, "Religious Naturalism: Oxymoronic Muddle or Future Spiritual Juggernaut?" p. 54.
[32] Crosby, *A Religion of Nature*, pp. 113–114.
[33] Ibid., p. 127.

all other concerns, not just those parts of nature that are of immediate use to humans. When you try to determine how to act, you should not ask: Is it good for me, my family, my kin, my country, or my species, but is it good for nature as a whole? And, presumably, if there is a conflict of interest, your loyalty should be toward nature. Such a form of environmentalism is very demanding and requires a radical reformation of people's lives. However, one can reject the view that Earth is merely the backdrop or setting for self-contained, self-regarding human enterprises without going as far as Crosby does. Still, what religious naturalists typically say requires a substantial change in human lifestyle and societal priorities. As we have seen, Rue, for example, maintains that religious naturalists have sympathy for all living things, feel guilt for enlarging ecological footprints, and take pride in reducing them. Hence, I will take another core belief of the religious–naturalist worldview to be:

(7) The sacredness of nature imposes significant moral obligations on us that exceed those obligations we have towards other living human beings or future human generations.

The most straightforward interpretation of this statement is that it implies the rejection of anthropocentrism and the adoption of some non-anthropocentric environmental ethics. Anthropocentrism is the view that of all things in nature, only humans (now living and future generations) have intrinsic or inherent value or are objects of moral concern. Consequently, nonhuman beings have merely instrumental value. Human beings are the sole source of moral concern, thereby occupying a unique place within ethics. Humanism adds to anthropocentrism the notion that humans do not simply possess moral worth but also have equal moral status, dignity, and rights (*human egalitarianism*). Non-anthropocentrism is the view that more things in nature than humans have intrinsic or inherent value or are objects of moral concern. Both humans and nature have *moral standing*; they count morally in their own right.

If non-anthropocentrism is the correct moral view, it significantly alters our moral obligations toward nature because it implies that we ought to consider the interests of other living beings when making decisions that affect them, regardless of whether these decisions serve human interests. But what moral obligations do religious naturalists believe we have toward nature because of its sacredness, and do things in nature, as humans, have equal moral worth; do they have equal moral status (*environmental egalitarianism*)? Just as one can, within human ethics, believe that all humans have moral worth but deny that they have equal moral status, one can, with environmental ethics, believe that other living things than humans have moral standing but deny that they have equal worth with each other or with humans. Thus, *moral status*, in contrast to moral standing, is a comparative notion, so two beings can have the same moral standing but different moral status or significance.

An egalitarian environmentalist like Paul W. Taylor admits that it is possible for living things to have different moral statuses. Still, he rejects this idea and maintains that "every species counts as having the same value in the sense that, regardless of what species a living thing belongs to, it is deemed to be prima facie deserving of equal concern and consideration on the part of moral agents."[34] J. Baird Callicott holds the opposite opinion. He writes, "The Land ethic manifestly does not accord equal moral worth to each and every member of the biotic community; the moral worth of individuals (including, take note, human individuals) is relative, to be assessed in accordance with the particular relation of each to the collective entity which Leopold called 'land.'"[35] On a more concrete level, this means that Taylor argues that we have a prima facie duty not to cause injury or suffering to other living beings, whereas Callicott does not believe we have such a duty. He instead maintains that we have a duty toward other species (not their individual members) not to threaten them with extinction by upsetting the sustainability of the ecosystems that make it possible for them to flourish. Another difference between Taylor and Callicott is that the former regards individual living things as the basic unit of moral concern, whereas the latter asserts that species, ecosystems, or the land are primary objects of moral consideration.

Callicott's environmental holism, or ecocentrism, appears to align more closely with religious naturalists' emphasis on nature and its sacredness than Taylor's environmental individualism. Religious naturalists can disagree about what ecocentric values and concrete moral duties their worldview supports, but they would presumably be more similar to Callicott's than Taylor's non-anthropocentric environmental ethic. Still, if nature is sacred, we have justification for nature's inherent worth that secular worldviews lack. Acknowledging something as sacred implies that one cannot treat it in any way one wants; it is to be treated with respect, care, awe, reverence, and devotion.

[34] Paul W. Taylor, *Respect for Nature*. Princeton University Press, 1986, p. 155.
[35] J. Baird Callicott, *In Defense of the Land Ethic*. SUNY Press, 1989, p. 28.

CHALLENGES FOR RELIGIOUS NATURALISM

What challenges does a religious–naturalist worldview face, such as the one I have identified? What would seem to be problematic aspects of it? Let me highlight some of these challenges without suggesting that there are no resources within religious naturalism to deal with them in a satisfying way.

First, I present an objection against God-talking religious naturalists; analogous arguments could be produced against other religious naturalists who embrace core belief (5) and participate in traditional religious gatherings. Recall that the belief is that some of the central traditional religious concepts are important or even essential metaphors or symbols expressing the sacredness of nature, the highest and most indispensable human ideals and values, and the central features of human flourishing.

It concerns, more precisely, those God-talking religious naturalists who want to remain a part of the Christian or, say, the Islamic community, who want to say, "I am a Christian" or "I am a Muslim." I will exemplify the problem by focusing on Christianity. Alvin Plantinga states this challenge quite bluntly. He maintains that the kind of radical reconstruction of theology a religious naturalist like Kaufman is involved in "encourages dishonesty and hypocrisy; it results in a sort of private code whereby one utters the same phrases as those who accept Christian belief but means something wholly different by them. You thereby appear to concur with those who accept Christian belief; in fact, you wholly reject what they believe."[36] This is a moral objection, which we can refer to as *the dishonest label objection.*

Perhaps there is a problem here, but things are not as straightforward as Plantinga suggests. Christianity, after all, is a pluralistic religion that has adapted to changing cultural contexts for more than two millennia. We have Christians who belong to different denominations and who emphasize, believe, and do different things. Moreover, we have more or less liberal and conservative Christians within these various denominations. We have, for instance, Christian fundamentalists who interpret Genesis literally, believing that God created the earth roughly 10,000 years ago and that there was a Noah's ark, which alone sailed the flooded earth. We have less conservative Christians who take these as religious stories to be interpreted metaphorically, but which still convey religious truths. Such people believe that Jesus Christ is the son of God, who was

---

[36] Alvin Plantinga, *Warranted Christian Belief.* Oxford University Press, 2000, p. 42.

raised from the dead by God, and that he had an important message from God to deliver to us. Liberals think that the incarnation should not be interpreted literally. Instead, we have in Jesus embodied, or incarnated, the ideal of human life lived in faithful response to God so that God could act through him. Accordingly, Jesus embodied a love that is a human reflection of divine love. Jesus makes God real to us, and his life and teaching challenge us to live in God's presence and to care for the poor and the oppressed. The statement that God is love and cares about us, especially about the poor and the oppressed, is believed to be literally true. Perhaps there is also a life after death in communion with God, in which every person, even those whose life on earth has been a living hell, will get a chance to flourish. Other liberals do not think that there is an afterlife. Heaven is a metaphor for our community with God here and now; to believe anything else is dangerous and a deviation from what is really important.

Often, these individuals attend different churches, but they can also be found in the same one. Who, then, is it that we should think exhibits Christian belief, and who is it, following Plantinga, that we should consider dishonest? This is not an easy question to answer. Do we get into even more trouble if we add radical theologians such as Kaufman to this picture – people who do not believe that Christians or anyone else can enter into a relationship with God through prayer or worship? We cannot interact with God since there is no God. God is, according to such thinkers, not the loving creator of the world or anything of that kind but is instead a symbol or metaphor for the sum of our values, representing to us their ideal unity, their claims upon us, and their creative power, or something of that sort; and this is what Christians should confess in their churches and express through rituals and sacraments.

You are, perhaps, dishonest if you are not explicit about your Christian religious naturalism. However, these individuals appear to be explicit about their views, at least in their academic writing, and I see no reason why we should assume that they would be any less so when in church. Notice, though, that the second group of religious naturalists does not face this challenge: those who reject God talk or the importance of traditional religious symbols and concepts. Instead, they emphasize that belief in the sacredness of nature suffices.

The core idea of religious naturalists is that it is possible and desirable to develop a worldview that is neither a form of supernaturalism (such as theism, Buddhism, or the new spirituality) nor a type of secular naturalism. In fact, they believe a religious–naturalist worldview is the most reasonable option available today. But is there logical space for such an in-between worldview? In particular, the reasons why the worldview of religious naturalists differs from that of secular naturalists seem unconvincing. Let us call this *the unique identity challenge*.

Consider, for instance, that Richard Dawkins, the well-known advocate of nonreligious or secular naturalism, is also known for expressing the wonder of living things, and he reckons that science inspires such wonder.[37] He maintains that real science does not diminish the enchantment of nature but rather enhances the poetry of experience by revealing the workings of the natural world in their full wonder. Dawkins says that, when it comes to feeling awe about living things, he has more in common with the Reverend William Paley than with atheists such as A. J. Ayer and David Hume. Nature, he thinks, is worthy of our awe and reverence. But why should we not classify him as a religious naturalist? If religious naturalists are to be known for their reverence for nature, Dawkins seems to qualify as one. But how could this be the case if he is a nonreligious naturalist? It appears that religious naturalists must offer better reasons for how their worldview differs from that of awe-affirming secular naturalists. What is it, more exactly, that makes a religious naturalist religious and is such that it does not, at the same time, make a secular naturalist religious?

Suppose that the answer to this question is simply that religious naturalists affirm the *sacredness of nature*; therefore, awe-affirming secular naturalists' reverence of nature is not enough. Indeed, there are good reasons to believe Dawkins would deny that nature is sacred. The belief that nature is sacred makes attitudes such as awe, reverence, and devotion appropriate ways to direct our minds toward nature. Dawkins has these or at least similar attitudes but lacks the belief in nature's sacredness; they have, in his case, a different evidential ground.

However, whether this is an adequate response to the unique identity challenge depends on what we mean by "sacred." We have seen that Wildman maintains that the "sacredness of nature expresses the self-transcendent potential of nature,"[38] and Kaufman highlights the unexpected creative power manifested in nature, as well as the serendipitous creativity of the natural processes that brought us and many other living things into being. But why would anyone deny the self-transcendent

---

[37] Richard Dawkins, *Unweaving the Rainbow*. Penguin Books, 1998.
[38] Wildman, "Religious Naturalism: Oxymoronic Muddle or Future Spiritual Juggernaut?" p. 54.

potential of nature or the serendipitous creativity of the natural processes? Is it not the evolutionary forces that began with the amoeba and have now led to the existence of more than a million species, some as complex as *Homo sapiens*, truly amazing? If the notion of sacred refers to this, we can probably assume Dawkins shares this belief with religious naturalists. Often, this property of natural processes is named "emergence."

This understanding aligns well with the views of other religious naturalists. Ursula Goodenough and Terrence W. Deacon write about the sacred emergence of nature and maintain that: "Religious naturalism, in this context, describes a person's interpretative, spiritual, and moral responses to ... our emergentist understandings of nature, where these spheres are ordinarily not experienced as separate categories, but rather as an overall orientation."[39] But then the original problem seems to reappear. If "sacred" is merely another term for "emergence," then there is only a verbal and not a real difference between religious naturalism and (some forms of) secular naturalism. Alternatively, if sacred emergence differs from nonsacred emergence, we would like to know what distinguishes them from each other.

Moreover, what is the actual justification for thinking that nature is sacred if it is supposed to contain something religious that goes beyond science and the discovery of emergent processes? Why hold such a belief? It cannot be that nature is sacred because it is identical to God, since religious naturalists reject pantheism. It cannot be that an unseen spiritual reality is the source of all visible things because they reject all forms of supernaturalism. It cannot be that nature has intrinsic or inherent value because I think that you have moral standing, even equal moral status, as I do, but that does not seem to give me a reason to believe that you are a sacred being. Lastly, nature is full of not just creativity and transcendence but also suffering and evil; thus, certain fundamental features of nature seem to make it a less appropriate object of sacredness.

---

[39] Ursula Goodenough and Terrence W. Deacon, "The Sacred Emergence of Nature." In *The Oxford Handbook of Religion and Science*, edited by Philip Clayton. Oxford University Press, 2006, pp. 864–865.

7

A Scientistic Worldview

Given that secular worldviews are not institutionalized in the same way as major religions, it is unclear what the range of beliefs and values of secular people might be and whether they are clustered in sets, as they often are in particular religions or faith traditions. However, in this study, I will distinguish between three such clusters. Indeed, I will express them so that they become coherent and distinctive nonreligious worldviews – scientism, secular humanism, and transhumanism – although combining them in different ways is possible. This chapter will focus on the first one, a scientistic worldview, but I will argue that they all share certain core naturalistic commitments in common, so we also need to take a closer look at naturalism.

However, I will begin by situating atheism within the framework of secular worldviews. Indeed, "scientific atheism" and "humanistic atheism" are terms sometimes used as alternative names for scientism and secular humanism,[1] not excluding that there are other possibilities that atheists could embrace. Both are highly influential but distinct ways of developing a secular outlook on life. The former is well known among philosophers and natural scientists, while the latter is more familiar to the general public and scholars in the social sciences and humanities. My purpose here is not to evaluate these alternative secular worldviews but to make their respective core commitments explicit and point out that they face different challenges and constitute two distinct worldviews, which should not be conflated or treated as the same.

---

[1] Stephen LeDrew, *The Evolution of Atheism.* Oxford University Press, 2016, p. 14.

ATHEISM AND NATURALISM

Atheism in modern Western history primarily manifests itself as a response to and rejection of theism, mostly as embedded in Christianity but by extension also in Judaism and Islam. Accordingly, I will take an atheist to be someone who disbelieves in God's existence or believe that God does not exist. In contrast, an agnostic neither believes that God exists nor believes that God does not exist but withholds judgment, and a theist believes that God exists. This mirrors the logical distinction between believing that p is true, disbelieving that p is true (i.e., believing that p is false), and not knowing what to believe about p. If we understand atheism in this way, it contains merely one ontological claim and says nothing about what else atheists believe about the nature of reality, their degree of certainty about the nonexistence of God, what their grounds are for holding this to be the actual state of affairs, or how they believe we should live our lives and think about life's significance or meaningfulness. Hence, there is more than one worldview option available to atheists. Atheists can combine their negative belief (that there is no God) with different affirmative beliefs about the nature of reality and our place in it.

If the substitution theory discussed in Chapter 1 is correct, we should not assume that atheists could avoid adopting, consciously or unconsciously, some or other affirmative beliefs about reality. Atheists, like everyone else, in their ways of thinking, talking, and acting, inescapably express a worldview of some kind. Atheism could be an element in all those worldviews that deny the existence of God. The notion of worldview provides an overarching framework into which both religious and nonreligious outlooks on life can be fitted, identifying features that can be compared and analyzed. I have suggested that secular worldviews share a commonality in denying the existence of a transcendent, divine, or spiritual dimension of reality and instead affirm or assume that reality has a different makeup. It is this structure that is important for understanding and living our lives. Secular people can understand this alternative outlook on reality in various ways. Still, I will assume that a commitment to naturalism is something that adherents to scientism, secular humanism, and transhumanism share in common.

Accordingly, I shall define naturalism so that it will contain as core beliefs no elements that advocates of these three secular worldviews cannot share. This is not standard procedure in philosophy, including the philosophy of religion. Instead, naturalism is often equated with scientism or scientific naturalism. My understanding of naturalism will include, as naturalists, also people who deny that the scientific method is the only method for acquiring knowledge or reliable information or that all reality can be captured using impersonal and valueless categories and concepts. Naturalism is more inclusive than scientific naturalism and is viewed as the main alternative to theism. David Macarthur writes, "Arguably, the basic philosophical motivation for naturalism is anti-supernaturalism, in particular, the denial that philosophy requires any *theistic* underpinnings of the sort that characterize the vast majority of the systems of Western philosophy throughout its 2500-year history."[2] Graham Oppy and N. N. Trakakis maintain, "Many atheists have been concerned to develop alternative worldviews to the kind of worldviews that are presented in the world's religions; and, in particular, many atheists have been concerned to develop naturalistic worldviews that leave no room for any kind of supernatural entities."[3] I believe this is correct: A naturalistic worldview would undoubtedly be the primary alternative for most secular intellectuals.

What, then, more exactly, is naturalism? We gave a partial answer in the chapter on a religious–naturalist worldview. We identified two core beliefs. The first one is as follows:

(N1) There is nothing beyond or beside nature or the natural order, and consequently, everything that exists is part of nature (*the naturalistic thesis*).

Nature is everything that exists, has existed, and will exist. Or, as Carl Sagan so elegantly put it in the TV series *Cosmos*: "The universe is all that is or ever was or ever will be." What, more precisely, nature consists of is still an open question: how naturalists understand (N1) will, as we shall see later in this chapter, have consequences for whether secular intellectuals embrace a scientistic or a humanistic worldview. Moreover, there is no explanation for why nature or the universe exists; it simply is. A related belief to (N1) is then as follows:

(N2) Nature (or the universe) and its natural laws are a brute fact in the sense that this is the place where explanations end.

---

[2] David Macarthur, "Liberal Naturalism and the Scientific Image of the World," *Inquiry*, 2018, 62/5, p. 573.
[3] Graham Oppy and N. N. Trakakis, "Late-Twentieth-Century Atheism." In *Twentieth-Century Philosophy of Religion*, edited by Graham Oppy and N. N. Trakakis. Acumen, 2009, p. 301.

Naturalists contrast this with the theistic belief that God is the most fundamental layer of reality and thus lacks an explanation. So, what appears to theists as something demanding an explanation (nature or the universe) appears to the naturalists as not needing any explanation, and vice versa.

Since, according to theists, God is the creator and sustainer of nature and its laws, the naturalistic thesis entails the rejection of a theistic worldview. All naturalists are atheists, although not all atheists are naturalists. Some Buddhists, for instance, deny that any God or gods exist, but they also believe that nature or the natural order is an illusion. Hence, they are not naturalists. Since naturalism entails atheism, it is incompatible with agnosticism. However, there might be gods immanent in the natural order, as well as ancestor spirits, angels, disembodied souls, immortal souls, or processes such as reincarnation, karma, or channeling, and spiritual energy in physical objects. But, as we have seen that Mario De Caro and David Macarthur, both naturalists, point out, "perhaps the most familiar definition [of naturalism] is in terms of the rejection of supernatural entities such as gods, demons, souls and ghosts," including "the Judeo-Christian God and the immaterial soul."[4] All these forms of being, properties, and processes are no part of the naturalistic conception of nature (and not merely the God theists believe is the creator and sustainer of the natural order). Naturalists have, in other words, a restricted notion of nature or the natural order. This means that naturalism goes beyond atheism in that naturalists not only deny the existence of God, as atheists do, but they also deny the existence of a transcendent, divine, or spiritual dimension to existence in general. Naturalists reject all forms of supernaturalism. Hence, another core claim is as follows:

(N3) There is no God, no gods, no beings such as spirits, angels, or demons, no processes like karma, reincarnation, and channeling, and no entities such as immaterial human or animal souls (*anti-supernaturalism*).

Naturalists take anti-supernaturalism to entail a rejection of all religions. (Remember that religious naturalists are an exception to this rule.) Typically, they believe science has undermined religious worldviews. For instance, Steven Pinker maintains that the worldview guiding the moral and spiritual values of an educated person today is the one presented to us

---

[4] Mario De Caro and David Macarthur, "Introduction: The Nature of Naturalism." In *Naturalism in Question*, edited by Mario De Caro and David Macarthur. Harvard University Press, 2004, pp. 2–3.

by science: "The findings of science entail that the belief systems of all the world's traditional religions and cultures – their theories of the origins of life, humans, and societies – are factually mistaken."[5] Alternatively, naturalists could think that science and religion, in some but not all forms, are compatible and acknowledge that they are different human practices with or without (significant) areas of contact. Secular intellectuals who are "irreconcilabilists" reject religion for scientific reasons, whereas those who, like Michael Ruse, are "reconcilabilists" reject religion primarily for nonscientific reasons. Ruse maintains that science and a theistic worldview are compatible. He writes: "These central [Christian] core claims by their very nature go beyond the reach of science. I do not say that you must be a Christian, but I do say that in light of modern science you can be a Christian. We have seen no sound arguments to the contrary."[6] Ruse himself rejects the existence of God for several reasons, but these, he tells us, have very little to do with science; the most important of them is the problem of evil: The existence of a massive amount of natural and moral evil in the world makes the existence of God highly unlikely.

What else are the distinctive features of a naturalistic worldview? A first element, sometimes referred to as the matter-first view, is based on scientific discoveries indicating that life and consciousness developed relatively late in the evolutionary history of the universe. Life and consciousness emerged from nonorganic materials, which constitute the fundamental elements of reality. If naturalism is correct, then the world, at the bottom, is wholly impersonal. Hence, a fourth core claim is as follows:

(N4) Matter or physical particles lie at the root of everything; consequently, the world, at the bottom, is wholly impersonal (*the matter-first view*).

The materialist or physicalist understanding of reality expressed in the matter-first view goes beyond the naturalistic thesis in that it says that, ultimately, nature consists of matter or physical particles in motion and that all that is nonmaterial, such as consciousness, thought, and purpose (if they do exist), is a consequence of particles that are fundamentally impersonal and without intentionality or consciousness. This means that the ultimate explanation of reality must, as John Searle says, be given in

---

[5] Steven Pinker, "Science Is Not Your Enemy," *The New Republic*, August 7, 2013, https://newrepublic.com/article/114127/science-not-enemy-humanities.
[6] Michael Ruse, *Science and Spirituality*. Cambridge University Press, 2010, p. 233.

terms of mindless, meaningless, unfree, nonrational, and brute physical particles.[7] Consequently, human behavior, just like the behavior of any other thing in nature, must be, in the end, traceable back to material causes and effects.

Naturalists also believe that nature is *self-organized*. Physical or non-living things have inherent tendencies; they exhibit specific behaviors. Iron, for example, expands when heated. Water turns to ice if the temperature goes below zero. Over time, through this self-organization, more complex material states have emerged in the universe. This has happened through the interaction of simple states and structures, resulting in the emergence of properties that the original parts themselves did not have. The processes of emergence that occurred when living things started to evolve from nonliving things are described by evolutionary theory.

Many naturalists point out that the discovery that made naturalism a live option for secular intellectuals and severely undermined the inherited theistic worldview was the discovery of natural selection, the key element of evolutionary theory. Gregory W. Dawes, in his defense of naturalism, writes, "Until 1859, …, it seemed that the diversity of living organisms could not be accounted for without reference to God, but Charles Darwin provided us with a natural alternative."[8] Richard Dawkins agrees, stating that before the appearance of evolutionary theory, people were more or less forced to believe in the existence of God. How else could such a diversity of living beings have emerged, and the various species function so effectively? Take the tiger as an example. It runs smoothly and catches its prey. It does not stagger here and there; it does not have useless legs sticking out here and there without function, ears that get in the way of its eyes so that it sometimes runs into trees, or tails sticking out that it trips over. But how does the tiger arise, and how can it be so apparently well-designed? Surely, all life forms could logically exist here, always, more or less as finished, almost perfect entities. They could have been a brute fact (just like the universe or nature as a totality is) that could not be explained. However, this idea was not entirely easy to digest, and the idea that God created the world with all its diverse life forms was much easier to understand and intellectually absorb. Naturalism or atheism did not have much going for them at that time. For Dawes and Dawkins, it is, therefore, almost obvious that

---

[7] John Searle, *The Construction of Social Reality*. The Free Press, 1995, pp. 4–5.

[8] Gregory W. Dawes, "In Defense of Naturalism," *International Journal of Philosophy of Religion*, 2011, 70/1, p. 15.

people before Darwin believed that there was a God behind the existence of all species and all life on earth.

While some philosophers have argued that David Hume, long before Darwin's time, refuted this kind of teleological argument for God's existence or the assumption that life in all its diverse forms is God's creation, Dawkins does not share this view. He points out: "But what Hume did was criticize the logic of using apparent design of nature as *positive* evidence for the existence of God. He did not offer any *alternative* explanation for apparent design, but left the question open .... I can't help feeling that such a position, though logically sound, would have left one feeling pretty unsatisfactory ..."[9] Dawkins's point is that a flawed hypothesis or explanation is always better than no explanation at all. While Hume may have shown that atheism was logically defensible, it was only with Darwin's theory of evolution that it became possible to be an "intellectually fulfilled atheist."[10]

For naturalists, evolution in some form is the only reasonable explanation for the diversity and complexity of life, and perhaps eventually for its origin. The theory of evolution thus has an extremely important role in shaping and justifying secular worldviews. It makes atheism and its accompanying worldview(s) reasonable; without it, naturalism is much more difficult to defend intellectually – no wonder some atheist associations celebrate Darwin Day. The secular philosopher Thomas Nagel maintains that evolutionary theory "enabled modern secular culture to heave a great collective sigh of relief, by apparently providing a way to eliminate purpose, meaning, and design as fundamental features of the world. Instead, they become epiphenomena, generated incidentally by a process that can be entirely explained by the operation of the nonteleological laws of physics on the material of which we and our environments are all composed."[11]

Before Darwin, naturalism was indeed one of several *possible* worldview options, but after 1859, it also became a *reasonable* worldview option, allowing one to be an intellectually fulfilled naturalist. Dawkins and many other naturalists argue that we should take one step further, because evolutionary theory demonstrates that naturalism is currently the only reasonable option for a scientifically informed person. This is because evolutionary theory shows that our world has not been designed by God or anyone else. We now, Dawkins writes, know:

[9] Richard Dawkins, *The Blind Watchmaker*. W. W. Norton & Company, 1986, p. 6.
[10] Dawkins, *The Blind Watchmaker*, p. 6.
[11] Thomas Nagel, *The Last Word*. Oxford University Press, 1997, p. 131.

All appearances to the contrary, the only watchmaker in nature is the blind forces of physics, albeit deployed in a very special way. A true watchmaker has foresight: he designs his cogs and springs, and plans their interconnections, with a future purpose in his mind's eye. Natural selection, the blind, unconscious, automatic process which Darwin discovered, and which we now know is the explanation for the existence and apparently purposeful form of all life, has no purpose in mind. It has no mind and no mind's eye. It does not plan for the future. It has no vision, no foresight, no sight at all. If it can be said to play the role of watchmaker in nature, it is the *blind* watchmaker.[12]

The evidence of evolution reveals a universe without design. This is *the blind watchmaker argument*. So, naturalists believe that evolution is an unguided and blind process, either because they, like Dawkins, think that science entails this or because it is the only reasonable interpretation of evolution that is compatible with the core beliefs (N1–N4) of the naturalistic worldview.

To summarize, naturalists believe that nature is self-organized. There are inherent tendencies in physical things that, over time, cause more complex things to emerge in natural history. In this way, nonlife (pure matter) can generate life, and unconscious life can evolve into conscious life through natural selection, random mutations, and similar processes. These qualitative changes have occurred without the input of any power existing outside or beyond nature, for instance, a God who has in some way directed and guided the evolution of life and matter.

Moreover, nature or the universe is not in any way intended to exist and presumably exists only by pure chance. So, there is no reason why the world happens to exist or why conscious life has arisen, and consequently, there is no ultimate meaning. If we put these two ideas together, yet another core belief of naturalism would be as follows:

(N5) Nature is self-organized, and the existence of nature, its properties, and their inherent tendencies to produce increased complexity over time result from purely unintended causal processes and natural laws that happen to exist (*the self-organized and randomness thesis*).

It means that naturalists deny the existence of natural teleology. The existence and structure of the cosmos are accidental or coincidental in the sense that they do not exist and evolve because of any underlying purpose. (*Teleology* means some things can be explained in terms of their

---

[12] Dawkins, *The Blind Watchmaker*, p. 5.

purpose or goal.) Nor do we, as a species, exist for a reason. But naturalists do not necessarily deny that personal or teleological explanations can be used to explain what people do, for example, that there is a purpose behind my writing this sentence and not another. We will see that for secular humanists, human teleology is crucial because, without its affirmation, they cannot distinguish between behavior and action, and the idea that we are persons risks being undermined, along with the affirmation of human dignity. But many scientific naturalists deny this possibility and reduce personal explanations to material explanations. However, the self-organized and randomness thesis does not involve a rejection of this possibility of human teleology, but what it does involve is a rejection that there is a purpose or plan for matter to exist and have the structure it has and that there is life, that there is conscious life, and that there is, even, self-conscious human life in nature. It implies a rejection of a plan for anything to exist at all.

Therefore, nature or the Universe is morally indifferent to our or other living things' existence. How, then, does the existence of *morality* and its normativity fit into a naturalistic universe? Even if it is unexpected that persons appear in such a universe, it is not surprising that, once such creatures exist, moral norms evolve. Evolutionary theory provides natural explanations for the emergence of morality, as well as other cultural phenomena. Roughly, the idea is that we humans, *Homo sapiens*, evolved from simpler life forms through natural selection, but life was (and is) difficult, so we needed (and need) each other's help to survive. That is why we live in groups together. However, we cannot live together in groups without rules or norms, such as "Don't kill others in our group," "Don't steal from them," and "Don't lie to them." With these needs, we develop our ability to express value judgments and, it seems, experience good (and evil) and not just experience pain and cold as many other organisms can. The basis of morality is specific human needs. We refer to these rules or norms as *morality* or *ethics*; over time, these obligations expand to include individuals outside our group. We can summarize this naturalistic genealogy as follows:

(N6) Morals or ethics are a special kind of social norms that arise from the human need to live together in groups, and there are no values, goods, or moral laws that exist independently of society and nature (*the naturalist genealogy of morality*).

Although moral norms can be seen as a form of social norms, they appear to be different. For social norms, in general, it is to my advantage to follow them provided that (a) enough other people in my environment expect me to follow them and (b) they also follow them. But a moral norm, we think, applies whether other people follow it or not. If slavery is immoral, then it is a moral norm that I should follow even if it turns out that a majority in the society I live in considers it legitimate to use enslaved people for labor. My willingness to follow the norm should not depend on whether enough other people in my group follow it. This is unlike social norms such as Swedes greeting people by shaking hands, as opposed to, for example, in China, where people greet each other by bowing. Simply put, we can say that the normativity of social norms is conditional (it depends on how willing other people are to behave as the norms prescribe). In contrast, the normativity of moral norms seems categorical (it applies to us regardless of whether acting according to them receives approval or disapproval from people around us).

Thus, there appears to be an interesting objectivity associated with moral norms that distinguishes them from other social norms. That it is wrong to murder other people or that all people have certain basic moral rights does not seem to be understandable solely based on the fact that those social groups that have developed such norms have been more likely to survive and reproduce. Nor does it seem possible to reduce these moral norms to a set of social norms expressing our likes and dislikes, which we have made most of the world's population follow through social rewards and punishments. As we will see in the following discussion, secular intellectuals understand this apparent objectivity of morality differently. In particular, we will observe an interesting difference in how morality is understood within a scientistic worldview compared to a secular–humanist worldview.

More could be said about naturalism in general, and some naturalists would prefer to express these core theses in slightly different ways. However, I believe this account provides a sufficient background against which we can explore the content of three distinct secular worldviews: scientism, secular humanism, and transhumanism.

SCIENTISM OR SCIENTIFIC NATURALISM

The first secular worldview we will examine is one that prioritizes science in all areas of life. Often, it has been referred to as scientism or scientific naturalism; other names used include "strict naturalism," "philosophical naturalism," "metaphysical naturalism," "scientific expansionism," or "scientific atheism." However, as already alluded to, often in philosophy, it is merely called naturalism. Since the possibility of a liberal form of naturalism is essential for developing a coherent form of secular humanism, as we will see in Chapter 8, we should reject this equation. Scientific naturalists maintain that secular people should rely on what science says about reality and then try to understand themselves, their lives, and society from that starting point. Science is the measure of all things. An important point to note, especially for those of us from non-English–speaking parts of the world, is that "science" in this context refers exclusively to the natural sciences, such as physics, chemistry, and biology.

"Scientism" is sometimes used as a pejorative label to indicate a misplaced faith in science. In contrast, this study will use the term descriptively, though it remains contested, similar to terms such as "feminism," "naturalism," "atheism," or "theism." After all, science is an evolving enterprise, and we cannot, therefore, a priori or once and for all, say that the proposed expansions are illegitimate or misguided. Advocates of scientism argue that we should take their claims seriously because science has, in the past, successfully addressed issues previously thought to be beyond its scope. Therefore, the dispute about the limits of science cannot be settled once and for all, and we should be optimistic simply because of science's great track record.

However, some people immediately say they are scientistic in their thinking. Michael Shermer simply embraces the view of scientism and proclaims:

We show deference to our leaders; pay respect to our elders and follow the dictates of our shamans; this being the Age of Science, it is scientism's shamans who command our veneration. ... [B]ecause of language we are also storytelling, mythmaking primates, with scientism as the foundational stratum of our story and scientists as the premier mythmakers of our time.[13]

Alex Rosenberg and Steven Pinker aim to reclaim the term away from their opponents and appropriate the pejorative for a position they are prepared to defend.[14] The overwhelming intellectual and practical successes of science have led them to think that there are no real limits to the competence of science, no limits to what can be achieved

---

[13] Michael Shermer, "The Shamans of Scientism," *Scientific American*, 2002, 286/6, p. 35.

[14] Alex Rosenberg, *The Atheist's Guide to Reality*. W. W. Norton & Company, 2011, p. 6; and Steven Pinker, "Science Is Not Your Enemy," New Republic, August 6, 2013, www.newrepublic.com/article/114127/science-not-enemy-humanities.

in the name of science (this is the Great Success of Modern Science Argument). There is nothing outside the domain of science, nor is there any area of human life to which science cannot successfully be applied. A scientific account of anything and everything constitutes the full story of the universe and its inhabitants. Or, if there are limits to the scientific enterprise, the idea is that science, at least, sets the boundaries for what we humans can ever know about reality. This is the view of scientism.

Several scientists, including Peter Atkins, Richard Dawkins, Carl Sagan, and Edward O. Wilson, have advocated for some form of scientism. Many philosophers, such as Patricia Churchland, Daniel D. Dennett, and Alex Rosenberg, also embrace scientism. These scientists, more so than these philosophers, have sold an enormous number of books, in addition to receiving prestigious scientific prizes and awards. The views of these scientists have been discussed in newspapers, on the Web, and broadcast on radio and television. If scientism has been around for a while, the significant impact these advocates of scientism have had on popular culture is new. They have brought not only science but also scientism right into the living rooms of ordinary people.

I will not treat scientism as a kind of religion but continue to use the notion of worldview. This understanding fits well with how one of the most reflected and consistent advocates of scientism expresses his outlook on life. Alex Rosenberg says,

we'll call the worldview that all us atheists (and even some agnostics) share 'scientism.' This is the conviction that the methods of science are the only reliable ways to secure knowledge of anything; that science's description of the world is correct in its fundamentals; and that when 'complete,' what science tells us will not be surprisingly different from what it tells us today.[15]

He adds, "Being scientistic just means treating science as our exclusive guide to reality, to nature – both our own nature and everything else's."[16]

In my rational reconstruction, I will assume that scientific naturalists or advocates of scientism accept the core beliefs of naturalism (N1–N5). Still, as we will see later in this chapter, they think there are more robust formulations of some of these available, and they prefer those.

[15] Alex Rosenberg, *The Atheist's Guide to Reality*. W. W. Norton & Company, 2011, pp. 6–7.
[16] Rosenberg, *The Atheist's Guide to Reality*, p. 8.

The Limits of Knowledge and Reality

Probably the most well-known claim of scientism expresses a particular idea about the limits of knowledge. It says that the only genuine knowledge about reality can be found through science and science alone. The only kind of knowledge we can have is scientific knowledge. Several scientists and scholars have adopted one version or another of this view. Patricia Churchland claims, "In the idealized long run, the completed science is a true description of reality; there is no other Truth and no other Reality."[17] Dawkins tells us, "Science is the only way to understand the real world."[18] R. C. Lewontin moves in the same direction, saying that people ought "to accept a social and intellectual apparatus, Science, as the only begetter of truth."[19] Stephen Hawking and Leonard Mlodinow maintain, "Most of us don't worry about these questions most of the time. But almost all of us must sometimes wonder: Why are we here? Where do we come from? Traditionally, these are questions for philosophy, but philosophy is dead. ... Scientists have become the bearers of the torch of discovery in our quest for knowledge."[20] In his essay, "The Limitless Power of Science," Peter Atkins advocates the "omnicompetence of science" and believes that "science, with its currently successful pursuit of universal competence ... should be acknowledged king."[21] Moreover, like Rosenberg explicitly connecting scientism to atheism, he writes, "There is no reason to suppose that science cannot deal with every aspect of existence. Only the religious – among whom I include not merely the prejudiced but also the underinformed – hope that there is a dark corner of the physical Universe, or of the universe of experience, that science can never hope to illuminate."[22]

Hence, one core belief of scientism is as follows:

(1) The only kind of genuine knowledge or understanding we can have is provided by science, and science sets the standard for justified or rational belief (the *scientistic–epistemic thesis*).

---

[17] Patricia Churchland, *Neurophilosophy*. MIT Press, 1986, p. 249.
[18] Richard Dawkins, "Thoughts for the Millennium." In *Microsoft Encarta Encyclopedia*, 2000.
[19] R. C. Lewontin, "Billions and Billions of Demons" (a review of Carl Sagan's book *The Demon-Haunted World*), in *The New York Review of Books*, January 9, 1997.
[20] Stephen Hawking and Leonard Mlodinow, *The Grand Design: New Answers to the Ultimate Questions of Life*. Bantam Press, 2010, p. 5.
[21] Peter Atkins, "The Limitless Power of Science." In *Nature's Imagination: The Frontiers of Scientific Vision*, edited by J. Cornwell. Oxford University Press, 1995, p. 132.
[22] Atkins, "The Limitless Power of Science," p. 125.

Claim (1) expresses a kind of epistemic exclusivism: Our beliefs are ultimately justifiable only by the methods of science. If one holds this epistemological view, then it is, of course, not difficult to understand that one would believe that everything, or at least as much as possible, could and should be understood in terms of science – because what we cannot understand and explain in terms of science is something that we cannot know anything about at all.

In that advocates of scientism treat science as the measure of all things, they are thereby interpreting the core doctrine of naturalism – that nature is all there is and ever will be – in one particular way. (Notice, again, that many scientific naturalists do not acknowledge this distinction but consider their view identical with naturalism.) Why does a scientific naturalist such as Jaegwon Kim ask, "What is it about intentionality or consciousness or content that require them to be naturalized? Why aren't they perfectly naturalistic as they are?"[23] It is arguable that people generally take it for granted that things like these are part of the furniture of the world. I think that the reason why these things are not "perfectly naturalistic as they are" is that a defining feature of the worldview that these naturalists embrace is the pride of place that they grant science. By "nature," they mean the space-time causal system that is studied and discovered by science and nothing more. As Wilfrid Sellars is famous for proclaiming, "Science is the measure of all things, of what is that it is, and of what is not that it is not."[24] However, this implies that (N1) of general naturalism is not precise enough to capture the core idea of scientism. What we need instead is something along the following lines:

(2) The only things that exist are the ones that the sciences can discover (the *scientistic–ontological thesis*).

I wrote in Chapter 1 that we can take ontology to be the inventory of all the things, properties, and relations that must exist for reality to be as it is. Scientific naturalists then maintain that science provides a complete inventory of all the things, properties, and relations that exist in the real world. "Natural" in the natural world means essentially the same as "natural" in the natural sciences. At the bottom, reality is what

---

[23] Jaegwon Kim, "The American Origins of Philosophical Naturalism," *Journal of Philosophical Research*, 2003, 28/Supplement, p. 85.

[24] Wilfrid Sellars, "Empiricism and the Philosophy of Mind." In *Science, Perception, and Reality*, edited by Wilfrid Sellars. London: Routledge, 1963, p. 173.

the natural sciences say it is and nothing more. Nature is equivalent to scientific nature. Daniel C. Dennett summarizes his naturalistic stance: "I declare my starting point to be the objective, materialist, third-person world of the physical sciences."[25] Core belief (2) goes beyond (1) in that it does not merely state that the only reality that we can know or can rationally believe anything about is the one to which science has access. It maintains further that only the reality that science can discover exists and nothing else.

The scientistic–ontological thesis encompasses the scientistic–epistemic thesis because we could not know anything about what does not exist. We cannot scientifically know something about a reality that science cannot access simply because it does not exist. However, the epistemic thesis does not entail the ontological one. If science only sets the limits for what we can know, then there may be nonscientific dimensions to reality. The epistemic core belief merely entails that we cannot know anything about such aspects of reality.

One way of stating the ontological thesis is to maintain that nothing but atoms or the matter they are composed of exists in the world. This is the idea that material objects are the only entities and causes in the world. Carl Sagan maintains:

I am a collection of water, calcium, and organic molecules called Carl Sagan. You are a collection of almost identical molecules with a different collective label. But is that all? Is there nothing in here but molecules? Some people find this idea somehow demeaning to human dignity. For myself, I find it elevating that our universe permits the evolution of molecular machines as intricate and subtle as we.[26]

Sagan argues that science has shown us that the only things that exist are material objects and their interactions. We are, consequently, merely "molecular machines" that are not essentially different from artifacts (i.e., machines). All this, Sagan thinks, is scientifically knowable, not perhaps when the scientific project will be fully developed or completed, but right here and now. Francis Crick calls these ideas the "Astonishing Hypothesis" and writes:

The Astonishing Hypothesis is that "You," your joys and your sorrows, your memories and your ambitions, your sense of identity and free will, are in fact no more than the behavior of a vast assembly of nerve cells and their associated

---

[25] Daniel Dennett, *The Intentional Stance*. MIT Press, 1987, p. 5.
[26] Carl Sagan, *Cosmos*. Ballantine Books, 1980, p. 105.

molecules. As Lewis Carroll's Alice might have phrased it: "You're nothing but a pack of neurons." This hypothesis is so alien to the ideas of most people alive today that it can truly be called astonishing.[27]

Unfortunately, according to Crick, most people's ideas have been shaped by prescientific illusions of religion. Still, only science can, in the long run, free us from the superstitions of our ancestors.

By now, it should be clear that the answer to Kim's question of why the things, properties, or relations that such words as "person," "the self," "intentionality," "consciousness," "agency," "beliefs," "reasons," "responsibility," and "values" refer to, need to be naturalized – and this no matter how natural they are taken by people in general to be – is that these phenomena do not line up neatly with any facts of the kind uncovered by science. They are difficult to locate in the third-person ontology of the sciences. Frank Jackson has referred to this as the "location problem."[28] Localizing a phenomenon means not only describing it but also attempting to explain and understand how it has arisen and fits within the possibilities and constraints of a particular worldview. The reason why free will, self-consciousness, the mental, and its products are questioned or appear to be anomalies has nothing to do with directly observing what humans do and say but with the difficulty of localizing these phenomena in a scientistic worldview. It is essential to understand that no one in the debate between advocates of the worldviews we study denies that, phenomenologically, it appears that humans possess self-consciousness or a self and have the rational ability to transcend physical–causal processes, forming beliefs, expressing intentions, and making value judgments, and that good and evil exist. Neither you nor I denies that the sun appears to revolve around the Earth, even though we know from what science has taught us that this is not the case. The Earth *appears to* be stationary when, in fact, it is rotating.

Since science is taken to be the arbiter of all reality, or at least all knowable reality, scientific naturalists will adopt a *skeptical attitude* toward all those things and properties that people believe exist but cannot be discovered and measured by science. Science is, after all, our exclusive guide to reality. Thus, this attitude extends beyond skepticism of theism and supernaturalism. Dennett exemplifies this attitude when he argues that Darwin's dangerous idea (i.e., evolution by natural selection)

[27] Francis Crick, *The Astonishing Hypothesis: The Scientific Search for the Soul.* Charles Scribner's Sons, 1994, p. 3.
[28] Frank Jackson, *From Metaphysics to Ethics.* Oxford University Press, pp. 1–5.

bears "an unmistakable likeness to universal acid: it eats through just about every traditional concept, and leaves in its wake a revolutionized worldview, with most of the old landmarks still recognizable, but transformed in fundamental ways."[29] "Darwin's dangerous idea is reductionism incarnate, promising to unite and explain just about everything in one magnificent vision."[30] Richard D. Alexander talks about the most recent discoveries in evolutionary biology as the greatest intellectual revolution of the twentieth century. He claims (just like Dennett) that these insights will profoundly impact our self-view, to such an extent that "we will have to start all over again to describe and understand ourselves, in terms alien to our intuitions."[31] Richard Dawkins is equally, if not even more, optimistic when it comes to what modern biology can deliver. He claims that we have "no longer ... to resort to superstition when faced with the deep problems: Is there a meaning to life? What are we for? What is man?"[32] According to him, science, particularly biology, can deal successfully with all these questions.

This skeptical attitude helps us understand why the *Online Medical Dictionary* defines scientism as the "concept that other areas besides science can and should be studied in a scientific manner, for example, the humanities."[33] Understood in this way, scientism is a standpoint within academic disputes about whether the social sciences and the humanities – such disciplines as psychology, sociology, anthropology, history, philosophy, literary studies, and religious studies – are genuinely autonomous and legitimate studies in their own right, like physics, chemistry, and biology. If one tends to answer "no" to this question, then one embraces scientism.

But we can now see that this attitude toward nonscientific academic studies merely results from embracing the scientistic–epistemic and the scientistic–ontological theses. So, one further scientistic thesis is as follows:

(3) The methods and theories of the natural sciences could and should be extended to the social sciences and humanities in such a way that these become the central methods and theories used, and thereby replace or at least marginalize previously used methods or theories considered central to these disciplines (*the expansionist thesis*).

---

[29] Daniel C. Dennett, *Darwin's Dangerous Idea*. Penguin Books, 1995, p. 63.
[30] Dennett, *Darwin's Dangerous Idea*, p. 82.
[31] Richard D. Alexander, *The Biology of Moral Systems*. Aldine De Gruyter, 1987, p. 3.
[32] Richard Dawkins, *The Selfish Gene*. Oxford University Press, 1989, p. 1.
[33] *Online Medical Dictionary*, "Scientism," October 9, 1997, www.mondofacto.com/facts/dictionary?scientism.

The expansionist thesis posits that academic studies not previously understood as part of the natural sciences can now become or need to be transformed into such a science. Steven Pinker, for instance, embraces this idea. He maintains that "scientism in the good sense" is not an imperialistic drive to occupy the humanities. Still, the humanities need to be transformed and enlightened by the sciences. He is surprised that scholars in the humanities are not delighted by the new ideas of science, that they resent the intrusion of science into the territories of the humanities, when in fact, "it is just the domain that would seem to be the most in need of an infusion of new ideas" and would in such a case "enjoy more of the explanatory depth of the sciences."[34] Hence, Pinker summons the humanities to a process of scientization. The sciences can give explanatory depth to the shallower understanding within the humanities. He aims to transform the nonscientific discourse of the humanities into a scientific one. Edward O. Wilson has made the same call: "It may not be too much to say that sociology and the other social sciences, as well as the humanities, are the last branches of biology waiting to be included in the Modern Synthesis."[35] We need to develop a Darwinian social and human science to obtain genuine knowledge and understanding of society and culture, not merely of physical nature. This mission is understandable in light of the core belief that our beliefs about reality are ultimately justifiable only by the methods of science.

The Everyday World and Ethics

Although advocates of scientism share a skeptical attitude toward everything that is not a proper part of science, they do not all draw the same conclusions about what to think about the nonscientific. This is because scientific naturalists essentially have two options to consider when assessing something that does not appear to be within the purview of science. They could either maintain that (a) the practice or phenomenon must be redescribed, reduced, or transformed into science (the *naturalization* or *scientization strategy*), or alternatively, they might maintain that (b) it must be explained away by science and treated as fiction, that is, it must either be taken as helpful but illusory belief or else be abandoned completely (the *elimination strategy*). They could try to either

---

[34] Pinker, "Science Is Not Your enemy," https://newrepublic.com/article/114127/science-not-enemy-humanities.
[35] Edward O. Wilson, *Sociobiology*. Harvard University Press, 1975, p. 4.

"naturalize" or "scientize" a phenomenon, that is, turn it into science, or reject it if that is not possible. But scientific naturalists disagree on what should be located in the first category and what should be placed in the second.

Let me illustrate this by revisiting what scientific naturalists think about the humanities before we proceed to consider the beliefs of everyday life. The humanities do not appear to be part of the sciences, so how should one think about this set of academic disciplines and their outcomes? Do the humanities have a place in a naturalistic world?

We have seen that Wilson argues that the humanities could and should be transformed or naturalized. He wants to find ways to incorporate them into a naturalistic, or more exactly, a scientistic worldview. Wilson maintains that the "only way to establish or to refute consilience [between the natural sciences and the humanities] is by the methods developed in the natural sciences ... [This idea's] best support is no more than an extrapolation of the consistent past success of the natural sciences. Its surest test will be its effectiveness in the social sciences and humanities."[36] Why would it be a problem if the natural sciences failed in undertaking this project? The answer given by scientific naturalists is that otherwise, there is a significant risk that there is no real content to the humanities since reality is at the bottom what science says it is and nothing more or, at the least, that there are no knowledge or justified beliefs in the humanities since our beliefs and our theories are justifiable only by the methods of the natural sciences.

Still, no such progress has been made yet, and many scholars in the humanities strongly oppose the scientization of their academic studies.[37] This response, of course, is irrelevant if one embraces a scientistic worldview. As Don Ross, James Ladyman, and David Spurrett phrase it, if it should turn out that science itself realizes that it cannot answer certain questions, then "we should [not] look to an institution other than science to answer such questions; we should in these cases forget about the questions."[38] Therefore, perhaps the elimination strategy is preferable. Rosenberg certainly thinks so; he maintains:

---

[36] Edward O. Wilson, *Consilience*. Alfred A. Knopf, 1999, p. 9.

[37] See, for instance, Leon Wieseltier's response to Pinker in Leon Wieseltier, "Crimes against Humanities," *New Republic*, September 3, 2013, www.newrepublic.com/article/114548/leon-wieseltier-responds-steven-pinkers-scientism.

[38] Don Ross, James Ladyman, and David Spurrett, "In Defense of Scientism." In *Everything Must Go: Metaphysics Naturalized*, edited by James Ladyman and Don Ross. Oxford University Press, 2007, p. 30.

There is only one way to acquire knowledge, and science's way is it. The research program this 'ideology' imposes has no room for purpose, for meaning, for value, or for stories. It cannot therefore accommodate the humanities as disciplines of inquiry, domains of knowledge. ... the humanities are a scientific dead end ... When it comes to real understanding, the humanities are nothing we have to take seriously, except as symptoms.[39]

Values, meaning, purpose, love, and beauty, studied in the humanities, are illusions: They are not within the purview of science and, therefore, have to be ruled out.

We have seen Crick argue similarly when it comes to who we are. In his view, we are nothing but a pack of neurons. As we also saw, Sagan proclaimed that we are nothing more than a collection of water, calcium, and organic molecules. This stance is quite reasonable if the core beliefs of scientism are taken to be true. What science cannot discover does not exist, or at least we know nothing about it. So, Jan Westerhoff argues that there is really no such thing as a self and my self. He writes, "many of our core beliefs about ourselves do not withstand [scientific] scrutiny. This presents a tremendous challenge for our everyday view of ourselves, as it suggests that in a very fundamental sense we are not real. Instead, our self is comparable to an illusion – but without anybody there that experiences the illusion."[40] He tells us that natural scientists have looked everywhere and cannot find the self. Given the scientistic assumption that what scientific methods cannot uncover does not exist, he concludes that our selves do not exist. There is an interesting overlap between scientific naturalism and Buddhism on this issue; both worldviews share a denial of the self (the no-self view) – even if the reasons why differ (see Chapter 4).

We can still *talk* as if there are persons, passports, and lovers, but they are not real features of the world. Daniel Dennett says he is committed to denying persons as substantive selves that essentially possess a first-person point of view because persons will not be part of the ultimate true scientific account of things.[41] However, he still thinks it is essential to talk about persons or human rights; it makes "*good* nonsense."[42] Folk language is inevitable; there is no way to translate what we say in

[39] Rosenberg, *The Atheist's Guide to Reality*, pp. 306–307.
[40] Jan Westerhoff, "The Self: The One and Only You," *New Scientist*, 2013, 217/2905, p. 37.
[41] Daniel Dennett, *Breaking the Spell: Religion as a Natural Phenomenon*. Penguin, 2006, p. 107.
[42] Dennett, *Darwin's Dangerous Idea*, p. 507.

it into the language of science. But we should not assume that when we use folk language, we are describing how things really are. Only when we use the language of science do we do that. That is why scientific naturalists can speak in folk language about selves, persons, morality, and human rights, as well as our beliefs about a mother's love and our sense of freedom, even though they (if they embrace the elimination strategy) do not believe these things exist.

Moreover, if morality or ethics cannot be made scientific, nihilism follows. Rosenberg is the scientific naturalist who is perhaps most explicit about this. He argues, "the biological facts can't guarantee that our core morality (or any other one, for that matter) is the right, true, or correct one. If the biological facts can't do it, then nothing can. No moral core is right, correct, true. That's nihilism. And we have to accept it."[43] We must accept it, Rosenberg acknowledges, despite the apparent risk that it might create a public relations nightmare for scientism.[44] According to Rosenberg, this is the bad news. *Nihilism* means that there is nothing that has intrinsic value, nothing that is morally right or wrong, but everything is just adaptations: "Our core morality isn't true, right, correct, and neither is any other. Nature just seduced us into thinking it's right. It did that because that made core morality work better; our believing in its truth increases our individual genetic fitness."[45]

We must be clear about what moral nihilism entails and what it does not entail. First, it differs significantly from *moral relativism*. Even if relativists and nihilists agree that morality is merely a human creation or social construction, relativists believe that there are moral norms and truths but that they are relative to individuals (individual relativism) or human societies or cultures (cultural relativism). So, what is morally true is not the same for all people, and cultural relativists believe that what moral norms we should embrace depends essentially on each culture's commitments. Each culture has the final say about what is morally right and wrong. Nihilists reject relativism simply because there are no moral truths, whether objective or relative ones, and consequently, no moral goodness, moral duty, or moral virtue. There are no moral qualities in the real world. As Richard Dawkins points out:

[43] Rosenberg, *The Atheist's Guide to Reality*, p. 113.
[44] Ibid., p. 95.
[45] Ibid., p. 109.

In a universe of blind natural forces and genetic replication, some people are going to get hurt, other people are going to get lucky, and you won't find any rhyme or reason in it, nor any justice. The universe we observe has precisely the properties we should expect if there is, at bottom, no design, no purpose, *no evil and no good*, nothing but blind, pitiless indifference.[46]

Nihilism is also not *moral skepticism*; it does not tell us that there are moral truths but that we cannot know which moral beliefs are correct. There are simply no moral truths, so there cannot be any justified moral beliefs or knowledge. Neither do nihilists say that everything is morally permitted because the ideas of morally permissible or forbidden are untenable nonsense. Nor cannot nihilists care deeply about others and oppose the torture and murder of innocent people. But they cannot regard such actions as immoral, even if they can find them distasteful, unappealing, or emotionally deeply upsetting.

Rosenberg believes that even though scientific naturalists must bite this bullet, the good news is that a million years of natural selection has ended up giving us all roughly the same core morality and fooled almost all of us into believing that these moral principles are binding on everyone because this illusion increases humans' biological fitness – our rate of survival and reproduction success. Letting our consciences be our guide enhances our fitness, but that does not make it morally right or wrong. Therefore, most people are nice most of the time, and that includes nihilists. Nothing is morally right about being nice, but we are stuck with it for the foreseeable future. "Scientism has to be nihilistic, but it turns out to be a nice nihilism after all."[47]

Rosenberg's nihilism is often referred to as the *error theory* in philosophy. The error theory is like atheism is concerning religion. Atheists believe there are no religious features of reality, so no religious claims are true. If we narrow the scope to theism, they maintain that theists try to speak the truth about God but always fail because there is no God. A careful scientific inventory of reality cannot find these theistic features, just as that inventory of reality cannot find any moral ones. Since science sets the boundaries for what exists, no religious, theistic, or moral truths exist. So, yet another scientific core belief seems to be as follows:

---

[46] Richard Dawkins, *River Out of Eden: A Darwinian View of Life*. Basic Books, 1995, p. 133 (emphasis added).

[47] Rosenberg, *The Atheist's Guide to Reality*, p. 144.

(4) When we make moral judgments, we are trying to say what is morally right and wrong, but since science cannot discover any moral features in the universe, there is nothing that is morally right or wrong – there are no moral truths, so our moral judgments are always mistaken (*the nihilist-error view*).

However, embracing *expressivism* is a different nihilistic option than the error theory, which is open to scientific naturalists.[48] Expressivism is a more complicated theory of morality than the error theory, and there are many different versions of it. Expressivists agree with error theorists that there are no moral features in the world, no moral judgments are true, and consequently, there is no moral knowledge, but deny that moral judgments try to describe (but always fail, according to error theory, and sometimes succeed according to theism) moral features or properties of things. We are not, as theists and error theorists assume, trying to speak the truth when making moral judgments; they serve a different function. Moral judgments say merely something about *us*, our emotions and desires, and express our commitments. For this reason, it is misguided to talk about moral beliefs because moral utterances can be neither true nor false. It is to misunderstand the language of morality if we think that when we say that torture is immoral, torture has a certain feature – being immoral, or that when we say that Hitler was an evil person, one thing that characterizes this person is being evil. What we are doing is instead expressing our opposition, indicating our disgust, encouraging others not to torture people, or urging others to say (but not believe or disbelieve) that Hitler was an evil person. Literally speaking, it is not true (or false) that Hitler was an evil person.

Still, expressivists can oppose the torture and murder of innocent people. Expressivists can regard such actions as immoral if they find them distasteful, unappealing, or emotionally deeply upsetting, simply because emotions or sentiments are what morality is all about, nothing else. Error theorists can have the same emotional response. Still, they cannot say that such action is immoral because they maintain that statements about torture tell us that torture has a certain feature – being immoral – but all such claims are false. Error theorists believe that our sincere moral claims are meant to state the truth, but since there are no moral truths,

---

[48] Notice that one can embrace the error theory or expressivism without accepting scientism. If you want to read more about these forms of moral nihilism, see, for instance, Russ Shafer-Landau, *The Fundamentals of Ethics*. Oxford University Press, 2024.

such claims are all mistaken. On the contrary, expressivists think this is
to misunderstand moral claims (they can acknowledge that many people
in ordinary life are confused about this) since they merely intend to say
something about our emotions, desires, sentiments, or commitments.

Expressivists see moral disagreement as a clash of emotions or cona-
tive attitudes. People value different things, but that is not a disagreement
in belief. Instead, it is a disagreement in attitude. A desire for world peace
or a preference for human rights is no more the sort of thing that can be
true or false than a command like "Shut up!" Error theorists would agree
that ethical judgments typically include emotional responses but claim
that they extend beyond that. When Anne says in an argument about
torture with Sarah, "No, what you believe about torture is false. In fact,
torture is always wrong," emotions are involved, but Anne still intends
to say that Sarah's belief about torture is mistaken. It is an example of
a disagreement in moral belief; it is just – adds scientific naturalists of
Rosenberg's kind – that science cannot discover such properties. Hence,
the universe is devoid of value; therefore, all moral beliefs humans hold
are false. Either way, scientific naturalists can reject the nihilist-error
view and instead embrace:

(4*) Science cannot discover any moral features of reality, but that does
not matter because moral judgments are not meant to state what is true
or false; instead, they express our emotions, desires, preferences, or sentiments (*the nihilist-expressivist view*).

The conclusion so far is that the scientific inquiry into the world's content
reveals all sorts of physical, chemical, and biological things and properties, but they do not uncover any moral features. But is this really so?
Some scientific naturalists are concerned about the unappealing implications that the scientistic–epistemic and scientistic–ontological theses
seem to have for ethics; neither error theory nor expressivism appeals
to them. These secular intellectuals have been searching for a scientifically respectable justification of morality. In other words, their objective
is to redescribe or transform ethics into science (the *naturalization* or
scientization strategy).

Wilson believes biologists will one day discover a "genetically accurate and hence completely fair code of ethics."[49] To achieve this goal,
philosophers should be given a long sabbatical: "Scientists and humanists
should consider together the possibility that the time has come for ethics

---

[49] Edward O. Wilson, *Sociobiology*. Harvard University Press, 1975, p. 575.

to be removed temporarily from the hands of the philosophers and biologized."[50] He thinks that no other domain of the humanities than philosophy is a union with the natural sciences more urgently needed. It is needed because "it is astonishing that the study of ethics has advanced so little since the nineteenth century. The most distinguishing and vital qualities of the human species remain a blank space on the scientific map."[51] So, Wilson is aware that ethics is a serious anomaly in a scientistic worldview; it does not fit well. But he has faith that science will eventually rise to this challenge, allowing moral knowledge to become a subset of biological knowledge. We will then be able to identify which moral beliefs are true. Thus,

(4**) Science will one day discover the moral features of reality, allowing it, in the near future, to determine what moral beliefs are true or false (*the scientific realist view of morality*).

Sam Harris thinks that science could actually deliver this here and now. Science can determine human values. His basic idea is that "questions about values – about meaning, morality, and life's larger purpose – are really questions about the well-being of conscious creatures. Values, therefore, translate into facts that can be scientifically understood" and justified.[52] Moral truths are simply facts about human well-being. Science can tell us what human well-being is and what kinds of actions promote it. There might be practical problems in doing this, but in principle, science can determine what is morally right and wrong.

It is undoubtedly correct that science can inform our moral choices (no advocates of any other worldviews we consider deny this). Given, for instance, that we do not want to jeopardize present human well-being or the well-being of future generations, science can offer us guidance on how to limit the severe climate changes that threaten our long-term well-being. But an obvious problem with Harris's proposal is that it remains unclear why we should consider human well-being our fundamental value. How does science know this is the correct value to embrace? Why human well-being rather than, say, the well-being of Earth's ecosystems? The answer to this value question could not be a scientific finding (not yet, anyway). Hence, the core value assumption of Harris's scientistic ethics does not

---

[50] Wilson, *Sociobiology*, p. 562.

[51] Edward O. Wilson, "The Biological Basis of Morality," *The Atlantic Monthly*, April 1998, p. 62.

[52] Sam Harris, *The Moral Landscape*. Free Press, 2010, p. 1.

come from science. So, for now, it seems more reasonable to accept moral nihilism than any scientific ethics if you embrace a scientistic worldview.

CHALLENGES FOR SCIENTISM

What challenges does scientism face? What would seem to be problematic aspects of it? Let me highlight some of these challenges without suggesting that there are no resources within the scientistic worldview to address them satisfactorily.

The first problem is the *challenge of incoherence*. One problem with the scientistic–epistemic thesis (the assertion that the only kind of genuine knowledge or understanding we can have is provided by science) is that it is not obviously a scientific claim. Is it biology, chemistry, physics, or any other scientific discipline that shows that this claim is true or at least reasonable? It seems far from clear. How does a scientist design a physical experiment or biological study to show that this thesis is true? Something like that is required because if science alone limits what we can know, we can only know that the scientistic–epistemic thesis is true if science can show that the only facts we can know anything about or rationally believe anything about are those it can detect and confirm. Critics argue that proponents of scientism contradict themselves on this point.

One possible response is to acknowledge that science cannot demonstrate that all genuine knowledge is scientific knowledge, but to argue that we could and should take this as our working hypothesis due to the successes of science. It is possible, but unlikely, that other kinds of knowledge exist. In this response, scientific naturalists want to place the burden of proof on those who claim that nonscientific knowledge exists. They merely maintain that we should be suspicious of all knowledge claims that are not scientific and that cannot be reduced to scientific knowledge. This weaker form of scientism appears not to be self-refuting. Hence, the idea is that it is rational to believe (or to accept as a working hypothesis) that our only kind of knowledge is scientific as long as there are no good reasons to believe otherwise.

The second challenge is that, indeed, nonscientific knowledge appears to exist, and some of this kind of knowledge is essential for being able to undertake the scientific project in the first place. This is the *epistemic challenge for scientism*.[53] Let us start with things that look most obviously

---

[53] See Mikael Stenmark, *Scientism: Science, Ethics, and Religion*. Ashgate, 2001, chapter 2 (reprinted by Routledge in 2016).

like scientific beliefs, for example, the belief that there is a tree outside the window or that people are walking down the street. These are just two examples of the observational or perceptual knowledge we acquire daily. But is observational knowledge, not scientific knowledge? One difficulty with classifying observational knowledge as scientific knowledge is that it would mean we are all scientists, and, further, that "science" existed long before the development of science as we now understand it. We all (or almost all of us, since some people are blind) would be scientists since we all have the means of acquiring these beliefs without seeking expert advice or undertaking scientific experimentation; that is, we must all be scientists because by perception alone we can come to know "There is a tree outside the window" and "People are walking down the street."

Compare these beliefs with what we would readily classify as scientific beliefs, such as "Genes are segments of chromosomes," "Chromosomes are composed of DNA," "Nuclear fusion causes the sun's energy," or "All particles of light travel with a velocity of 300,000 km/sec." In contrast to observational beliefs, these beliefs are obtained through scientific inquiry and experimentation. Scientific knowledge presupposes the development of specific methods and advanced experimental procedures; however, not everyone is a scientist, as most of us do not possess the necessary skills required. Thus, science aims to provide us with knowledge about the natural world in realms that are too small, too distant, or too far in the past to be directly experienced. This is done by developing theories about, for instance, the transmission of diseases, the motions of planets and stars, the succession of fossils, and the similarities among organisms.

Another related problem is that scientific knowledge appears to require at least one type of knowledge beyond perceptual knowledge to emerge at all, namely, memory knowledge. Beliefs of memory are beliefs about things we have previously experienced or thought about. For instance, I remember being married to Anna and have been writing about a scientistic worldview today. Furthermore, I do not merely believe these things; I also reckon that I know these things. But for scientists to develop and test scientific hypotheses against a certain amount of data, they must be able to remember the content of their hypotheses, the previous test results, and, even more fundamentally, that they are scientists and where their laboratories or research institutes are located. Their scientific practice appears to presuppose memory knowledge, but then there is knowledge beyond scientific knowledge. The truth appears to be that unless we could trust our memories (and obtain knowledge), we could never reason at all or do any science whatsoever because, in any inference, we must remember the premises on our way to the conclusion.

Suppose I enter a café in Stockholm and sit at a table. The waiter comes, and I utter a fragment of a sentence in Swedish. I say, "Kan jag få en öl, tack?" The waiter brings the beer, and I take a drink. I read a book and noticed a Coca-Cola sign on the wall, as well as cars outside the window. I put some money on the table and left the café. This sounds simple, but as John Searle and others have pointed out, its ontological complexity is staggering.[54] More importantly, in this case, its significant features fall outside the scope of science. The critics of scientism maintain that we cannot capture the features of the description I have just given in the language of physics and chemistry or any other of the natural sciences. There is no physical–chemical–biological description adequate to define "café," "waiter," "sentence in Swedish," "money," or even "chair" and "table," even though cafés, waiters, money, chairs, and tables are physical phenomena. Since no physical–chemical–biological description can be given of these phenomena, no scientific knowledge of the social world seems to exist. But we think we know these things; a large chunk of our knowledge is about the social world we inhabit. Where science can only see masses of metal in linear trajectories, we can see cars being driven along the road. We can see dollar bills where science only sees cellulose fibers with green and gray stains. The critics maintain that further examples of nonscientific knowledge are then hermeneutical knowledge (I know what "Drink Coca-Cola" means), intentional knowledge (I know that someone had the intention to convince me to buy Coca-Cola), and social knowledge (I know that I am sitting in a Café and that there are such things as waiters).

Science can explain the lit billboard "Drink Coca-Cola" in terms of the strength of the steel posts that support the sign, the current of electricity that causes the lights to glow, and so forth. However, meaningful phenomena such as intentions are nothing that scientists can obtain knowledge about by merely applying the methods and instruments of physics, biology, or any other natural science. Therefore, critics argue that advocates of scientism are forced to deny the existence of intentions or purposes, and consequently, must maintain that our purported knowledge about them is an illusion. In this case, they have to deny that the billboard contains a dimension of reality undetectable by their scientific methods, namely, that the sign expresses an intention to persuade us to

<hr />

[54] Searle, *The Construction of Social Reality*, pp. 1–29.

buy a particular product and, furthermore, that we can obtain knowledge about this. Therefore, the critics conclude that we have good reasons to believe that the world is bigger than the world of the sciences and that we can obtain knowledge about this bigger world that cannot be reduced to scientific knowledge. Scientific naturalists can acknowledge that there are problems here. Still, they could maintain that they have faith in science and its progress, so eventually, this kind of nonscientific knowledge can be transformed into scientific knowledge or be shown to be redundant.

If the second challenge for a scientistic worldview is that its epistemology seems too limited, the third focuses on the ontology of scientism, maintaining that reality is richer in content than the things and properties within the purview of science. Let us refer to this as the *ontological challenge for scientism*. We can say that nonscientific things (if they exist) do not depend on being advanced by a scientific theory, and they cannot be reduced to scientific entities. When discussing the epistemic challenge, I provided some examples of nonscientific entities, such as tables, chairs, waiters, and cars. We could also add to this list professors, law courts, countries, and universities. To develop this line of challenge of scientism, let me focus on something of utmost importance for (religious and secular) humanists, namely, persons. What characterizes *persons* is that they are beings who have a robust first-person perspective of the world, and this is acknowledged as such by other beings who are also persons (second-person interaction). To have a perspective is to be disposed to perceive the world from a particular spatiotemporal location, and to be able to do so robustly is to conceive of oneself as oneself – to have a self-conception and a self-understanding.[55] As Macarthur points out, it is appropriate to ask a person why they acted the way they did, expect a reason in reply, assume that their action is intelligible, and apply normative notions like responsibility, praise, and blame.[56] Persons can enter into relationships of responsibilities – epistemic, ethical, and legal – and thus be acknowledged as such by other persons. Persons are agents who can intentionally open doors, invite friends to parties, and become scientists. They exhibit a rational intelligibility that involves a responsiveness to reasons and meanings not reducible to scientific intelligibility of law-like or merely physical causal happenings.

---

[55] Lynne Rudder Baker, *Naturalism and the First-Person Perspective*. Oxford University Press, 2013, pp. 30–47.
[56] Macarthur, "Liberal Naturalism and the Scientific Image of the World," p. 575.

Of course, a person can be studied from a scientific point of view as a particular collection of water, calcium, and organic molecules called Carl Sagan.[57] Still, the concept of a person will not be invoked in the explanatory vocabulary of science. But if we want to explain scientific practice (and many other human activities), we need the concept of a person. Science becomes intelligible first when we understand that scientists are persons, rational agents capable of making and being moved by judgments about reasons, capable of correcting the inferences they drew between evidence and theory. They try to convince other scientists of the reasons to favor one theory over another. They are engaged in the practice of searching for evidence to determine the best scientific explanation of certain natural phenomena. According to these critics, the mistake that scientific naturalists make is to focus solely on the object of scientific research and overlook the *subject* conducting this research. As Stan Klein maintains, "Timing devices, neuroimaging technologies, electroencephalographs, and a host of modern means of obtaining objective knowledge about mind are useless absent an experiencing [and reasoning] subject."[58] Without persons, there is no science, but persons with self-conception and reason-giving are not accessible from the third-person perspective of science. Hence, the critics argue that a nonscientific entity must exist for science to be rationally intelligible: persons. We need a richer ontology than the one science provides. In Chapter 8, we will focus on intellectuals who consider this a core commitment of their secular–humanist worldview, as it is essential for grounding the idea of human freedom and dignity.

Whereas the previous challenges for scientism have been raised by religious and secular intellectuals alike, the fourth objection comes primarily from theists and concerns the blind watchmaker argument. However, let me start by laying out some of the implications of scientism for the debate about whether we should embrace a secular or a religious worldview, as this is relevant to understanding the blind watchmaker argument and its validity. What counts as evidence or good reasons in such a debate is significantly shaped by whether people embrace a scientistic or non-scientistic secular worldview. Scientific naturalists must stick to the evidence that science can produce because science is the measure of everything. The atheist William Rowe would have serious problems with

---

[57] See the previously given quotation from Carl Sagan in Section "The Limits of Knowledge and Reality."

[58] Stan B. Klein, "A Defense of Experiential Realism: The Need to Take Phenomenological Reality on Its Own Terms in the Study of Mind," *Psychology of Consciousness*, 2015, 2/1, p. 43.

this line of argument. He writes that it was a keen sense of the lack of God's presence in his life, the existence of meaningless evil or horrible suffering in our world, along with his conviction that morality need not be grounded in God's nature (since Moore's argument that moral truths are not merely true but necessarily true is cogent) that were the decisive evidence in his case.[59] However, these are existential and philosophical arguments and evidence of a sort that arguably fall outside the purview of science. If that is the case, it would entail that people who justify their secular worldview based on the kind of reasons Rowe gives would lack rational ground. It would also imply that those who embrace scientism could not appeal to this kind of evidence in support of their secular worldview and against religious worldviews.

Science then becomes a double-edged sword. Suppose secular people view science as the only acceptable source of knowledge and justified belief. In that case, such an epistemology does not merely require, in this case, that theists provide scientific reasons why they believe in God and believe that nature is God's creation; it also requires that of themselves that their atheism, and in fact, their whole secular worldview, would have to be scientifically justified. In this regard, liberal naturalists are in a better position, as their evidence base does not consist solely of scientific evidence (see Chapter 8). They could just as well ground their rejection of theism, or other forms of religion, on reasons of a kind other than scientific, for instance, on philosophical, political, moral, or existential ones, or, for that matter, on reasons that the social sciences and the humanities can generate.

Recall that the blind watchmaker argument concludes that the evidence of evolution reveals a universe without design (see Section "Atheism and Naturalism"). Evolutionary theory shows that our world has not been designed by God or anyone else. Why, according to Dawkins, should we believe this? The reason is that the evidence of evolution establishes that all living things have evolved from some elementary form of life. Moreover, in *The Blind Watchmaker*, he argues against the idea that blind, unguided evolution could not have caused complex organic systems, such as the mammalian eye or the wing, and suggests how a blind, unguided process of evolution over millions of years could have developed these.[60] But how could this line of argument establish that evolution

---

[59] William Rowe, "Friendly Atheism Revisited," *International Journal for Philosophy of Religion*, 2010, 68/1, pp. 10–11.

[60] Dawkins, *The Blind Watchmaker*, chapters 2–4.

is blind? The critics argue that the scientific evidence is compatible with the belief that God has directed and overseen the process of evolution. All Dawkins has established is that it is biologically feasible to believe that all living things, in all their complexity, are the result of an unguided, blind natural process. It is a genuine possibility. A conclusion that enables one to be an intellectually fulfilled atheist, like Dawkins. However, the conclusion that is supposed to follow is that evolution reveals a universe without design, so science establishes that the world has not been designed by God or anyone else. Thus, evolutionary theory is also taken to show that it is not possible to be an intellectually fulfilled theist. For this reason, religious intellectuals, such as theist Alvin Plantinga, have pointed out that the blind watchmaker argument is invalid (even if the argument's premises are true, the conclusion does not follow) because there is a significant gap between what is possible and what is actual.[61]

As far as it goes, this criticism is probably correct, but since Dawkins presumably embraces a scientistic worldview, it does not present his entire case. If we add the scientistic–epistemic and the scientistic–ontological theses, the argument becomes valid. Since science cannot discover any design in the evolutionary processes, it can explain the development of life without teleological explanations, *and* science sets the boundaries for what we can know and what exists. It follows logically that evolution reveals a universe without design. Or, more precisely, it follows that evolution reveals life on Earth to be without design – no God or anyone else has directed or overseen the process of evolution on our planet. Of course, theists reject these scientistic theses, so whether the argument is not merely valid but also sound depends on whether this additional scientistic premise is true. As we will see in Chapter 8, secular intellectuals who are liberal naturalists – many of whom embrace secular humanism – do not think science sets the boundaries for what we can know and what exists. Consequently, they must reject the blind watchmaker argument or construe it differently than Dawkins does.

---

[61] Alvin Plantinga, "The Dawkins Confusion: Naturalism 'ad absurdum,'" *Christianity Today* (Books and Culture), 2007.

8

A Secular–Humanist Worldview

It is not unusual for scientific naturalism and secular humanism to be conflated and assumed to express essentially the same worldview, or at least that they are obviously compatible.[1] However, one can be a scientific naturalist and reject the core idea of humanism of human freedom, autonomy, and dignity simply because one thinks that scientific naturalism implies moral nihilism or because one thinks that human freedom is an illusion or that persons do not exist – the carrier of dignity in a humanistic worldview. So, as will be seen in more detail, there are good reasons to distinguish between the two. Just as scientific naturalism (or scientism) and humanism can mean different things, secular humanism can also have multiple interpretations. I will offer a rational reconstruction of it, which distinguishes it from the other worldviews in this study. Other plausible understandings are, of course, possible.

I view humanism's central ingredients as encompassing a particular perspective on human nature, certain core values, and an emphasis on culture as something irreducible to nature, thereby highlighting the importance of the humanities for understanding ourselves and the world we inhabit. Humanists emphasize the uniqueness of human beings and human life, as well as the essential product of that uniqueness, culture. Humans are unique because they are persons born free and equal in dignity and rights. For this reason, humanists are suspicious of all attempts to reduce human beings to mere physical things or instruments of a divine will, to protect human agency and dignity. To these general

[1] See, for instance, Michael Shermer, "Scientific Naturalism: A Manifesto for Enlightenment Humanism," *Theology and Science*, 2017, 15/3, pp. 220–230.

189

characteristics of humanism, secular humanists add certain elements such that there are no good reasons to believe that any religious worldview is true, and, in particular, they embrace naturalism.

It is illuminating to adopt Thomas Nagel's terminology and characterize a scientistic worldview as a way of understanding reality, our place in it, good and evil, and our significance in the scheme of things, as a secular construal of life from the *outside in*, that is, starting from the cosmic point of view delivered to us by science.[2] A secular–humanistic worldview would instead attempt to answer these big existential questions from the *inside out*, starting from the human point of view. As a community, we give sense to our lives; there is no need for a higher (divine or naturalistic) order to give sense to us. We should build our worldview from the basis of our uniqueness – our personhood, freedom, and dignity – and think of ourselves as representatives of humanity and of nothing else, and live accordingly.

In this chapter, I will first provide an account of humanism that both religious and secular individuals can embrace. Humanism has likely existed in one form or another for a long time. However, in the West, it can at least be traced back to the humanistic movements of the fifteenth and sixteenth centuries, specifically to what is known as Renaissance humanism. These humanists celebrated the individual as a rational and political being created by God to think and act for themselves. They advocated for developing the humanities as valuable academic disciplines in their own right. In particular, Renaissance humanism is closely tied to a renewed interest in classical Greek culture. The term "humanist" was likely first used to describe a segment of the "academic" curriculum – the humanities (*Studia humanitatis*), which included the study of language, grammar, poetry, rhetoric, and philosophy.

Second, I will identify the additional beliefs, values, and attitudes that shape humanism into a secular worldview. Understandably, secular organizations want to claim the term "humanism" for their purposes, referring to their worldview simply as "humanism" rather than "secular humanism." However, since the roots of humanism are found in Renaissance Christianity, and considering that there are religious forms of humanism, such as Christian humanism, along with the fact that scholars in the humanities are referred to as humanists, it would be inadequate and somewhat misleading, in the academic study of worldviews, to refer to the worldview as humanism and its practitioners as

---

[2] Nagel, *Secular Philosophy and the Religious Temperament*, p. 6.

humanists. Therefore, I will use the terms "secular humanism" and "secular humanists" to identify the core beliefs, values, and attitudes that characterize this particular secular worldview. The term "secular" preceding "humanism" is used to underscore the rejection of religious belief and practice.

HUMANISM

Humanism is a mode of thought and action that emphasizes the rational agency, freedom, dignity, and thus uniqueness of human beings and human life, as well as the essential product of that uniqueness, namely culture. It is here that the relationship between humanism and the humanities becomes evident: humanism takes for granted that the explanations and understandings given by the humanities and the social sciences tell us very much about human culture, whereas the explanations of the natural sciences tell us much less about it. For humanists, what differentiates human beings from the rest of the animal world is that they are without a rigidly fixed form and have the ability to make of themselves what they will or the potential to be molded by our social environment into many different forms in a much shorter timeframe than is necessary in the case of nonhuman animals.

There is something exceptional about us, and to grasp this and what this uniqueness has produced, which is culture, we need methods and theories of a qualitatively different kind from those that the natural sciences can offer. Curtis White maintains:

When hominids became capable of symbols (which is to say, when they became human), they entered upon a new kind of evolution, one that became ever more complex, more self-knowing, and more independent of biology. ... they hallucinated a "parallel" world because, strangely, they could better survive the real world if they first worked out the details symbolically. Eventually, the symbolic world discovered a kind of autonomy. It discovered its own concerns beyond the imperatives of biology and atoms (whatever it is that they want).[3]

This symbolic world, this extra-material reality, is the focal point of the humanities: "The scientist [*as* scientist] is insensible to the nuance of what-it's-like to be human, while in art a harmonic shift, an unexpected rhythm, will seem to say so much and so convincingly."[4] So, one thing humanists share with theists is the uniqueness thesis:

---

[3] Curtis White, *The Science Delusion*. Melville House, 2013, pp. 77–80.
[4] White, *The Science Delusion*, p. 185.

(1) Human beings are unique in that they are persons; that is to say, they are self-aware, autonomous, rational, and moral beings who can choose what to believe and do freely, at least sometimes, and are, therefore, responsible animals (*the human uniqueness thesis*).

However, humanists do not have to ground the uniqueness thesis in the belief that humans are created in God's image, as Renaissance humanists did; instead, they can ground it in a particular view of human nature – a view that posits that we possess the properties stated in the uniqueness thesis. Hence, to believe in human *self-awareness* or *self-consciousness* is to take it to be true that we have the ability to identify ourselves through reflection and introspection, and to distinguish between ourselves and other selves. Through self-awareness, an individual experiences and understands their own character, feelings, intentions, reasons, and desires. In other words, humanists, in contrast to scientific naturalists, believe that we have an irreducible first-person perspective. A human person can not only have thoughts about herself, but she can also conceive of herself as the subject of such thoughts. I can not only wonder how I will die, but I can also realize that I am having that thought. You, as a person, did not exist until there was something that it was like to be you, which happens around two years after your birth. Only beings with inner lives are persons. Consequently, the death of a person can occur before she dies as a human being. It occurs with the permanent loss of her first-person perspective, for instance, when she cannot physically recover enough after an accident to entertain a thought like "Am I dying?"[5]

To believe that humans can *freely choose* is to affirm that when faced with a choice between competing options, we typically feel it is up to us which way we choose and take for granted that this feeling is not mistaken. Sometimes, at least, we can decide what to do and believe. We can perhaps say that free will is the capacity unique to persons that allows them to control their actions and sometimes choose differently than they did.

I am not saying that humanists must affirm that humans have libertarian freedom. You have *libertarian* free will if more than one option was open to you, given everything as it actually was at the time. Some humanists embrace that view, but others are *compatibilists*. They believe

---

[5] Lynne Rudder Baker, *The Metaphysics of Everyday Life*. Cambridge University Press, 2007, pp. 67–85.

that free will is compatible with causal determinism, that is, the thesis that the course of the future is entirely determined by the conjunction of the past and the laws of nature. Compatibilists maintain that an agent can be determined in all her choices and actions and still make some of her choices freely. The truth of causal determinism would entail that the laws of nature are not merely probabilistic, for if they were, then the conjunction of the past and the laws would not entail a unique future. Humanists might instead think that causal indeterminism is true. Alternatively, if some entities within the world are not entirely governed by the laws of nature, then even if those laws are themselves deterministic, that world would not be deterministic. However, most humanists have presumably not given much thought to these deeper philosophical issues. The idea here is that humanists affirm something special about humans that makes them unique so that we, for instance, can genuinely talk about human actions and not merely human behavior. Consequently, we can hold people, but not nonhuman animals, morally responsible for their actions. Hence, *incompatibilism* – the thesis that there is no free will due to causal determinism – is irreconcilable with humanism.[6]

Because we have free will, humanists emphasize our *autonomy* or self-determinacy, which means that we, as individuals, can and should decide what to do and believe, and not always submit to others' will or external authorities. We should think for ourselves! We need "bildung" or lifelong education to make these choices wisely. For humanists, a multifaceted education and lifelong self-cultivation are essential for becoming mature human beings.

To believe that humans are *rational* agents is not to think that humans always make rational decisions, but rather that they possess reason or intelligence; they have reliable cognitive faculties that can process experiences and information and evaluate arguments to come to conclusions. They are rational, not a-rational creatures. Because of this, they, in contrast to elephants, can take responsibility (be blameworthy or praiseworthy) for their actions and beliefs. Unlike elephants, humans can act morally or immorally and be rational or irrational in their beliefs. Because humans can give and respond to reasons and arguments, many things they do have an *intention* behind them. I get out of my chair and vote because I believe in democracy. Therefore, not

---

[6] A helpful introduction to these tricky but vital questions is Kevin Timpe, "Free Will," *The Internet Encyclopedia of Philosophy*.

all causes are merely physical. Some are mental. The mind has causal powers that are not reducible to the laws and regularities investigated by science. For this reason, in a humanistic worldview, it is essential to distinguish between *behavior* and *action*. In contrast to mere behavior, actions have an intention and mental motivation behind them. Our actions are causally explained by the reasons why we do them. To perform the act of voting, the reason that I believe in democracy is part of the causal explanation of the action. There is both physical and mental causation in a humanistic universe, while there is merely physical causation in a scientistic universe.

Humanists do not think that any other animals on earth are *persons* (the technical philosophical term for a being with these characteristics) but are open to the possibility that other beings in other places in the universe have them. Humanists believe that humans are, in this way, special; they embrace the uniqueness thesis or what is sometimes referred to as "human exceptionalism" without denying that humans and other animals share the same evolutionary history or being committed to the idea that there exists a soul independently of the physical body (so-called mind–body dualism). Instead, their personhood, including their capacity to act for reasons, justifies this belief in human uniqueness.

These humanistic convictions about human nature are not the result of scientific inquiry, but rather the product of our experiences of ourselves and other humans. Humanists (in contrast to many scientific naturalists) view those experiences as revealing something true about who we are. Whether science can confirm them or not is irrelevant. Roger Scruton maintains that we are able to see each other I-to-I, and from this, all judgment, all responsibility, all shame, pride, and fulfillment arise. We are persons, and personality is of our essence:

Hence there are concepts that play an organizing role in our experience but which belong to no scientific theory because they divide the world into the wrong kinds of kind ... the kind to which we fundamentally belong is defined through a concept that does not feature in the science of our nature. Science sees us as objects rather than subjects, and its descriptions of our responses are not descriptions of what we feel.[7]

Persons are not describable impersonally. Therefore, the subject, the person, is, in principle, unobservable to science, for "if I look for it in the

---

[7] Roger Scruton, "Scientism and the Humanities." In *Scientism: The New Orthodoxy*, edited by Richard N. Williams and Daniel N. Robinson. Bloomsbury, 2015, p. 138.

world of objects, I shall never find it. But without my nature as a subject nothing is real for me. If I am to care for my world, then I must first care for this thing, without which I have no world – the perspective from which my world is seen."[8]

Culture is the unique product of that extraordinary nature, and here, we can find a great divide between humanists and non-humanists. As Charles Taylor writes:

Here we see a big watershed in our intellectual world. There are those who hope to anchor an account of human nature below the level of culture, so that cultural variation, when it is not trivial and negligible, can be explained from this more basic account. ... And then there are those who find this account of human life unconvincing, who see it as an evasion of the most important *explananda* in human life, which are to be found at this level of cultural difference.[9]

Humanists view culture as something that cannot be reduced to nature. This explains their rejection of scientism or scientific naturalism. Leon Wieseltier's response to Pinker's invitation to the scientization of the humanities (which I referred to in Chapter 7) illustrates this skeptical attitude well. He maintains:

"The question of the place of science in knowledge, and in society, and in life, is not a scientific question. Science confers no special authority, it confers no authority at all, for the attempt to answer a nonscientific question. ... Nor does science confer any license to extend its categories and its methods beyond its own realms, whose contours are of course a matter of debate."

But "now science wants to invade the liberal arts." He responds, "Don't let it happen." We should reject scientism and its "crimes against the humanities."[10] Hence, humanists, in contrast to advocates of scientism, can and frequently do question the results of science when it comes to claims about society and culture (but not nature). For instance, Thomas Hylland Eriksen writes that evolutionary theory is, of course, accepted today by virtually all social scientists and scholars in the humanities, including himself as a social anthropologist. Still, he maintains that there are many who:

feel a deep sense of unease about Darwinism. I dare to say that this does not merely depend on the fact that it is misunderstood, that it is hard to reconcile oneself with its ruthless and amoral nature, or, for that matter, that many of us

---

[8] Scruton, "Scientism and the Humanities," pp. 137–138.

[9] Charles Taylor, "Understanding the Other," In *Dilemmas and Connections*. Harvard University Press, 2011, p. 27.

[10] Leon Wieseltier, "Crimes against Humanities," *New Republic*, September 4, 2013.

are demolished and brainwashed Christians. The animosity also stems from the fact that there are many things between heaven and earth that Darwinism cannot adequately explain, and there are important questions it lacks the tools to address. Certain interpretations of Darwinism conflict with a humanistic worldview, and there is little room in the grey zone between these outlooks.[11]

There is a tension between a humanistic worldview and a Darwinian worldview, and Eriksen, like many other humanists, seriously doubts that Darwinian explanations are adequate for understanding human culture and society. They reject scientistic beliefs such as Dennett's that "Darwin's dangerous idea," that is, evolution by natural selection, bears "an unmistakable likeness to universal acid: it eats through just about every traditional concept, and leaves in its wake a revolutionized world-view, with most of the old landmarks still recognizable, but transformed in fundamental ways."[12] Hence, another humanistic core belief is as follows:

(2) Culture goes beyond nature and is of a different kind; therefore, its central features are not detectable by science, and we need humanistic studies to understand ourselves and our life-world (*the irreducibility-of-culture-thesis*).

Knowledge and Reality

By relying on our ordinary senses and assuming that they are truth-apt, humanists take the real world to contain persons, self-consciousness, colors, sounds, music, smells, languages, beauty, good, evil, intentions, beliefs, purposes, virtues, moral and aesthetic values, legal laws, social norms, table, chairs, professors, universities, and countries. They have a quite rich ontology that encompasses both social and cultural things and properties, as well as natural things and properties, including organisms, metals, mass, electrons, oxygen, and genes. Humanists view the deliverances from our ordinary senses, the humanities, and the sciences as complementary. Even if they sometimes conflict with each other, they each make significant contributions to our understanding of the world.

One way of expressing this complementary view is to say that the sciences and the humanities do not tell us what exists, but rather what

---

[11] Thomas Hylland Eriksen, *Charles Darwin*. Nya Doxa, 1999, p. 86 (my translation from Swedish).
[12] Daniel C. Dennett, *Darwin's Dangerous Idea*. Penguin Books, 1995, p. 63.

else exists besides the things and properties we already know to exist through our everyday life practices. For instance, I know I had breakfast this morning, that it tasted delicious, and that breakfast is a part of the furniture of the world. However, I do not need the sciences or the humanities to know these things; I need them to tell me what else exists besides such things and properties. On this account, the sciences and the humanities give us theories to explain or help us understand things that are not directly accessible to us in our everyday lives. For example, we know that earthquakes and volcanic eruptions happen and are more common in some places than others. However, science (through the theory of continental drift) gives us something beyond what we already know, namely, that the Earth's continents move in relation to each other, which explains phenomena such as earthquakes and volcanic eruptions. We all know what violence is and have probably seen people use violence against other people. However, the humanities (through the theory of structural violence) tell us that there is a different form of violence than individual violence, violence that is not directly visible, that lacks an identifiable subject, namely, structural violence, and it can take a variety of forms on an economic, political, social, and cultural level.

It is essential to realize that not all of us share such an essentially complementary view of the relationship between our everyday lifeworld, the humanities, and the sciences. Some people would rather say (or what they say entails) that even if our everyday lifeworld, the sciences, and the humanities can sometimes be in harmony with each other, there is, in fact, a far-reaching tension or even conflict between what is held to be true in these three parts of people's worldview. Science and science alone should be at the center of our worldview. As we have seen, this stance takes secular individuals who embrace scientism. Since science is taken to be the arbiter of all reality, or at least all knowable reality, and since it is our exclusive guide to reality, these individuals will or have to adopt a skeptical attitude toward the other two elements of people's worldview. Ideas and views that can be justified by science are acceptable; those that cannot be justified by such means and thus cannot be transformed into scientific findings or knowledge should be rejected or, at the very least, treated as second-class citizens in our worldviews. For this reason, they reject the complementary view, and here is one reason it is crucial to understand that a scientistic worldview is radically different from a humanistic worldview. It makes no difference whether we add that it is a secular worldview we are trying to depict.

These consequences of scientific naturalism worry not merely religious but also some secular intellectuals. It worries those nonreligious individuals who believe that the world of persons, intentionality, agency, self-consciousness, social institutions, and morality is real and cannot be reduced to the world of science. They think that we can know things about these phenomena and that they matter for how we should understand and live our lives. Mario De Caro and David Macarthur, for instance, maintain that "all attempts to reduce, eliminate, or reconceive these concepts [such as intentionality, agency, freedom, meaning, reference, rationality, and personal identity] in terms of supposedly more scientifically legitimate notions do not just fail – they entirely miss the kind of importance that these notions have in our lives and experiences."[13] These naturalists want to develop a more liberal naturalistic worldview than the scientistic one. They embrace *liberal naturalism*. Secular thinkers like these believe that science is essential for developing a secular way of life, but not as important as scientific naturalists do, since there are other forms of knowledge beyond scientific knowledge. De Caro and Macarthur still maintain that liberal naturalists are atheists since they reject theism and supernaturalism. Therefore, they aim to explore and develop a distinct secular worldview that excludes religious outlooks on life.

Perhaps we could say they believe that a secular construal of human life and flourishing should be guided by, but not necessarily derived from, science, as scientific naturalists do. This means that their epistemic stance is: There are other forms of knowledge and understanding, but science provides the most reliable one and sets the standard for rational belief (*the epistemic-privileged view*). Secular thinkers, such as De Caro and Macarthur, among others, believe that the defining feature of naturalism is the pride of place it grants science. On this account, naturalism is best understood as the philosophical companion to science, and an interesting question is, of course, how far you can deviate from that companionship and still be a naturalist. When might a secular person be better described as a humanist than a naturalist?

I think the answer to that question is that one can be a humanist and accept the privileged view. However, such epistemology would not typically reflect the importance granted to the deliverances of our ordinary

---

[13] Mario De Caro and David Macarthur, "Introduction: The Nature of Naturalism." In *Naturalism in Question*, edited by Mario de Caro and David MacArthur. Harvard University Press, 2004, pp. 16–17.

senses and the humanities in a humanistic worldview. One option Petar Lukić and Iris Žeželj offered those who answered their questionnaire on scientism is that "science is a good way to reach reliable knowledge in certain domains, but other ways are equally good for other fields such as law, ethics, or art."[14] This is arguably more in line with the kind of answer humanists would give than De Caro and Macarthur's. De Caro and Macarthur's stance seems closer to Lukić and Žeželj's fourth option: "Science is by far the best way to reach reliable knowledge, all other ways have a lot less to offer." However, they would, presumably, want to delete "a lot" from that statement. Either way, I would suggest that the epistemic stance of humanists is best captured in this statement:

(3) Our ordinary senses and the humanities offer us a different kind of knowledge or understanding than do the sciences (i.e., interpersonal knowledge), a knowledge that might even be more important than what science provides us with (i.e., thing or third-person knowledge) since this knowledge arises from our unique capacity of seeing each other I-to-I, as persons and not as merely objects (*the epistemic-pluralist view*).

Humanism, we could say, expresses a worldview that aims to be *consistent* with science but not *guided* by science (as in liberal naturalism) or *derived* from science (as in scientism). Instead, it is guided by a belief in human freedom, autonomy, and dignity, as well as the priority of culture over nature in our understanding of human life and its significance. Claim (3), which is a form of epistemic pluralism, entails a rejection of both epistemic exclusivism (the scientistic–epistemic thesis) and epistemic privilegism (the privileged view).[15] A consistency-with-science thesis is part of humanism, but we must take into account that it comes with a crucial qualifier: It is *granted* that science stays within its proper domain of inquiry.

Expressing the general ontology of humanism is trickier. I guess that De Caro and Macarthur would favor something along these lines: The notion of nature must be extended beyond the scientific realm to fully capture social reality, mental events, and the normative dimensions of

---

[14] Petar Lukić and Iris Žeželj, "Delineating between Scientism and Science Enthusiasm: Challenges in Measuring Scientism and the Development of a Novel Scale." *Public Understanding of Science*, 2024, 33/5, p. 574.

[15] This may provide a reason to differentiate a liberal naturalist worldview from a secular humanistic one, although I will not explore that here. See Chapter 7 for a discussion of the scientistic–epistemic thesis.

human life, but not so far as to allow any theistic or supernatural elements, processes, or agents into the natural order. Perhaps this is sufficient if we omit the last part of the statement when characterizing the general ontology of humanism and retain it when specifying the ontology of secular humanism. However, I worry that it still privileges science too much when it comes to determining what exists – if we, indeed, live in a humanistic universe. Humanists' point of departure is ordinary life, values, society, and culture, rather than the world of the natural sciences. I would, therefore, suggest we express the general features of the humanistic ontology along these lines:

(4) Reality, at least, includes all those things, properties, and relations that we can discover and justify by using our cognitive faculties as they are applied in everyday life, the humanities, and the social and natural sciences (*the humanistic-ontological thesis*).

The crucial point is that we recognize that humanists believe the social and cultural world is just as important in developing a feasible worldview as the natural world, and the former cannot be reduced to the latter. They worry that if the epistemology and the ontology of science are taken to be the measure of all things, we would create an inhumane world in which humanists would not like to live.

Human Dignity and Rights

At the very core of humanism is a particular moral stance: *human beings are persons born free and equal in dignity and rights*. I assume this is what most people directly associate with when they hear the word "Humanism." In his short introduction to humanism (which he takes to be identical with secular humanism), Stephen Law maintains that "humanism involves a commitment to the existence and importance of moral value."[16] I think that this is correct, but it is more substantial than that since humanists affirm the particular values that the idea of human freedom and dignity implies. The part of the conviction that human beings are persons born *free and equal in dignity* has been central to humanistic thought for a long time. I would say that if one does not embrace the idea of human dignity, one is not a humanist. It is a necessary condition that one must fulfill to be considered an advocate of a humanistic worldview.

---

[16] Stephen Law, *Humanism*. Oxford University Press, 2011, p. 2.

The latter part, that we have *equal human rights*, is a more recent conviction added to humanism. It is based on the ideas expressed in 1948 when the United Nations adopted the Universal Declaration of Human Rights, which set out fundamental human rights to be universally protected.[17] These include, for example, the right to life and liberty, freedom of speech and expression, the right to work and education, freedom from torture and degrading treatment, freedom of religion, and the right to a fair trial. These rights are not derived from any institution, such as the rights of a citizen, a professor, or a judge, but rather rights that we have solely in virtue of being human; they are natural rights. The connecting idea is that these human rights are grounded in the worth or the dignity of the right-holder. It is by virtue of our dignity as human beings that we possess these rights. Rights are what respect for dignity requires.

Human dignity can be understood in various ways, and not all humanists agree on how to interpret the concept. In my analysis of this core humanistic doctrine, I will develop it along Kantian lines. Immanuel Kant (1724–1804) maintains that one should, "Act in such a way that you always treat humanity, whether in your own person or in the person of any other, never simply as a means, but always at the same time as an end."[18] His stance contrasts sharply with Thomas Hobbes's (1588–1679) understanding of the value of humans. He writes, "The value, or WORTH of a man is, as of all other things, his price: that is to say, so much as would be given for his power."[19] According to Kant, dignity is above price. It is an unconditional and incomparable worth that admits of no equivalent, which elevates us above animals and mere things. Therefore, we cannot treat people as if they merely had a price. To do so would be morally wrong. The idea is that all human beings are valuable in themselves, irrespective of the use that other people or society can derive from them. They have intrinsic value, not merely instrumental value.

We can say that someone has dignity if they resist a valuation in terms of usefulness, so their worth is intrinsic. All humans possess the property of being human intrinsically. Humanists add that all humans possess the property of dignity intrinsically. They believe that all people possess a unique value tied solely to their humanity or personhood.

---

[17] Universal Declaration of Human Rights | OHCHR.
[18] Immanuel Kant, *Groundwork of the Metaphysics of Morals* (English translation). Harper & Row, 1964, p. 96.
[19] Thomas Hobbes, *Leviathan*. Hackett, 1994. Part I, chapter 10, para. 16.

It has nothing to do with their class, race, gender, religion, abilities, or any other factor, except that they are human or persons. It is the conviction that all humans deserve respect and ethical treatment, regardless of their status, abilities, or circumstances. If people have dignity, they ought to be valued for their own sake, even if, in fact, they are not. In the terminology developed in Chapters 3 and 6, this means that all humans have *moral standing*.

However, one is not a humanist – at least not in the contemporary sense – if one believes that all humans have moral worth but denies that they have equal worth with each other. In a humanistic worldview, humans do not merely have moral standing; they have equal *moral status* or *significance*. Human dignity denotes a worth that humanists maintain belongs to all persons equally. In this sense, dignity is not a worth one can earn by, for instance, living up to social standards of character and conduct or by inhabiting an elevated social position or rank. Moral standing is different from social standing.

Kant believes that animals, in contrast to humans, have merely instrumental value, but humanists can deny this and grant that other beings, besides humans, also have intrinsic value. So, some human rights can be shared with nonhuman animals, but not all rights. What people cannot do, and remain *human*ists, is to maintain that other species or members of other species have equal moral status or that some other animals have a higher moral status than some humans do, because the idea is that no nonhuman animal has the property of dignity. As George Kateb writes: "The core idea of human dignity is that on earth, humanity is the greatest type of being"; we are "the highest species on earth – so far."[20] Humans are supremely valuable.

To summarize, the belief in human dignity contains at least three ideas: first, that all human beings have value in themselves (intrinsic value); second, that all human beings have equal value; and third, that humans have greater value than nonhuman animals living on earth. We can then say that another core belief of humanism is as follows:

(5) All human beings have value in themselves, and all of them have equal value and, therefore, should be treated with unique moral respect, which we express by abiding by certain limits in our treatment of others and in terms of accepting their natural rights (*the principle of human dignity*).

---

[20] George Kateb, *Human Dignity*. Harvard University Press, 2011, pp. 3–4, 17.

At the core of a humanistic worldview is the conviction that human beings are persons born free and equal in dignity and rights. Humanists believe in the dignity and rights of all humans. As we have seen earlier, many who embrace a scientistic worldview have no problem with dignity; instead, they might even encourage talking about human dignity and rights, but they do not believe in them. Their view is a form of *moral fictionalism* that suggests we should not eliminate moral considerations from our minds, as we have done with beliefs in mermaids and witches. Why? Because moral language or practice provides us with useful fiction. We should pretend that people have dignity and rights because such talk is practically useful in our society. This, in a similar way to how we have seen that some religious naturalists think, we should continue talking about God and performing religious rituals, even if they do not believe that God exists, because God-talk can help us overcome, for instance, existential anxiety. This is *religious fictionalism*. In contrast, humanists are not merely talking about human dignity; they believe that humans have a unique intrinsic value. Humanists think it is true that we possess moral dignity and rights. It is, for them, an ontological and not merely a linguistic feature of our world.

Why do humanists believe in human dignity? Religious humanists might ground dignity in a belief that humans are created in the image of God or that they are a special manifestation of the divine order of the cosmos. We will revisit this issue when we discuss one of the challenges for secular humanism toward the end of the chapter, but is there a ground for human dignity available, whether a humanist embraces a religious or secular worldview? A striking feature of the UN documents is that, although they affirm that all humans possess dignity and that human rights are grounded in that dignity, they refrain from providing any reasons for embracing the belief in human dignity. But why do humanists think that we have dignity and natural rights, other than that it is politically correct to affirm that this is the case?

A frequently given answer is that it is something that humans are born with;[21] it is something that every human being possesses by virtue of being human and which characterizes them permanently and fundamentally from conception to death. All people have equal intrinsic value simply due to their humanity. No matter how severely impaired a human

---

[21] This seems to be the typical answer you get when searching on the web; see, for instance, "What Is Human Dignity?" Common Definitions | Human Rights Careers.

may be, they retain their human nature. People suck deep into dementia, who suffer from severe brain injury, or who are in a permanent coma still have a human nature and still belong to the kind of animals we call *Homo sapiens*. So, possessing human nature is ineradicable from human beings and is uniquely human. Since humans share the same nature, they possess equal worth and the same moral status.

Another grounding provided by humanists is that humans have dignity and rights by virtue of their capacity for or exercise of *rational agency*; they are capable of self-governance, having the capacity to make free and deliberate choices and form, implement, and revise a plan of life.[22] They are able to act for a reason, not merely out of instinct or due to environmental pressure. These are remarkable features that give those who possess them great worth. But we are more than that; we are centers of hope and despair, love and hate, emotions, intentions, and self-reflections. We are *persons*, and that is truly remarkable. So, personhood is to be treasured wherever we find it, and those who possess it have great worth. Moreover, we lack good reasons to believe that nonhuman animals are persons. Presumably, once upon a time in evolutionary history, there were others who also were persons living on earth (such as Neanderthals), and perhaps there will be – see Chapter 9 – post-human persons, but for now, we are alone. Being persons is perhaps the deepest fact about us, at least if we live in a humanistic universe, and it bestows us with dignity.

Here, we find the answer to why some humanists find scientific naturalists' idea that material objects are the only entities and cause in the world, in Carl Sagan's words, "demeaning to human dignity." Remember (see Chapter 7) that Sagan maintains:

I am a collection of water, calcium, and organic molecules called Carl Sagan. You are a collection of almost identical molecules with a different collective label. But is that all? Is there nothing in here but molecules? Some people find this idea somehow demeaning to human dignity. For myself, I find it elevating that our universe permits the evolution of molecular machines as intricate and subtle as we.[23]

Now, one possible answer to the question of what human uniqueness is, about what is ineradicable from human nature, is a particular set of

---

[22] Thomas E. Hill, "Kantian Perspectives on the Rational Basis of Human Dignity." In *The Cambridge Handbook of Human Dignity*, edited by Marcus Düwell, Jens Braarvig, Roger Griffinsword, and Dietmar Mieth. Cambridge University Press, 2015, pp. 215–221.
[23] Carl Sagan, *Cosmos*. Ballantine Books, 1980, p. 105.

molecules or a specific genetic makeup (the human genome). But humanists find it baffling to suggest, like Sagan seems to do, that human dignity
is merely grounded in a set of organic molecules. What on earth does that
have to do with dignity?[24] In contrast, being a person is a truly remarkable feature we can intuitively see could ground dignity. Therefore, belief
in human dignity would not seem to be a natural part of a worldview that
denies the existence of persons. That humans are persons explains why
we should treat them with a unique form of respect, allowing them to
make their own choices and ensuring they have the freedom to live their
lives as they see fit.

These Kantian-inspired accounts of human dignity and rights do
not align naturally with utilitarian humanists. *Utilitarianism* is the
ethical theory that right actions are those with good consequences for
as many humans as possible. What rights actions should have good
consequences for is something they have different ideas about; in classical utilitarianism, it is about the increase in pleasure (and the decrease
in pain). Hedonism is added to consequentialism. Perhaps the most
well-known formulation of the ethical theory is in terms of happiness:
Human actions are right if they promote the greatest happiness for the
greatest number of people. Because good consequences are the bedrock of their ethical outlook, utilitarians could argue that we should
believe in human dignity and rights because doing so benefits society.
The idea is that respecting human rights can lead to the greatest overall
happiness. For example, protecting freedom of speech and the right to
a fair trial can foster a more stable and just society, ultimately benefiting everyone. The dignity and rights of human persons ought to be
defended because of social utility.

Even if the founder of utilitarianism, Jeremy Bentham (1748–1832),
famously stated that natural rights are "nonsense on stilts," John Stuart
Mill (1806–1873) argues that affirming human dignity and rights is compatible with utilitarianism. The reason Mill gives in his classical work
Utilitarianism is: "To have a right, then, is, I conceive, to have something
which society ought to defend me in the possession of. If the objector
goes on to ask, why it ought? I can give him no other reason than general
utility."[25] Still, it seems there can be tension when the dignity and rights

---

[24] Nicholas Wolterstorff, "Why Naturalism Cannot Account for Human Rights," In *The
Blackwell Companion to Naturalism*, edited by Kelly James Clark. Wiley-Blackwell,
2016, p. 453.

[25] John Stuart Mill, *Utilitarianism*. Hackett, 2001, p. 54.

of individuals conflict with the greater good. In such cases, utilitarians might prioritize overall happiness over individual dignity and rights. However, I will assume that utilitarian humanists can overcome these challenges and embrace the idea of human dignity.

SECULAR HUMANISM

Given this understanding of humanism, there are religious and secular people who are humanists, just as there are religious and secular people who are non-humanists. What do we have to add to humanism to get secular humanism?

We obtain secular humanism by incorporating the core beliefs of naturalism into humanism (see the first part of Chapter 7). Hence, one affirms or at least assumes that there is nothing beyond or besides nature or the natural order, and consequently, everything that exists is part of nature (*the naturalistic thesis*); nature (or the universe) and its no God, no gods, no beings such as spirits, angels, or demons, no processes like karma, reincarnation, and channeling, and no entities such as immaterial human or animal souls (*anti-supernaturalism*); matter or physical particles lie at the root of everything; consequently, the world, at the bottom, is wholly impersonal (*the matter-first view*); and that nature is self-organized, and the existence of nature, its properties, and their inherent tendencies to produce increased complexity over time result from purely unintended causal processes and natural laws that happen to exist (*the self-organized and randomness thesis*). Andrew Copson takes the term secular humanism – he prefers to talk merely about humanism – "to denote a non-religious, non-theistic, and naturalistic approach to life."[26] We can say that if these core beliefs are true, we live in a naturalistic universe. Thus, we can say that secular humanists believe the following:

(6) We live in a naturalistic universe.

A Secularly Grounded Ethics

However, I think that there is more to secular humanism than simply incorporating these naturalistic core beliefs. In particular, secular humanists, like all humanists, take ethics or values to be of utmost importance

[26] Andrew Copson, "What Is Humanism?" In *The Wiley Blackwell Handbook of Humanism*, edited by Andrew Copson and A. C. Grayling. Wiley-Blackwell, 2015, p. 4.

because, at the core of their worldview, is the belief in human dignity: People have equal moral worth and should be treated with unique moral respect. This commitment does not seem to be compatible with moral nihilism, neither in the form of error theory nor expressivism. This nihilism better fits the previous secular worldview we consider: scientism. So, secular humanists need an alternative theory about ethics to those provided by moral nihilists.

Recall that according to the *error theory*, people, including humanists, when they make moral claims, mean to state the truth. Still, they are systematically mistaken because there are no moral truths, so all moral beliefs are false (see Chapter 7). Accordingly, it is false that human beings have dignity and equal worth; however, it may be convenient for various reasons to pretend that this statement is true (moral fictionalism). Thus, advocates of a scientistic worldview, who think that ethical truths cannot be scientifically determined, may pretend that people have dignity and rights. But it would be awkward, to say the very least, to assume that secular humanists are engaged in make-believe when they affirm that human beings are persons born free and equal in dignity and rights.

What about expressivism and secular humanism? Why would they be strange bedfellows, but perhaps less so than the error theory? Recall that *expressivism* is the theory about ethics that agrees with error theorists that there is no moral truth and, consequently, no moral knowledge, but disagrees with them that we are trying to speak the truth when making moral judgments (see Chapter 7). Instead, moral statements express our feelings, emotional attitudes, desires, or preferences; they have a practical or performative function rather than a cognitive one. Like the statements "Please, open the door" and "Shut up!" the statement that "Humans have equal dignity and rights" cannot be true or false. Simply put, the expressivist idea is that humanists express a negative emotion toward those who do not respect people's dignity and rights (and a positive one toward those who do), and since that is what morality is about, they can criticize non-humanists. This is a complex matter in philosophy because expressivism can be developed in many different ways; however, the problem for humanists with this theory about ethics still appears to be at least twofold.

First, on an expressivist account, those opposing human dignity and rights merely hold different emotions or preferences regarding the value of human lives. It is an emotional disagreement or a disagreement about preferences. But if that is all, how can humanists coherently maintain that their emotions or preferences should count for more than those of the non-humanists? Second, in Section "Human Dignity and Rights," we saw that humanists attempt to ground moral dignity in certain characteristics that define us: It could be the kind that we belong to (humankind), having the capacity for rational agency, or being persons. However, this sounds like humanists maintain that humans possess a property or set of properties that grounds their intrinsic worth. They are the feature or combination of features on which dignity that grounds rights supervenes, and they are uniquely human features. Therefore, the most straightforward interpretation of the humanist stance is to take them as saying that *it is true* that humans have moral dignity and natural rights. Moral realism, rather than expressivism, seems to be the theory about ethics that humanists presuppose when they maintain that all humans have value in themselves. All of them have equal value and, therefore, should be treated with unique moral respect. (Notice, though, that I do not want to deny that some humanists embrace expressivism or claim that it is impossible to develop a coherent expressivist form of humanism. I merely suggest that other theories about ethics fit better.)

Advocates of *moral realism* agree with the error theorists that moral claims should be taken at face value. People are trying to speak the truth when making moral judgments, but in contrast, moral realists argue that at least some moral claims are true.[27] Humanists, for instance, hold that it is true that humans possess moral dignity and natural rights. It is true that genocide is immoral, so some moral views are better than others. We can and do make moral mistakes, but moral progress is also possible; our ethical views can, over time, become better attuned to what is objectively true. Slavery was once morally permitted, but we now know it is morally wrong. Hence, a secular humanist core belief seems to be:

(7) Moral claims can be objectively true or false, and if true, they express normative facts that track the moral features of the world existing independently of us, and we can have moral knowledge (*moral realism*).[28]

---

[27] Russ Shafer-Landau, *Moral Realism: A Defense*. Oxford University Press, 2009.
[28] It is essential to recognize that the term "naturalism" in metaethics refers to a specific set of theories within moral realism. Very simply, moral naturalism says there are objective moral facts, and these facts are facts about natural things. Moral non-naturalism posits that objective moral facts are a distinct kind of fact that we must discover through ethical thought and deliberation. So, moral truths are fundamentally different from natural

However, some secular thinkers have questioned whether moral realism is a reasonable position to adopt, given that we live in a naturalistic or nonreligious universe. Because we live in such a universe, Sharon Street and others have argued that the evolutionary process is unlikely to generate beings capable of discovering moral truths. This type of argument has been referred to as *the evolutionary argument against moral realism.*

Humans are a pure product of evolution and natural selection, as are their moral judgments. Natural selection has led us in an evolutionary direction that has nothing at all to do with moral truths. This is so because natural selection selects only behaviors that benefit our survival and reproduction, not what we believe to be morally true. Street suggests that our predicament when making moral judgments, given our evolutionary history, can be compared to going to Bermuda and letting the wind and tide determine the course of the boat. She continues:

just as the push of the wind and tides on your boat has nothing to do with where you want to go, so the historical push of natural selection on the content of our evaluative judgments has nothing to do with evaluative truth. Of course every now and then, the wind and tides might happen to deposit someone's boat on the shores of Bermuda. Similarly, every now and then, Darwinian pressures might have happened to push us toward accepting an evaluative judgment that accords with one of the realist's independent evaluative truths. But this would be purely a matter of chance, since by hypothesis there is no relation between the forces at work and the "destination" in question, namely evaluative truth.[29]

According to Street, this means that our moral capacity, that is, our ability to generate moral truths, is far from reliable. If we manage to do this in a naturalistic universe, it is more a matter of luck than skill. Now, it is true that we have developed certain instincts and attitudes, and based on these, we have formed certain value judgments. However, we would have a very different morality if our evolutionary history had taken a different course. Therefore, there can be no objective moral truths (what is good is good whether or not we take it to be), or more precisely, if there were, it would be extremely unlikely that we could discover them except by sheer luck, just as an occasional boat drifting by chance can arrive in Bermuda.

---

truths. Both naturalists and theists, in the sense that these notions are given in Chapters 3 and 7, can embrace or reject any of these metaethical theories. Therefore, we must not confuse these two understandings of naturalism, and I will only use the more general concept of moral realism.

[29] Sharon Street, "A Darwinian Dilemma for Realist Theories of Value," *Philosophical Studies*, 2006, 127/1, pp. 121–122.

Religious intellectuals have been quick to point out that the existence of objective values or moral truths, as well as our ability to discover them other than by sheer luck, is much less surprising if we live in a theistic universe.[30] In such a universe, it would come as no surprise that God influenced or directed evolution toward the emergence of self-conscious, rational, and moral beings capable of discovering moral truths. Returning to Street's analogy, there would then actually be a relationship between the forces at work and the "destination" in question, namely, moral truth. So, at least certain forms of religious humanism seem not to be undermined by Street's argument. Other secular intellectuals have questioned this evolutionary argument against moral realism, arguing that moral realism is compatible with a naturalistic understanding of evolution.

However, and this is the important point here, Street suggests an alternative, non-realist way in which secular humanists can still maintain that *it is true* that humans have moral dignity and rights. Secular people can and indeed must grant that we have developed certain instincts and attitudes and, based on these, formed certain value judgments, and we would have a very different morality if our evolutionary history had taken us in a different direction. However, according to humanists, we are reflective and self-conscious beings who can act for a reason. We are capable of noticing any evolutionary or culturally inherent evaluative tendencies we have, stepping back from them, and deciding to disavow rather than endorse them. Therefore, our moral judgments are also influenced by rational reflection, and we can come to the conclusion that it is morally right to confer moral dignity on people and grant them human rights. This metaethical theory is called *moral constructivism*. Constructivists argue that moral truth is conferred, not recognized. Moral claims are capable of being true or false, but their truth or falsehood depends on our needs and informed decisions. Ethical facts are "constructions" of rational and practical reasoning.[31]

Secular humanists can thus, without embracing moral realism, maintain that it is true that there are human rights, not only as legal rights but also as moral rights. This is because, as John R. Searle writes, a "completely naturalistic conception of human life and society is consistent

---

[30] See, for instance, Mark D. Linville, "The Moral Argument." In *The Blackwell Companion to Natural Theology*, edited by William Lane Craig and J. P. Moreland. Wiley-Blackwell, 2009, pp. 391–448.

[31] Matthew Chrisman, *What Is This Thing Called Metaethics?* Routledge, 2023, pp. 126–128.

with a belief in the existence of universal human rights, in the same way that it is consistent with a belief in the existence of money, private property, and governments."[32] So, taking our human inherent "proto" evaluative attitudes as an unavoidable starting point, we can still go way beyond them and come to a conclusion in a rational deliberation that it is true that there are human rights, in a similar way that we can come to the conclusion that it is true that there is money, private property, and governments. Moral truths express normative facts that depend on us (on our evaluative attitudes and collective intentionality) for them to be true or false. Hence, secular humanists could be either moral realists or constructivists, and if they are the latter, they affirm:

(7*) Moral claims can be intersubjectively true or false, and, if true, they express normative facts that we confer to them through our rational, practical reasoning so that we can have moral knowledge (*moral constructivism*).

Progress, Secularism, and the Meaning of Life

Humanists typically look to the future, believing that if they work together, human beings can build a better, more humane world. However, faith in human progress is more pronounced in secular humanism. The reason for this is that secular humanists see themselves as defending a worldview that, over the last centuries, has freed us from the chains of religion and superstition. This is not merely good in the sense that we have left these untruths behind but also in the sense that a secular society led by autonomous persons guided by reason, the humanities, and the social and natural sciences alone can prosper in a way that a religious society never can. As David Kline maintains, "Religion, as dominantly interpreted in the West, suppresses ideas and orientations of complete human autonomy and agency as it imposes onto the human imagination systems of outside determination preventing human beings from freely and consciously constructing their own systems of meaning and purpose."[33]

This optimism is profound in *the Humanistic Manifesto I* (1933) but is more moderately expressed in *the Humanistic Manifesto II* (1973) and *the Humanistic Manifesto III* (2003). Still, the last one begins by stating, "Humanism is a progressive philosophy of life that, without

---

[32] John R. Searle, *Making the Social World*. Oxford University Press, 2010, p. 198.
[33] David Kline, "Humanism against Religion." In *The Oxford Handbook of Humanism*, edited by Anthony B. Pinn. Oxford University Press, 2021, p. 225.

supernaturalism, affirms our ability and responsibility to lead ethical lives of personal fulfillment that aspire to the greater good of humanity."[34] Bill Cooke acknowledges secular humanism's tendency toward optimism but argues that a more pessimistic attitude toward life and society is, at the very least, compatible with this worldview. He even talks about the tradition of pessimistic humanism.[35] Today's secular humanists are not nearly as optimistic as their predecessors that a society free from religion, merely guided by human reason, the humanities, and the sciences, will be a society that steadily progresses toward increased freedom, respect, justice, and peace. Still, I will take them to affirm that a society in which significantly more people are secular than religious has a better future ahead of it than if the opposite were true. Secular humanists believe that, overall, religion is an obstacle to human progress and flourishing.

A core commitment of secular humanists is that the state and religion should be separated. If we embrace a secular–humanist worldview, we are, says Law, "secularists" in the sense that we "favor an open, democratic society in which the state takes a *neutral* position with respect to religion, protecting the freedom of individuals to follow and espouse, or reject and criticize, both religious and atheist beliefs."[36] Both religious and secular people can affirm this idea of a secular state. I previously called it a worldview-independent state because, as Law stresses, the state does not align itself with any anti-religious point of view either. Both secular and religious people can reject it, but I will take it as a necessary requirement for being a secular humanist that one affirms this political doctrine. This idea is often called secularism. Law points out that it does not mean the state should publicly silence religious people, only allowing them to express their religious views privately. Instead, he maintains that it merely denies that religious voices should be given a privileged status.

It is possible to understand secularism in the way Law does (and not as I did in Chapter 2). In such a view, society is better off without religion because it is not merely false but is also dangerous to human well-being and a democratic society. We should, therefore, actively push history forward toward the goal of a nonreligious world. Secular people

---

[34] *Humanism and Its Aspirations: Humanist Manifesto III, a Successor to the Humanist Manifesto of 1933* – American Humanist Association.

[35] Bill Cooke, "Must Humanism Be Optimistic?" *Free Inquiry*, 2021, 41/6.

[36] Law, *Humanism*, p. 3.

could, on this issue, have different political agendas, and some secular humanists could be closer to embracing one or the other account of secularism. I will, however, express this core belief of secular humanism in line with Law's more modest understanding:

(8) The state must be neutral regarding religion, not privileging any religion or antireligious point of view but protecting citizens' freedom to be or not to be religious (*political secularism*).

One can have a more ambitious understanding of political secularism and be a secular humanist, but one must at least embrace it, as stated in (8). (Many religious individuals also accept (8) but would presumably reject more ambitious forms of secularism.)

What about the question of whether life has any meaning? What options do secular people have, and can we say that secular humanists answer the question in a specific way? Advocates of a secular worldview take their outlook on life to imply the rejection of any ultimate purpose or meaning to life (cosmic meaning). Typically, this is understood as rejecting the *telos* thesis central to a theistic worldview. Recall that it is the belief that we exist for a reason because God intended creatures like us to emerge in the process of evolution. God also had a particular purpose for us to fulfill: to love and obey God, to love each other, and to be God's deputies on Earth (see Chapter 3). As we also saw in the chapter on theism, some secular intellectuals, such as Kurt Baier and Jean-Paul Sartre, think that this is a good thing because, contrary to what appears, if there is a cosmic meaning, our life would be meaningless (see Chapter 3). Others mourn this loss, something that even threatens life's meaningfulness (if God does not exist, life is meaningless), whereas yet others do not think it matters one way or the other.[37]

The characteristic secular humanist response emphasizes that our lives can have meaning without it being bestowed by God or grounded in a divine, transcendent, or spiritual dimension of reality. Human life can be worthwhile or filled with purpose even if we live in a naturalistic universe of the kind that secular humanists take our actual universe to be like. One can say that these humanists believe there is meaning *in* life, but not meaning *of* life. Caring about and loving someone confers meaningfulness to life, and so do being happy, doing morally good work such as helping others in need, being creative in the artistic sense or in

---

[37] In Joshua W. Seachris, ed., *Exploring the Meaning of Life*. Wiley-Blackwell, 2013, all these stances, as well as theistic ones, are exemplified and discussed.

the sense of setting up companies or hospitals, or solving practical, scientific, and philosophical problems. Many things in life can contribute to its meaningfulness. It can vary from person to person, but presumably, not just anything can confer meaning to life; it must be something worthwhile, and stated negatively, at least not something that undermines human dignity.

Here, we find another difference between scientific naturalism and secular humanism. For scientific naturalists, values and meaning can be an essential part of their secular worldview, provided they fall within the purview of science or are a proper part of the reality that science can discover. To the extent that this is unlikely, nihilism follows. It denies that a meaningful *or* meaningless life is possible because, literally, nothing has any value. In Chapter 7, we saw that Rosenberg maintains that value, meaning, love, and purpose are illusions. Science has ruled them out. We, therefore, must say "farewell to the purpose-driven life."[38] For secular humanists, science is not the source of values, and it is irrelevant whether science can determine what is worthwhile in life. For them, the world is bigger than the world science can detect. Perhaps we can say that secular humanists believe that the existence of values and meaning is independent of both a divine order and the natural order that science can discover, but for different reasons. A meaningful life is independent of a divine order because there is no such order, but we can still find meaning in life. The natural order that science discovers is real, but science is the wrong tool to use to detect life's meaningfulness (or meaninglessness). Hence, one further central belief of secular humanism is as follows:

(9) While there is no cosmic or ultimate meaning to the existence of nature and life, our human lives can still have meaning, and this is so irrespective of whether this meaning can be discovered by science.

Just as faith in progress and the optimism that accompanies it, affirming life's meaningfulness in a naturalistic universe is a strong tendency among secular humanists. However, it is not required to count as an adherent of a secular–humanist worldview. Just as there are those with a more pessimistic attitude who look upon human progress with skepticism, there are secular humanists who lean toward the idea of life's meaninglessness, absurdity, or insignificance.[39]

---

[38] Rosenberg, *The Atheist's Guide to Reality*, pp. 194f.
[39] See, for example, Thomas Nagel, "The Absurd," *Journal of Philosophy*, 1971, 69/20, pp. 716–727.

Philip Kitcher emphasizes that the role religion fulfills in human lives regarding meaning-making and belonging constitutes a challenge for secular humanism or what he calls secularism.[40] He criticizes the so-called new atheists (intellectuals such as Dawkins, Dennett, Harris, and Hitchens) for failing to consider that religious beliefs are of deep moral and existential value.[41] They ignore that for religious people, their beliefs play a critical role in making their lives bearable and in providing answers to the question of why their lives matter. Consequently, the choice between a religious or secular worldview is not merely *intellectual* but just as much *existential*. He even thinks that secularists must provide religious people with equal or greater resources for making sense of their lives, or else the latter are rationally entitled to stick to their beliefs. Therefore, a future secular society without religious people must ensure that its citizens suffer no loss or diminishment in their moral and existential resources; it must secure that life in such a society is not only endurable but also meaningful for its citizens. So, Kitcher stresses that secular humanism must be responsive, just as religion is, to our deepest impulses and needs. Secular worldviews have to offer something to replace the existential and social aspects of traditional religions, to provide "secular surrogates" for them.

One such challenge is the community that religious organizations offer people, which gives them a sense of belonging, participation, coherence, and a common aspiration to create the Kingdom of God on earth or whatever other vision of life they endorse. So, developing secular communities and contexts that can fulfill this function in people's lives is essential. Another challenge is that religious people should be able to give up their faith in God without losing an overall meaning or purpose to their lives. Kitcher maintains that secular humanists could argue that our lives are more meaningful if we choose our paths and own life projects, thereby determining the meaning and purpose of our lives. He acknowledges that the hope secular life can provide is less grand than religious people imagine. Still, while life in a completely secular world is always vulnerable, it is not bleak and hopeless. Still, secular humanists have more work to do in the future when it comes to fulfilling the social and existential needs that religion has been responsive to and sought to

---

[40] Philip Kitcher, "Challenges for Secularism." In *The Joy of Secularism*, edited by George Levine. Princeton University Press, 2011, p. 24.
[41] Philip Kitcher, "Militant Modern Atheism," *Journal of Applied Philosophy*, 2011, 28/1, pp. 1–13.

address over the millennia. It is a major challenge, but it is not a reason to choose a religious life over a secular one. He writes: "Many – perhaps most – human lives do not go well. Death often removes those we love, and shatters our projects. Secular humanism is committed to the attempt to decrease the frequency with which people's aspirations are frustrated and broken, despite recognizing that it can never expect to turn back all the reversals our mundane existence brings."[42]

Secular organizations have also started to offer not just the possibility of being formal members of those associations but also to provide, in Kitcher's terminology, secular surrogates for religious ceremonies or rituals. There are, for example, secular naming ceremonies, weddings, and funerals that are offered as replacements for religious ones. Still, most nonreligious people are *secular nones*; they are individuals who self-identify as secular but have no affiliation with an organized secular community. This contrasts with the religious worldviews, where most adherents are organized and belong to particular communities. The number of *religious nones* (individuals who self-identify as religious but have no affiliation with an organized religious community) is much lower than that of secular nones. However, this might change in the future, and if Kitcher is correct, such a development is necessary.

Secular humanists reject the hegemony of science and base their secular outlook on other sources of knowledge and justification besides those provided by science. In particular, the belief in human uniqueness and human dignity is at the core of their worldview. However, secular humanists can and frequently do assume that religion is incompatible with science and that this, at least for some of them, constitutes an important reason why they attempt to develop a secular alternative. Many would argue that the theories and findings of anthropology, sociology, history, philosophy, and religious studies have been just as important in undermining the religions of the world as science. Still, contrary to scientific naturalists, their secular worldview does not flow out of, find its basic building blocks in, or is constrained to what science says reality is, and basically nothing more. Secular humanists certainly respect and are impressed by science, but they do not believe that science is the measure of all things; we humans, as a community of persons, are instead the measure of all things. It is belief in our freedom and dignity, not faith in science, which is at the core of their worldview.

---

[42] Kitcher, "Challenges for Secularism," p. 49.

CHALLENGES FOR SECULAR HUMANISM

What challenges does secular humanism face? What would seem to be problematic aspects of it? Let me highlight some of these challenges without suggesting that a secular–humanist worldview lacks the resources to deal with them in a satisfying way.

Due to the development of environmentalism, in particular biocentric worldviews, humanists have received criticism for their elevated view of humanity and have been accused of advocating "speciesism." Let us refer to this as *the challenge of speciesism*. Humanists believe that humans possess dignity and that only humans on Earth are capable of possessing this dignity. Many of them maintain that all people possess a unique value tied solely to their humanity. It has nothing to do with their class, race, gender, religion, abilities, or any other factor, except that they are human. However, critics object that if dignity is essentially connected to being an individual of a specific species, *Homo sapiens*, then that makes brute species membership enough to confer a unique worth. It is entirely arbitrary, a rest from the Judeo-Christian heritage of thinking that humans are created in God's image – a justification of human dignity not available to secular humanists. Instead, the critics argue that it is a form of discrimination favoring those who belong to a particular species against individuals who belong to other species. It is speciesism and similar to racism, where members of one race claim superiority over another race simply due to their membership in their particular race. The idea of human dignity and superiority is based on the invalid assumption that species difference alone is a sufficient justification for separate treatment or differentiation in moral worth. Therefore, the critics conclude that secular humanists should reject humanism, embrace *egalitarian environmentalism*, and become *egalitarian environmentalists*.

However, if every species and every member of each species has equal worth or even dignity, then it seems impossible to live and flourish as a human being. An axiom in ethical theory is that *ought implies can*. That is to say, nothing can be morally required of an individual if it is impossible for that individual to do so and stay alive. I cannot be blameworthy for not jumping into the river and trying to save the child who is drowning if I cannot swim. Such action could be praiseworthy, but not one's moral duty. Some egalitarian environmentalists are aware of this problem but respond that it is a particular property that grounds equal value among individuals of diverse species. Typically, this property is taken to be *sentience*, the ability to experience feelings and sensations such as pleasure or pain.[43] It is sentient beings, no matter which species they belong to, that make them deserve moral consideration and provide grounds for equal moral worth. Such a form of egalitarian environmentalism is livable and does, therefore, not violate the axiom that ought implies can.

Many secular humanists acknowledge that if the idea of human dignity – that all people hold a unique and equal value – is tied solely to their humanity, then the charge of speciesism might be warranted. However, they maintain that they have an answer available that does not require them to abandon their secular–humanist worldview. Even if sentient nonhuman animals hold a morally significant property to an equal degree (sentience), it remains the case that humans possess further valuable properties that those living creatures lack or do not possess to an equal degree. We have seen that humanists maintain that human beings are also persons; they are self-aware, autonomous, rational, and moral beings. These are properties that nonhuman animals either lack or possess to a much lesser degree, but which confer on humans a moral status that is superior to that of nonhumans. Hence, the challenge of speciesism states a forceful objection to some, but presumably not all, forms of secular humanism.

We previously saw that Street and Searle challenged whether secular humanists could reasonably embrace moral realism. Instead, they propose that since we live (as they believe) in a naturalistic universe, social constructivism about ethics offers a much more plausible understanding of the nature of moral beliefs. Other thinkers have criticized social constructivists for making morality too relativistic. Let us name this *the challenge for social constructivist metaethics*. The core idea of the constructivist theory about ethics is that taking our human needs and motivations as a starting point, we can, after informed and rational deliberation, come to a conclusion that it is true that there is human dignity and rights in a similar way that we can – as Searle points out – conclude that it is true that there is money, private property, and governments. Moral and societal progress is possible. However, if communists or radical socialists succeed in persuading us by rational argumentation that we should abolish private property, then it is no longer true that there is private property. Likewise, critics argue that an altered, rationally based social agreement or contract could threaten human dignity and moral

---

[43] Peter Singer, "Speciesism and Moral Status," *Metaphilosophy*, 2009, 40/3–4, pp. 567–581.

rights. That possibility undermines the moral objectivity that many secular humanists attribute to human dignity and rights. British citizens, through a process of deliberative democratic procedure, concluded in 1975 that they should become members of the European Union (EU); it then became true that the UK was no longer a country that was not part of the EU. However, in 2016, they reversed this decision and left the EU. Before 1997, it was true that the UK was not a member of the EU; after 1997, it became true that they were a member; and then, after 2016, it became false again. The critics argue that we do not want this kind of relativity of social truths regarding moral truths; therefore, a social constructivist theory about ethics should be rejected.

As we saw in Chapter 3, many theists are aware that the amount of evil in the world is a problem for their religious worldview or, more specifically, their belief in God. Similarly, some naturalists acknowledge that one of the most profound problems with a naturalistic worldview is how it can account for the appearance, through the operation of the laws of physics and chemistry, of conscious beings like ourselves, capable of discovering those natural laws and, moreover, the truth of naturalism itself. Nagel concedes that a theistic understanding explains how science is possible because there is a coherence between the natural order and our consciousness in such a worldview. God intentionally creates both phenomena. Naturalists (such as himself) have much more difficulty explaining this coherence: "Once the question is asked, atheists must consider whether their view of how we got here at all makes it likely that our cognitive abilities would enable us to discover the laws of nature."[44] This challenge is not merely directed at secular humanism but at all secular worldviews that contain the core beliefs of naturalism. This challenge is similar to the one that Street directed against secular humanists who embrace evolutionary theory and moral realism. Likewise, it targets secular people who embrace evolutionary theory and naturalism. It is often called *the evolutionary argument against naturalism*.[45]

The core idea is that it is unlikely that natural selection, unguided by God or something like God, has generated beings with the capacity to

[44] Thomas Nagel, "A Philosopher Defends Religion," *The New York Review of Books*, September 27, 2012, www.nybooks.com/articles/archives/2012/sep/27/philosopher-defends-religion.
[45] See Alvin Plantinga, *Where the Conflict Really Lies*. Oxford University Press, 2011, pp. 307–350; and Thomas M. Crisp, "On Naturalistic Metaphysics." In *The Blackwell Companion to Naturalism*, edited by Kelly James Clark. Wiley-Blackwell, 2016, pp. 61–74.

discover by reason the truth about a reality that extends vastly beyond the initial appearances. Natural selection is interested in behavior, not the truth of belief, except when the latter relates to behavior. So, it is presumably reasonable to assume that our reason is reliable about matters of survival and reproduction, generating beliefs, for example, about the presence of predators, food, or potential mates. But what about beliefs that go far beyond anything with survival value? What about physics or evolutionary theory? Or, as in Street's argument, what about moral realism or, as these critics add, atheism, materialism, and naturalism? If we live in a naturalistic universe, the probability that the cognitive faculties we inherited from our Pleistocene ancestors reliably produce truths about things that go way beyond what we need for feeding, flying, fighting, and reproducing is very low. However, science reveals truths about the world far beyond its initial appearances. Therefore, we should reject naturalism and embrace some form of non-naturalism, such as theism, a worldview in which it would not be extremely unlikely that we could reason our way to scientific truths except by sheer luck, just as (in Street's analogy) an occasional boat drifting by chance can arrive in Bermuda. Instead, the critics argue that in a theistic worldview, we can understand the deeper dimensions of the world because God has guided evolution to produce creatures that are made in God's image. Hence, critics conclude that theism offers a better explanation for why science produces knowledge successfully than secular humanism or any other naturalistic worldview does.

Notice that an adequate response to the challenge is not to think that, since our reason obviously is reliable, the evolutionary argument against naturalism is unconvincing. To think in such a way would be analogous to arguing that there is obviously much evil in the world, so the argument from evil against theism is unconvincing. It is not the existence of evil that critics question, but rather whether the amount of evil is compatible with theism or should be expected if we live in a theistic universe. Similarly, it is not the reliability of our cognitive faculties that the critics question, but whether such reliability is compatible with or to be expected if we live in a naturalistic universe in which evolutionary theory is true. Because of the discrepancy between evil and what to expect as a theist, critics conclude that we are unlikely to live in a theistic universe. Likewise, the idea here is that due to the discrepancy between our reliable reasoning abilities and what to expect as a naturalist, critics conclude that we are unlikely to live in a naturalistic universe. Nor should we trust the arguments that we do live in such a universe. Given naturalism and evolutionary theory, it is highly unlikely indeed that our cognitive faculties should be reliable when conducting science or arguing for a naturalistic worldview.

In what way would advocates of a scientistic worldview criticize secular humanists? Their primary criticism would be that secular humanists believe in many things that are not within the purview of science, in particular, things about ourselves. Searle states the challenge in this way: "How can we square this [humanistic] self-conception of ourselves as mindful, meaning-creating, free, rational, etc., agents with a [naturalistic] universe that consists entirely of mindless, meaningless, unfree, non-rational, brute physical particles?"[46] Secular humanists, including Searle himself, hope that at least parts of this self-conception can be preserved in a naturalistic worldview. Scientific naturalists, such as Paul Churchland and Alex Rosenberg, are not nearly as optimistic.[47] The challenge is about whether the ontology of naturalism is rich enough to accommodate secular humanists' conception of themselves or whether, in the end, it forces them to partially or entirely abandon it. This is a huge question; let us raise it here concerning humanists' belief in free will. Some scientific naturalists argue that neuroscientific findings on how the brain functions in human decision-making provide strong evidence to conclude that prior unconscious events predetermine our decisions, and thus, free will is an illusion. This is *the incompatibilist challenge against free will*. Incompatibilists are individuals who believe that being free is incompatible with being causally determined.

It is natural to think that we have free will on a given occasion, just if we could have done otherwise, just if it were within our power, in that situation, to act differently from how we did act at the time. Suppose I lie about my salary to make myself look important and boost my prestige. Typically, we assume that I could have refrained from telling that lie and that I am morally responsible for telling it. It was within my power to refrain from lying, but I did not, and I am therefore guilty of lying and blameworthy for my actions. Secular humanists, like almost everyone who believes in free will, take for granted that the brain plays an indisputable role in generating decisions of this sort, so that is not the issue. However, critics point out that neuroscience provides good reason to believe that our brains produce our decisions unconsciously, and we become aware of them only after the fact. (They base their case

---

[46] John R. Searle, *Freedom and Neurobiology*. Columbia University Press, 2007, pp. 4–5.

[47] Paul Churchland, *Matter and Consciousness*. MIT Press, 1984; and Alex Rosenberg, *The Atheist's Guide to Reality*. W. W. Norton & Company, 2011.

on a certain interpretation of research, such as the famous EEG experiments conducted by the physiologist Benjamin Libet and others in the 1980s and the experiment by C. S. Soon and others in 2008.) Since our decisions are made unconsciously, it is not up to us to decide what we choose. Instead, our brains have already determined what we will do, so free will is an illusion. Everything we have done could not have happened any other way, and everything we do will be decided for us without any input from our conscious selves (if we have any). So, I could not have avoided lying about my salary; instead, I was determined to lie on that occasion. But on other occasions, I may be determined to tell the truth. I do not have the freedom I think I have. I have no choice in how I act. I have a will, but it is not free.

Sam Harris maintains that the conclusion of this argument – that our choices matter but that we cannot choose them – has profound consequences for our ideas about personal and moral responsibility, and consequently, for our social and legal systems. If it is not possible for me, on that occasion, to refrain from lying, then I cannot really be responsible for that wrongdoing. He writes: "The men and women on death row have some combination of bad genes, bad parents, bad environments, and bad ideas (and the innocent, of course, have supremely bad luck). Which of these quantities, exactly, were they responsible for?"[48] None is Harris's answer. Not only are criminals "nothing more than poorly calibrated clockwork" who do not deserve any punishment for their deeds, but also "those of us who work hard and follow the rules would not 'deserve' our success in any deep sense."[49] Likewise, Rosenberg maintains that "science shows that no one acts with free will. So, no wrongdoer ever earns punishment. This is an unavoidable conclusion that scientism draws from applying determinism to core morality."[50] Hence, these critics conclude that the humanistic conception of ourselves as mindful, meaning-creating, free, rational agents is incompatible with a naturalistic universe that consists entirely of mindless, meaningless, unfree, nonrational, brute physical particles.

[48] Sam Harris, *Free Will*. The Free Press, 2012, p. 54.
[49] Harris, *Free Will*, p. 1.
[50] Rosenberg, *The Atheist's Guide to Reality*, p. 293.

9

A Transhumanist Worldview

Transhumanism originated as an elite worldview but has gained a vast audience through popular films and books and has even been described as the new religion in certain parts of the world, such as Silicon Valley in California. Its significance in today's highly technological society is profound and will undoubtedly be even more so in the future. In 1998, philosophers Nick Bostrom and David Pearce founded the World Transhumanist Association (WTA). The WTA changed its name to Humanity+ in 2008.[1] Other organizations also play a role in the transhumanist movement, including the Extropy Institute, the Lifeboat Foundation, the Immortality Institute, the Singularity Institute for Artificial Intelligence, and more academically oriented organizations such as the Institute for Ethics and Emerging Technologies and the Singularity University. One thing of particular interest with this worldview is that besides "lay" people, so to say, there is one group of transhumanists that stand out in a way that is not typically of the other worldviews: There are, of course, the intellectuals, often prominent academic spokespersons such as Nick Bostrom, Max Moore, Natascha Vita-More, and Stefan Lorenz Sorgner, but there are also the wealthy transhumanists or tech entrepreneurs such as Aubrey de Gray, Ray Kurzweil, Peter Thiel, and Elon Musk. This second group of individuals typically does not feature as front figures in a worldview. We will examine the arguments presented by individuals from both groups.

Transhumanists do not speak with one voice; we will analyze some areas where they diverge. Nonetheless, I will identify some of the core

[1] For more on WTA, visit www.humanityplus.org/.

beliefs of this new and evolving secular worldview, doing so in a manner that distinguishes transhumanism from the others surveyed in this book, without denying that elements of it could be incorporated into the other worldviews. The term transhumanism was coined in 1957 by Julian Huxley. He considered it a key concept of an entirely new outlook in life, "a new ideology," in that it actively promoted a deliberate effort by humanity to transcend itself entirely.[2]

TRANSHUMANIST VALUES

Transhumanism is an outgrowth of secular humanism, but it also differs in a fundamental way from it, to the extent that it is reasonable to identify it as a rival secular worldview. Bostrom says it has "roots in secular humanist thinking, yet it is more radical."[3] It is more radical because transhumanists are actively striving to accelerate an end to the human condition as we know it. Since its roots are in secular humanism and the Enlightenment, rather than Renaissance humanism, I will not refer to it as "secular transhumanism" but simply as "transhumanism." Thus, I will take its default version to be secular without denying that it is possible to develop religious transhumanism. The difference in historical roots provides my rationale for using the qualifier "secular" when discussing the nonreligious version of humanism, but not when discussing transhumanism. Hence, whenever we want to talk and write about a non-secular version of transhumanism, I propose adding "religious" to transhumanism. This interpretation aligns with Bostrom's remarks that "transhumanism is a naturalistic outlook," but that certain forms of religiosity may be compatible with transhumanism.[4] He also acknowledges that it is a worldview: "While not a religion, transhumanism might serve a few of the same functions that people have traditionally sought in religion. It offers a sense of direction and purpose and suggests a vision that humans can achieve something greater than our present condition."[5]

Other transhumanists have been less open to the possibility that transhumanism and religion are compatible. Some even think that

---

[2] Julian Huxley, *New Bottles for New Wine*. Chatto & Windus, 1957, pp. 17 and 255.

[3] Nick Bostrom, "Transhumanist Values." In *Ethical Issues for the 21st Century*, edited by Frederick Adams. Philosophical Documentation Center Press, 2003, p. 4.

[4] Stefan Lorenz Sorgner writes that "most transhumanists hold naturalistic views." Stefan Lorenz Sorgner, *On Transhumanism*. The Pennsylvania State University Press, 2021, p. 2.

[5] Nick Bostrom, "Transhumanist FAQ: A General Introduction." Version 2.1, 2003, p. 46. https://nickbostrom.com/views/transhumanist.pdf.

religion, or at least a theistic worldview, is the major obstacle to a posthuman future. For instance, Simon Young maintains that the "greatest threat to humanity's continuing evolution is theistic opposition to Superbiology."[6] Kurzweil writes that a "primary role of traditional religion is deathist rationalization – that is, rationalizing the tragedy of death as a good thing."[7] But we need to overcome this deathist rationalization. We need to leave traditional religion behind and move forward. Still, Kurtzweil recognizes that we need "a new religion."[8] In my terminology, his idea is that we need a new worldview.

Consequently, I will assume in my rational reconstruction of transhumanism that the transhumanists accept the core beliefs of naturalism. Hence, they believe that there is nothing beyond or beside nature; that there is no God, no gods, and no transcendent, divine or sacred dimension of reality; that matter, physical particles or fields of energy lie at the root of everything and that consequently the world, at the bottom, is wholly impersonal; and that nature is self-organized and the existence of nature, its properties, and their inherent tendencies to produce increased complexity over time is the result of purely unintended causal processes and natural laws that just happen to exist. If these core beliefs are true, we live in a naturalistic universe. Thus, we can say that transhumanists believe the following:

(1) We live in a naturalistic universe (*naturalism*).

While seeing *Homo sapiens* as the product of natural selection and chance (a chance event is not part of anyone's plan) alone, transhumanists maintain that, in our hands, evolution might have a purpose after all. We, not God, will gain, for the first time since the Big Bang, the ability to control evolution in a conscious way. If we dare to act in such a way, the evolutionary processes can go from being unguided to becoming guided. To be *transhuman* is to be in a conscious transition to the next evolutionary phase of what counts as human; to be *posthuman* is to be a member of a new, consciously designed species.

What, then, makes transhumanism a distinct worldview from secular humanism and scientism? Bostrom, arguably the leading philosopher of transhumanism, maintains that it is "a way of thinking about the

---

[6] Simon Young, *Designer Evolution: A Transhumanist Manifesto*. Prometheus Books, 2006, p. 324.
[7] Ray Kurzweil, *The Singularity Is Near: When Humans Transcend Biology*. Penguin Books, 2005, p. 372.
[8] Kurzweil, *The Singularity Is Near*, p. 374.

future that is based on the premise that the human species in its current form does not represent the end of our development but rather a comparatively early phase."[9] Nevertheless, it is more than that empirical claim or prediction (which could or could not become true in the future) because what really defines transhumanism is a normative claim. The value commitment that this claim reveals cannot be found in humanism or, indeed, in any of the other worldviews we have considered so far. It is that we ought to enhance humanity radically – physically, cognitively, and emotionally. Within information technology, an enhancement is any product change or upgrade that increases software or hardware capabilities beyond the original client specifications. An *enhancement* within the transhumanist worldview is any biotechnological change or upgrade that increases people's physical, cognitive, or emotional capacities beyond or far beyond the limitations set by human nature. This could be achieved, for instance, by altering the genetic makeup of humans in the future. Essentially, then, enhancement means elevating human capacities beyond or far beyond a baseline of normal human limitations. Transhumanism goes beyond humanism also in the sense that transhumanists aim to create something that is no longer human but posthuman.

At the core of transhumanism is the idea of reevaluating the entire human situation as traditionally conceived. We should actively try to create transhumans and, eventually, posthumans. Transhumans (or Humanity 2.0) are transitional humans, who are moderately or significantly enhanced, with capacities that fall somewhere between those of unaugmented humans (or Humanity 1.0) and full-blown posthumans.[10] Transhumans could be people with implants (microchips and nanobots) to monitor and prevent some diseases or gene-edited babies. Posthumans are individuals who have undergone such radical changes that they can be classified as a new species of persons that have evolved from *Homo sapiens*. It is not possible to draw any sharp line between transhumans and posthumans. Still, the latter could be humans who have uploaded their brains to computers or become cyborgs with added neural circuitry that enhances their cognitive powers so radically that they become superintelligent. (So, "posthuman" does not denote anything that happens after the human era and does not imply that there are no humans anymore.) Hence, the transhumanist core value consists of the following normative claim:

---

[9] Bostrom, "Transhumanist FAQ," p. 4.
[10] Bostrom, "Transhumanist Values," p. 5.

(2) Using biotechnology and AI, we should change, improve, or refine humanity radically, even to the extent that we create a new species, the posthuman (*the idea of radical enhancement*).

The stance is that improving human nature through the means of biotechnology is morally valuable; we ought to create transhumans and posthumans. Transhumanism entails that we should prefer transhumans over humans, but it does not necessarily require that we favor posthumans over transhumans. We may favor them if they lead lives that are more worthwhile than the alternative human lives would be, but whether that will be the case may be hard for us, with our limitations, to fully comprehend. Still, most transhumanists prefer posthuman life over both human and transhuman life and think we ought to create them. They, in the words of Bostrom,

wish to follow life paths which would, sooner or later, require growing into posthuman persons: they yearn to reach intellectual heights as far above any current human genius as humans are above other primates; to be resistant to disease and impervious to aging; to have unlimited youth and vigor; to exercise control over their own desires, moods, and mental states; to be able to avoid feeling tired, hateful, or irritated about petty things; to have an increased capacity for pleasure, love, artistic appreciation, and serenity; to experience novel states of consciousness that current human brains cannot access.[11]

Not only would some posthuman modes of being be very good, but more importantly, it would be very good for us (or most current human beings) to become posthuman. If we allow it, biotechnology can provide the means to obtain radical human enhancement.

Transhumanism is like scientism in that science also plays a key role in this worldview. Science and advanced technology will make the ideas of transhumanism possible to actualize. They make a dream into a realistic vision for the future. However, it differs from scientism in that transhumanists are not skeptical of philosophy, a nonscientific form of inquiry. Bostrom writes, "our human brains may cap our ability to discover philosophical and scientific truths. It is possible that failure of philosophical research to arrive at solid, generally accepted answers to many of the traditional big philosophical questions could be due to the fact that we are not smart enough to be successful in this kind of inquiry."[12] He even describes transhumanism as a philosophy and, consequently, not as a science, and is upfront with that the transhumanist

[11] Bostrom, "Transhumanist FAQ," p. 5.
[12] Bostrom, "Transhumanist Values," p. 6.

idea of uploading our consciousness into virtual reality presupposes "certain philosophical assumptions about the nature of consciousness and personal identity."[13]

Most importantly, transhumanists believe that science can never justify its core value commitment. It tells us, as we have seen, that we ought to radically enhance humanity. The same holds for other central values of transhumanism, such as emphasizing individual freedom and choice in enhancement technologies. Regarding the sixfold typology of understanding the relationship between our worldview and science (see Chapter 5), we can say that the transhumanist worldview is guided by science in its formation. Still, it nevertheless goes beyond science on certain crucial matters. Transhumanism is not taken to be entailed by science; it does not (as scientism) proclaim to start from and stop with science.

Most transhumanists are keen to emphasize that they are humanists and thus embrace humanism and its core idea that all humans as individuals have the same intrinsic worth (the doctrine of human dignity). We have seen that they go beyond humanism in maintaining that we should radically change, improve, or refine humanity, even to the extent of creating a new species, the posthuman (the idea of radical enhancement). Transhumanists maintain that these two core value commitments are compatible. Still, as we will see when discussing the challenges that transhumanism faces, some humanists have questioned whether that is the case.

It is through developments in genetics, nanotechnology, robotics, and artificial intelligence (AI) that radical human enhancement can be obtained. Therefore, crucial to transhumanists is the relaxation of laws surrounding innovative biotechnology and AI, so that these technologies can be developed and widely made available. The justification of such "bioliberal" laws is ultimately based on the ideas of human autonomy, morphological freedom, and reproductive freedom. Transhumanists value human autonomy, that is, the ability and right of individuals to plan and choose their own lives. Hence, if some people want to modify their bodies using enhancement technologies, they have a moral right to be able to do so.

Anders Sandberg sees *morphological freedom* as "an extension of one's right to one's body, not just self-ownership but also the right to

---

[13] Bostrom, "What Is Transhumanism?" 2001, https://nickbostrom.com/old/transhumanism.

modify oneself according to one's desires."[14] It goes beyond merely passively maintaining the body as it is and extends its potential. But it also implies that nobody may force us to change in a way we do not want to. Not only should individuals have broad discretion over which enhancement technologies to apply to themselves, but parents should also usually decide which technologies to use when having children. This type of freedom is sometimes called *reproductive freedom*, but in the transhumanist case, it goes way beyond the right to have or not have a child, to have or not have an abortion. It is about the right to design one offspring. A designer baby is an embryo that has been genetically modified to produce a child with specific traits. In some cases, unfavorable characteristics (such as genetic diseases) may be removed, or favorable traits (like enhanced intelligence, musicality, or strength) might be added.

By editing embryos or enhancing our nature, we can alter the course of evolution for generations and thus create transhumans and eventually posthumans, simply because these changes are inherent and transmissible via reproduction to subsequent generations. Hence, another central transhumanist value consists of the following normative claim:

(3) We as individuals should be free to decide and radically modify who we are, who we might want to become, and who our children should become by using biotechnological means (*morphological* and *reproductive freedom*).

Transhumanists believe that people should have the right to choose which enhancement technologies, if any, they want to use on themselves and their children. They acknowledge that in cases where such free choices have a substantial impact on other people, this right may need to be restricted.

HUMAN NATURE

The idea of radical human enhancement is only possible to achieve if one thinks that human nature is malleable or, at least, will be in the near future. Human nature is a "work-in-progress," a half-baked beginning that we can and should learn to reshape in desirable ways.

---

[14] Anders Sandberg, "Morphological Freedom – Why We Not Just Want It, but Need It." In *The Transhumanist Reader*, edited by Max Moore and Natasha Vita-More. Wiley-Blackwell, 2013, p. 56.

Transhumanists take for granted that human nature is foremost a product of natural selection and other biological processes, and is, therefore, innate. Who we are is the product of unguided evolution, but we essentially have the same nature (or genotype) as our ancestors, stemming from our long-enduring existence as hunter-gatherers. Still, we are more than our genetic and biological makeup, so our current extended phenotypes differ from those of hunter-gatherers. We read and write, live in cities, buy food at supermarkets, drive cars, vote in elections, and women give birth in hospitals, whereas our ancestors did none of those things.

Transhumanism challenges the view that human nature is not up for grabs, an idea Bostrom seems to assume to be explicit in most contemporary theories of human nature and implicit in practically all of today's political thinking.[15] However, this is not entirely true and is worth emphasizing and reflecting on in relation to the other worldviews. There are indeed politicians and researchers in the natural and social sciences and the humanities that, as Helena Cronin claims, "Certainly, human nature is fixed. It's universal and unchanging – common to every baby that's born, down through the history of our species"[16] or as Steven Pinker thinks that human nature is stable and is the "endowment of cognitive and emotional faculties that is universal to healthy members of *Homo sapiens*."[17] However, as the subtitle of Pinker's book highlights, there is also the "Modern Denial of Human Nature." Accordingly, how we behave and think is purely a matter of social conditioning and owes nothing to our biological nature. Human nature is, rather, a myth that aims at imposing one particular set of male Eurocentric values on the rest of the world.

These thinkers take the idea that there is no universal essence of human nature to be a core claim of contemporary research within the social sciences and the humanities. Pinker refers to this as the Blank Slate; some of its other critics have dubbed it the Standard Social Science Model. In contrast, its advocates today typically refer to it as either *anti-essentialism* or *social constructivism*. This idea can be interpreted as a rejection of human nature. However, I would rather interpret it as denying a robust biological human nature; human nature is essentially social

[15] Bostrom, "What Is Transhumanism?"

[16] Helena Cronin, "Getting Human Nature Right: A Talk with Helena Cronin," *Edge* 73, 2000 [www.edge.org].

[17] Steven Pinker, *The Blank Slate: The Modern Denial of Human Nature*. Allen Lane, 2002, p. 142.

and thus flexible or malleable.[18] The core belief of social constructivism would then be that (a) human nature is primarily the product of culture or learning and socialization, and (b) it is not fixed but quite plastic or malleable. Humans are social constructions like money, professors, and countries.

Transhumanists, on the other hand, are not social constructivists but *biotech constructivists*. Using biotechnologies, we can (re-)construct ourselves in radically new ways to obtain physical and mental capacities that far exceed what is now possible. Hence, a third core belief of transhumanism is the following:

(4) Human nature – our innate biological faculties and propensities – is not fixed but changeable and flexible, essentially receptive to biotechnological interventions and modifications (*the malleability thesis*).

The idea of radical enhancement presupposes the truth of the malleability thesis. We can significantly change, improve, or refine humanity, even to the extent of creating a new species, the posthuman, because human nature – our innate faculties and propensities – is not fixed but changeable and flexible, essentially receptive to biotechnological interventions and modifications.

Why radically enhance humanity? Not because we can or because it is inevitable, but because transhumanists believe such life is more worthwhile than our present one. Transhuman and posthuman lives would be better than human lives because three limitations – mortality, ignorance, and suffering – will no longer define their lives. Those lives are worth striving for because they, in contrast to ours, are characterized by superlongevity, superintelligence, and super-wellbeing (or at least one or two of these great-making properties). The idea is that these limitations can be conceived as essentially biotechnical problems, and thus, problems that can be overcome using genetic engineering, nanotechnology, and robotics.

SUPERLONGEVITY AND THE SINGULARITY

Over the past 250 years, the average life expectancy in many developed countries has gone from 40 to 80 years. The chance of these individuals

---

[18] I have attempted to explicate these rival theories of human nature in Mikael Stenmark, "Is There a Human Nature?" *Zygon: Journal of Religion and Science*, 2012, 47/4, pp. 890–902; and Mikael Stenmark, "Three Theories of Human Nature," *Zygon: Journal of Religion and Science*, 2009, 44/4, pp. 894–920.

living to see their 100th birthday has increased. However, the average life expectancy does not rise because humanity as a species has managed to extend its lifespan. It increases because more individuals live to older ages. Improvements in public health at all stages of life have had a clear impact on average life expectancy, primarily by reducing child mortality rates, which has significantly contributed to the increase in average life expectancy. But what about the maximum lifespan? The official world record for the longest lifespan is held by Jeanne Calment, who died in 1997 at the age of 122. Since then, no one has come close to reaching that age; however, let us assume that 125 years is the maximum human lifespan. (One of the living animals with the longest lifespan on earth is the Aldabra giant tortoise, which can live around 200 years.) Given this situation, the transhumanist stance on what to do can be contrasted with that taken by those sometimes referred to as "healthspanners."

Healthspanners are individuals, typically in the medical sciences and healthcare, who conduct research and actively promote a way of living that aims to provide a healthy and extended lifespan, followed by a quick and painless death. They are seeking to identify and block the causes of terminal diseases. Applying this research and health advice will not significantly extend the maximum lifespan: If we cure cancer, we will add a little more than three years to the average life, and solving heart disease will give us an extra four years. Healthspanners aim to slow the aging process, enabling a longer and higher-quality existence. Within 200 years, these measures might increase our maximum life span by, say, twenty years. Still, the primary aim should be an extended health span: to create a future in which people over seventy years are healthy, active, and free from severe diseases, and then can die quickly and painlessly (so-called compressed morbidity).

Transhumanists reject the assumption of healthspanners that aging is something natural and their acceptance of the inevitability of death. We should not see death as a natural and inevitable part of human life. Instead, biotechnology offers us an opportunity to remedy nature's unfortunate mistakes. They question the necessity of death and want to make mortality a question of choice. The picture of the human predicament that healthspanners paint is accurate in that such a life is the best we can hope for, unless we are willing to enhance our human nature radically. Transhumanists believe that biotechnology can lengthen the maximum life span to range anywhere from 500 years to practically forever, or make death optional. If we merely allow it, relaxing laws around innovative biotechnology is crucial. We will be able to grow old without aging and remain young forever, or as young as we wish, for as long as we wish. Alternatively, some transhumanists are more modest, thinking that if we continue aging at the current rate in the future, we would have a maximum life span of a thousand years. Transhumanists are committed to believing in *superlongevity* or *radical life and health-span extension*. They take mortality to be a curable disease. Once we have developed an efficient cure, we will have a radically enhanced capacity to stay alive and healthy.

Essentially, two approaches are available to transhumanists. They could either (as Aubrey de Grey suggests) endlessly repair and enhance the human body or (as Ray Kurzweil proposes) eventually upload the human mind to a computer system or a new biosynthetic body. De Grey, the chief science officer of Silicon Valley's SENS Research Foundation,[19] compares the body to a car, and in doing this, he exemplifies the typical mindset of transhumanists that human limitations can be conceived as *technical problems* and, thus, problems we can overcome utilizing genetic engineering, nanotechnology, and robotics. The human body is reconceptualized as a complex physical machine. It can be understood as essentially a computer composed of overwritable data and updatable applications. De Grey believes that if we can repair seven types of physical damage to our bodies, we will be on the path to living for more than a thousand years.[20] To start, if we can restore tissue suppleness, replace cells that have stopped dividing, and remove those that have grown toxic, avert the consequences of DNA mutations, and mop up the gunky by-products of all of the above, we should gain thirty years of healthy life. This procedure would give us the time needed to make further advances, allowing us to begin growing biologically younger. We have then achieved "longevity escape velocity." *Longevity escape velocity* is the future state of affairs when one's remaining life expectancy (not life expectancy at birth) is extended longer than the time that is passing. It is the point where, for every year one survives, one gains an extra year. Alternatively, the longevity escape velocity will be reached when genetic and nanotechnological therapies add more years to one's life than the time it takes to research and develop them. From then on, people with relatively healthy bodies can extend their

---

[19] SENS is an abbreviation for "Strategies for Engineered Negligible Senescence."

[20] Aubrey de Gray and Michael Rose, *Ending Aging. The Rejuvenation Breakthroughs That Could Reverse Human Aging in Our Life-time.* St. Martin Press, 2007.

lifespan by undergoing regular treatments that regenerate deteriorating tissues and improve the health of their skin, eyes, and brain. De Gray even thinks (in an interview published in 2021) that there is a 50 percent chance that we will reach longevity escape velocity by 2036.[21] These predictions are not essential, but worth mentioning because they say something about how close many transhumanists think radical enhancement is.

Kurzweil (who has been a chief engineer at Google) talks about crossing four bridges. Bridge 1 is the effort to slow aging using current technology, including exercise, a proper diet, and nutrient supplements. Kurzweil himself takes 250 pills a day and receives six intravenous therapies each week to increase muscle strength and keep his skin supple.[22] Bridge 2 is when we are at the stage where we are offered personally tailored immune therapies for cancer, as well as organs grown from our own DNA. When we reach this stage of adopting biotechnological enhancements, we reach the breakpoint of longevity escape velocity. Bridge 3 is when superintelligent nanobots are developed, specifically blood-cell-size devices that will roam the body and brain, cleaning up all the cellular damage. Since technological growth is exponential rather than linear, future changes to the human body and intellect will occur much faster than they do now. When we cross Bridge 4, these nanobots will connect our brains to a neocortical annex in the cloud, and our intelligence will expand rapidly by a billionfold. Once that transformation happens, the Singularity occurs. Kurzweil famously predicts that it will happen before 2050.

Thus, we need to preserve the body long enough to reach the point where, if we want to, we can transition from being cyborgs to becoming completely synthetic AIs or uploading our consciousness into the cloud. *Cyborgs* are artificial humans (or animals) where biological and technical elements are integrally attached, making mental and physical capabilities far beyond those of humans possible. They are examples of what Kurzweil refers to as mostly original substrate humans (MOSHs). Completely synthetic AIs are a step beyond cyborgs, as they do not contain any biological components. This step is desirable because our biological parts are too fragile to ensure our survival against all accidents and mayhem over very long periods of time. *Uploading* (utilizing,

---

[21] For more on this, see https://longevity.technology/news/longevity-escape-velocity-by-2035-and-it-will-be-free/.

[22] Kurzweil, *The Singularity Is Near*, p. 211.

for example, *whole brain emulation*) to create a substrate-independent mind is the process of transferring a mind from a biological brain to a computer or creating an AI by replicating the human brain's functionality in software. Still, the idea is not that posthumans necessarily have to be disembodied once they are uploaded. A substrate-independent mind could have a virtual (simulated) body or interact with others by buying or renting a synthetic body to experience physical reality. Perhaps one could say that, just as in some traditional forms of mind–body dualism, embodiment is the principal problem of the human condition for transhumanists.

For Kurzweil, as we have seen, the Singularity is the time in the future when humans or transhumans will merge with AI and entirely transcend their biological limitations. He describes the development up to the point of the Singularity by saying that "for a time, we'll be a hybrid of biological and nonbiological thinking, but, as the cloud keeps doubling, the nonbiological intelligence will predominate … and it will be anachronistic, then, to have one body."[23] We, or those who have followed this path of radical enhancement, will no longer be transhumans but posthumans. Bostrom phrases it differently. He writes that the Singularity is as follows:

a point in the future when the rate of technological development becomes so rapid that the progress curve becomes nearly vertical. Within a very brief time (months, days, or even just hours), the world might be transformed almost beyond recognition. This hypothetical point is referred to as the Singularity. The most likely cause of a singularity would be the creation of some form of rapidly self-enhancing greater-than-human intelligence.[24]

On this issue, I will follow Bostrom and understand the Singularity as a thesis, not about us and our possible transformation into substrate-independent minds but about a particular point in the development of technology. Thus, it is the belief:

(5) In the near future, there will be a moment when artificial intelligence becomes smarter than humans, and the rate of technological development becomes so rapid that the progress curve becomes nearly vertical (*the Singularity thesis*).

---

[23] The quotation from Kurzweil is from Tad Friend, "Silicon Valley's Quest to Live Forever," *The New Yorker*, April 3, 2017, www.newyorker.com/magazine/2017/04/03/silicon-valleys-quest-to-live-forever.

[24] Bostrom, "Transhumanist FAQ," p. 19.

Transhumanists also have a backup plan that would be implemented if the biotechnological progress during their lifetime is not fast enough or is hindered by political decisions, so they cannot reach longevity escape velocity due to age or accident. *Cryonics* is an experimental medical procedure of preserving humans at cryogenic temperatures (usually at −196°C or −320.8°F) in the hope that future science can restore them to healthy living conditions and rejuvenate them.[25]

For centuries, the default position of naturalists has been that there is no afterlife. To say that there is an *afterlife* (of any kind) is the same as saying that biological death is not a definitive end to human existence. Hägglund even considers this default position the defining feature of what he calls "secular faith" in contrast to religious faith.[26] This life is all we have; when we die, our lives end, and, he adds, this is a good thing. All naturalists or secular people would then embrace what we can call the *death-is-the-end theory*, which says that bodily death is the complete and definitive end of our existence as human beings or persons. Religious people could also embrace that theory, but typically opt for a reincarnation, immortality, or resurrection theory. According to the *reincarnation theory*, our bodies die and decay, except for an essential or immaterial part of us (such as a soul, spirit, or consciousness) that continues to exist and, at some point, is reborn in a new body, a process that occurs repeatedly. The *immortality theory*, on the other hand, assumes that our bodies die and decay, but an essential or immaterial part of us continues to exist, without any further bodily incarnation in this world, in an immaterial or spiritual realm. Finally, we have the *resurrection* or *reembodiment theory*, which says that our bodies die and decay. Still, God will, at some point in the future, intervene and recreate us (or some of us) as living embodied beings and simultaneously create the Kingdom of God. It is interesting to reflect on how transhumanist ideas about immortality or superlongevity relate to these more traditional theories. Do they offer us a new kind of theory, or is their theory a variant of one of these existing theories?

Initially, transhumanists advocate for a *life extension theory* rather than an afterlife theory. They believe, as we have seen, that if we can overcome our biological limitations and stop the aging process, we can extend our lives almost indefinitely or as long as we want. We can end

[25] For more on cryonics, see www.alcor.org/.
[26] Martin Hägglund, *This Life: Secular Faith and Spiritual Freedom*. Anchor Books, 2020, p. 5.

our lives when we feel satisfied after a few thousand years, or die earlier if we have an accident, which means our lives cannot be saved. We are mortal beings with the potential for almost eternal life. Similarly, if humans cannot save their entire body from aging and death, they can opt for becoming cyborgs instead. However, the organic parts (such as our brain) that persist over time must manage to preserve our identity so that it is we, and not someone else, who become these cyborgs. As we incorporate more biotechnology into our bodies, we become increasingly machine-like and indestructible.

Hence, another core belief of transhumanism is as follows:

(6) In the near future, we will be able to radically enhance our lifespan in this life so that we can live and stay healthy for thousands of years (*the life extension thesis*).

Only if we can change our bodies in the future by obtaining a new biosynthetic body in which we can place our self or consciousness, can we talk about an afterlife. Our original biological body is then dead, but we (our personality) live on in another body. The film series "Altered Carbon" (2018) is based on the idea that we can upload or move our consciousness into a new carbon-based shell or casing, which becomes our new body. Another option is reaching the final phase of Kurzweil's vision of the future, where we humans (if we want to) completely leave our old or biotechnologically enhanced bodies behind and become substrate-independent minds. The idea is that in the near future, we will be able to upload our consciousness to the virtual world, made possible by future supercomputers. We then leave our physical bodies behind and enter an afterlife where our bodies die and decay, but we live on, not in the Kingdom of God, but in a virtual world.

Transhumanists argue that such an afterlife is possible because human identity is not dependent on the body. Our self can survive outside the body as long as there is a continuity between the memories of our "then-self" and our "now-self." Kurzweil refers to this view as "patternism." He writes: "Since the material stuff of which we are made turns over quickly, it is the transcendent power of our patterns that persists."[27]

The transhumanists' backup plan must be seen as a new variant of the resurrection or reembodiment theory. Recall that this plan is that if we die before the longevity escape velocity is reached, our dead bodies can be frozen and preserved so that when the necessary

---

[27] Kurzweil, *The Singularity Is Near*, p. 388.

biotechnology is available in the future, our bodies can be brought back to life (not by God but by future scientists or AI). The faults that caused us to die can then be repaired, allowing us to continue living as resurrected persons. We can then add one more core conviction to the transhumanist worldview:

(7) In the near future, we will be able to radically enhance our lifespan beyond this life so that we, as substrate-independent minds, can live and stay healthy virtually forever (*the uploading and afterlife thesis*).

The idea is that death is just one more frontier to defeat. Some transhumanists talk about conquering death.

In transhumanism, we are witnessing the emergence of a new kind of secular worldview. A secular outlook that rejects what has previously been the default position of naturalism: that there is no afterlife. In this way, the borderline between secular and religious worldviews is blurred. One crucial difference between them is that a transhumanist afterlife is voluntary, whereas a religious afterlife (typically) is not. According to reincarnation, immortality, and resurrection theories, we will enter an afterlife, whether we like it or not. Instead, transhumanists maintain that we ourselves decide whether to radically extend our life, even to the extent that it practically becomes immortal, given that some AI in the future would not hinder us from dying.

SUPERINTELLIGENCE AND GENERAL AI

Transhumanists do not merely aim to use biotechnology to challenge mortality and radically enhance our health. They also aim to overcome human ignorance and significantly enhance our cognitive abilities. Enhancing the human brain's cognitive capacities and even creating a superintelligence are other crucial goals of transhumanism. They believe there are biotechnological solutions to limitations in cognition, allowing us to radically enhance our general reasoning abilities, study skills, critical thinking, and problem-solving capacity.

According to Bostrom, a *superintelligence mind* (whether completely artificial or a hybrid with both biological and artificial components) is a mind that can radically outperform the best human minds of today in practically every field, including theoretical reasoning, practical wisdom, and social intelligence.[28] It is more intelligent than the human

[28] Bostrom, "Transhumanist FAQ," p. 12.

mind in both quantitative and qualitative senses. For instance, it thinks faster and in a more creative way. It is also more sensitive to people's needs and an outstanding exemplar of moral virtues; its moral character far exceeds that of the best humans. It is brighter than Newton, Einstein, and Darwin, and more virtuous and compassionate than Jesus, Gandhi, and Mother Teresa. It is an artificial mind that is unsurpassable by the human mind in terms of theoretical reasoning, practical wisdom, and social skills.

Before proceeding, we must consider that there are different ways of understanding AI, general AI, superintelligence, and similar notions in contemporary academic and public discourse. This ambiguity is confusing, and in what follows, I will stipulate how I will use the terms and introduce the distinction between weak and strong AI. Let us say that *human intelligence* is the (a) process of thinking and reasoning about something or everything that people possess, which makes it possible for them (b) to plan, learn, and improve so that they can respond to challenges or opportunities in (c) a wide range of practical and theoretical situations.

The core idea behind AI is that such intelligence can be produced artificially to some extent. Human intelligence is an example of natural intelligence. However, the idea of AI is that intelligence would not have to be the product of natural or biological processes. AI are technological entities, such as computers or robots, that can perform theoretical or practical tasks that would otherwise require human intelligence. However, an AI that satisfies the intelligence requirement in the full human sense would require much more. It would involve a process of thinking and reasoning about something or everything that enables AI to plan, learn, and respond to challenges or opportunities in a wide range of practical and theoretical situations. In this more demanding sense, AI is referred to as *artificial general intelligence* (AGI). AGI is an AI system that can learn and perform all the intellectual tasks that a human can. Such a technology has not yet been created, and some people do not believe it can be created; however, transhumanists firmly believe that it will be created and that it will happen very soon.

As the notion of AI is used today, what is required for a machine to be "intelligent" is much less demanding than it must have AGI. It is sufficient that it performs specific intellectual tasks well to count as AI. AI is, more exactly, equivalent to *artificial narrow intelligence* (ANI), which is the process of thinking and reasoning about something that machines or technologies possess in a limited domain or "microworld."

Thus, AI does not have to satisfy condition (c). A computer performs a specific task when it plays chess. Today, AI often outperforms the best of humans in a limited domain, but it operates under far more constraints than even the most basic human intelligence. Google would be another more sophisticated example. It is a search engine that utilizes an algorithm designed to retrieve and organize search results, providing the most relevant and dependable data sources possible. This example reveals more about how AI makes decisions. It utilizes algorithms that either follow established rules or, in the case of machine learning, analyze large datasets to identify and recognize patterns. Because machine learning involves multiple layers and machines develop their own learning patterns, it is more opaque compared to traditional rule-following computing. Thus, more sophisticated examples of narrow AI can also learn and apply new things to new situations in its microworld. Thus, to some extent, condition (b) is satisfied.

ChatGPT (GPT stands for Generative Pre-trained Transformer) is an example of another class of AI. A natural language processing tool enables us to engage in human-like conversations, answer questions, and assist with tasks such as writing an essay or composing a speech. ChatGPT is not as limited in scope as the more traditional AI. This type of transformer can perform various functions at an impressive level. It have passed nearly every major standardized academic test at remarkable levels, can "understand" natural language, not merely code and math, reason fairly deeply about what it knows, and "understand" some of the contexts that are only implicit in our use of language, and it can explain its reasoning, self-learn, and correct itself (often imperfectly). (It does not really understand because it is not conscious.) Due to these improvements, these transformers represent a step toward AGI, the ability to understand and learn any intellectual task humans can. This new class of AI is a powerful technological tool that scientists and scholars can utilize in their research. Still, these transformers cannot replace them or be artificial scientists and scholars, nor can they be our new politicians, lawyers, or physicians. If they could, as transhumanists believe, it will soon be the case, we would have examples of AGI.

One last distinction of importance is the one between weak and strong AI. Sometimes, the distinction is believed to be the same as between artificial narrow and general intelligence, but it is not. *Weak AI* refers to intelligent-acting machines, that is, artificial creatures that appear to possess the entire mental repertoire of human persons. It can pass for a human in all thinking and behavior. It thus satisfies all three conditions for intelligence above. *Strong AI*, on the other hand, is an artificial person – a designed entity with all our mental powers, including consciousness, the capacity for experiences, and self-awareness; it has a robust first-person perspective. To manifest a robust first-person perspective, one must be able to consciously conceive of oneself as oneself, to be aware of one's own identity and continued existence over time.

Strong AI, if possible, would then satisfy a fourth condition of human intelligence: (d) it has *personhood*. What it means more exactly to have personhood or to be a person is a complicated and controversial issue, not the least because it is closely tied to legal, political, and moral concepts of citizenship, equality, liberty, and dignity. Nevertheless, it is sufficient for our purpose to say that besides being intelligent, one must have consciousness, self-awareness, moral agency, and the ability to perform intentional and self-motivated actions. Moral agency is an individual's ability to make choices based on a notion of right and wrong and be held accountable for these actions.

We are aware of examples of narrow AI that outperform the best human minds in a specific domain. So, it seems possible that future AI could outperform the most brilliant of us in many domains, perhaps one day even in all domains. No matter which situation we enter, we can then ask AGI how to solve intellectual, political, legal, ethical, religious, and relational problems, and the answer it provides will be far better than anything that the brightest, most virtuous, and socially competent human could possibly come up with. It is perhaps not omniscient as God is, if we live in a theistic universe, but AGI outperforms the best human minds in practically every field and situation. If AGI could reach such heights, it would be an example of superintelligence in Bostrom's terminology. Moreover, creating superintelligence may be the last invention humans will ever need to make, as superintelligences could themselves take care of further scientific and technological development, as well as artistic, moral, political, and spiritual advances. Still, superintelligence would be an example of weak general AI. It would be an intelligent-acting machine or a synthetic substrate that *appears* to have the entire mental repertoire of human persons. The AGI would not (yet) be an artificial person.

The lack of a strong AGI would not be a problem for transhumanism because we are persons. The idea is that one day, *we* (or at least some of us) can merge with the AGI either by (a) connecting our human brain to the AGI and wirelessly upgrading our memory, reasoning capacity, practical wisdom, and social skill implants or by (b) uploading, that is, transferring our intellect from our biological brain to the AGI and become substrate-independent minds. Transhumans (Humanity 2.0) would not merely be more energetic and stronger, with much extended life and health spans, than we (Humanity 1.0) have. They will also be significantly better than we are at concentrating on complex tasks, remembering names, seeing connections between things, following intricate lines of argument, learning languages, understanding mathematical proofs, and recognizing why certain ways of acting are morally wrong and why complicated political reforms are necessary. They will be like us; they might even be you and me, but they are significantly cognitively upgraded. Our cognitive capacities have improved massively, but they are still, so to speak, within the natural human range. On the other hand, posthumans' cognitive capacities will far transcend those limitations and will radically outperform even the best of transhumans. It is hard for us even to imagine what their cognitive capacities might be.

Hence, another core belief of transhumanism is as follows:

(8) In the near future, we will be able to radically enhance our cognitive capacities, such as perception, memory, reasoning, imagination, and introspection, to such an extent that they significantly exceed the maximum attainable by any current human being (*the superintelligence thesis*).

In this sense, a superintelligence is a transhuman or posthuman person with intelligence far surpassing that of today's brightest and most gifted humans. Hence, the superintelligence thesis differs from the singularity thesis in that the latter maintains that there is a point in the near future when AI surpasses human intelligence, and the rate of technological development becomes so rapid that the progress curve becomes nearly vertical. Presumably, the Singularity is a precondition for superintelligence, at least if this transhuman or posthuman intelligence is supposed to exceed significantly the maximum attainable by any current human being. The type of intelligence the two theses predict is also different because strong superintelligence is required in (8), whereas weak superintelligence is enough in (7).

SUPER-WELLBEING OR RADICAL EMOTIONAL ENHANCEMENT

The core idea of transhumanism is that we should radically change, improve, or refine humanity, even to the extent of creating a new species, the posthuman. We have seen that the idea of radical enhancement means, more concretely, that the human health span – the ability to remain alive and fully healthy, both physically and psychologically – will be radically enhanced. In our biological but augmented bodies, we, as transhumans, can live for hundreds, if not thousands, of years. As posthumans, with substrate-independent minds, we might live almost forever. Second, it means that we will become much smarter than we are now. Our cognitive capacities will be radically enhanced to such an extent that they greatly exceed the maximum attainable by any current human being. Transhumans, and even more so posthumans, will possess superintelligence. The third area of improvement of human nature that transhumanists emphasize is *well-being* or our *emotional life*. It is "the capacity [we have] to enjoy life and respond with appropriate affect to life situations and other people."[29]

What super-wellbeing or radical emotional enhancement, more exactly, amounts to is more elusive than what superlongevity and superintelligence are. To begin with, *well-being* refers to the value that a life holds for the individual whose life it is. It has to do with how well life goes for a person. Different human lives go differently well; in this sense, they have different values, but well-being does not refer to the intrinsic worth of people. Their lives could have the same intrinsic worth and dignity but differ in how well their lives unfold. One person may die very young, another live in extreme poverty, yet another might be deeply depressed throughout life. The idea is that a person who lives a very long life full of joy, love, relative prosperity, and friendship is more valuable than the lives of those who have lived shorter lives, everything else being equal. They all have the same moral status, but they differ in well-being.

Thus, one way to cash out radical emotional enhancement is in terms of well-being. A life filled with joy, comfort, sensual pleasures, fun, positive interests, and excitement has a higher degree of well-being than one with fewer of these features. Some transhumanists, like the co-founder (with Bostrom) of the WTA, David Pearce, embrace hedonism and equate well-being with the balance of pleasure over pain or suffering. So, people would be in a state of super-wellbeing if all (physical and mental) suffering and pain were completely eradicated, by biotechnological means, from their lives and replaced with gradients of bliss or all-pervasive happiness.[30] However, as Bostrom points out, one does not have to be a hedonist to appreciate pleasure as a critical aspect of the good. He stresses that an essential aspect of emotional enhancement is also responding appropriately to situations and other people. In both respects, one's assessment depends on one's normative beliefs of what a good life is. Still, people are engaged in improving, or trying to improve, their emotional lives, personalities, or characters. Bostrom gives the following examples:

We may seek to reduce feelings of hate, contempt, or aggression when we consciously recognize that these feelings are prejudiced or unconstructive. We may take up meditation or physical exercise to achieve greater calm and composure. We may train ourselves to respond more sensitively and empathetically to those we deem deserving of our trust and affection. ... Many of us expend life-long effort to educate and ennoble our sentiments, to build our character, and try to become better people. Through these strivings, we seek to achieve goals involving modifying and improving our emotional capacities.[31]

Well-being would have to incorporate all these goals, but still probably allow for a wide range of different ways to improve our emotional capacities, again depending on our normative beliefs. Crucially, however, whether such dependence will remain hinges on whether our radically improved cognitive capacities or superintelligence would make it possible for us to discover what is morally true, objectively good, or at least come to an informed consensus about these things. After all, the present plurality of conceptions of the good or differences about what a virtuous life amounts to could be a consequence of our limited cognitive capacities. Either way, we could perhaps say that *super-wellbeing* is achieved when the quality of life radically surpasses the best emotional and virtuous life humans can currently have. Hence, another core belief in the transhumanist worldview is the following:

(9) In the near future, we will be able to radically enhance our emotional capacities and wellbeing to such an extent that they greatly exceed the maximum attainable by any current human being (*the super-wellbeing thesis*).

What emotional capacities posthumans may have is harder to say. Nevertheless, Bostrom and other transhumanists are open to the possibility that there might be "entirely new psychological states and emotions

---

[30] David Pearce, *The Hedonistic Imperative*, www.hedweb.com/.
[31] Bostrom, "Why I Want to Be a Posthuman When I Grow Up," p. 37.

that our species has not evolved the neurological machinery to experience, and some of these sensibilities might be ones we would recognize as extremely valuable if we become acquainted with them."[32]

To sum up, the idea of radical enhancement of human nature is expressed in terms of superlongevity, superintelligence, and super-wellbeing. Health, cognition, and emotion can all be radically enhanced to such an extent that they greatly exceed the maximum attainable by any current human being. Alternatively, we could perhaps say that transhumanism aims to eliminate or radically reduce mortality, ignorance, and suffering from the human condition.

Posthumans have at least one of these great-making capacities (superlongevity, superintelligence, or super-wellbeing) that radically exceed the maximum attainable by any currently living human being. They could have all three, but it is sufficient that they have one to be posthuman. For instance, persons with our level of intellect and emotional life would be posthumans if they could live a healthy life for thousands of years. Consequently, transhumans lack these radically enhanced capacities. But what is then required to be transhuman, to be a member of Humanity 2.0 and not of Humanity 1.0? It is hard to say. Recall that the idea is, after all, to increase human lifespan, cognition, and well-being gradually until they presumably one day become exponential in growth. Nevertheless, perhaps we could say that if one of these capacities increases by a factor of 2, that suffices for being a transhuman. For instance, if the maximum lifespan of current human life is 125 years, and let us say that the maximum health span is 90 years, then someone is considered a transhuman if their lifespan is 250 years and they remain fully healthy for 180 years. A factor of 2 improvement in humans can be called a *major* enhancement, in contrast to the radical ones we discussed earlier. A *moderate* enhancement would be something less; it would be something that just falls beyond what is currently possible.

If the transhumanist worldview turns out to be true, then one day, our universe, and in particular the Earth, would at the same time be populated by humans, transhumans, and posthumans. The reason might be that some individuals have consciously chosen to remain merely humans, while others have chosen to become either transhumans or posthumans. Alternatively, the reason might be economic, so only some people can afford to become members of Humanity 2.0 or join the new species,

---

[32] Ibid.

posthumans. It might also be for political reasons, if the ruling class wants to retain most of these privileges for themselves.

CHALLENGES FOR TRANSHUMANISM

What challenges does transhumanism face? What would seem to be problematic aspects of it? Let me highlight some of these challenges without suggesting that there are no resources within the transhumanist worldview to address them in a satisfying manner.

The first challenge is the *problem of unfair distribution and increased inequalities*. A frequently raised objection is that enhancing human nature will inevitably lead to increased social injustice and inequality. Enhancement technology will be expensive, so most people will not be able to afford to enhance their own human nature and that of their off-spring. Only wealthy people will have the resources to upgrade their intellect, significantly extend their life and well-being, and genetically enhance their children. As the gap between the rich and the poor continues to widen, we should reject major and radical enhancements of human nature. This is a serious problem, but the question is whether it is a new or more severe challenge for enhancement technologies than more traditional forms of technology. Initially, new technology has been expensive, and those with access to it have been those with economic resources. However, the typical pattern with new technology is that it becomes cheaper over time. Medical procedures and medicine have gradually become more affordable, benefiting both the rich and the poor, for instance, through the development of vaccines and the discovery of penicillin. Transhumanists believe that determining the degree of income redistribution that is desirable is a political, not a technological, problem. If so, it is not a problem intrinsic to transhumanism. Still, one may argue that enhancement technology might create a greater problem than the old technology because the old technology is external to human nature. In contrast, the new biotechnology will be internal to us. Hence, the competitive advantages of being smarter, faster, stronger, never depressed, and always mentally strong would give enhanced individuals a crucial edge over non-enhanced individuals, one they would want to maintain to secure the best opportunities in life.

Francis Fukuyama is one of the most well-known critics of transhumanism. He even thinks transhumanism may be the most dangerous idea in the world. Instead, he embraces what has been called *bioconservatism*. Bioconservatives advocate that biological research and biotechnological applications must be significantly limited. We should not use technology to change human nature in any significant way. Why? Fukuyama argues that transhumanism comes at frightful moral costs because it undermines human dignity and equal human rights. He writes, "Underlying this idea of the equality of rights is the belief that we all possess a human essence that dwarfs manifest differences in skin color, beauty, and even intelligence. This essence, and the view that individuals therefore have inherent value, is at the heart of political liberalism. But modifying that essence is the core of the transhumanist project."[33] This is because they aim to transform human nature into an upgraded transhuman nature and ultimately replace it with posthuman nature. Therefore, the biotechnological enhancement of human nature must be significantly limited.

However, many academic activists, such as many feminists, embrace social constructivism and deny the existence of a human essence; yet, they empathetically defend human dignity and equal human rights. For this reason, it is not apparent that equality of rights presupposes that there is such a thing as a common human nature. There may be alternative ways of defending human dignity beyond grounding it in a common human nature. A constructivist account of dignity may regard the special status of humans as something we humans decide to extend to each other. But the *problem of undermining human dignity or dehumanization* may still be a challenge for transhumanism to overcome because radical enhancement may lead to a relative loss of moral status for human beings. Posthumans might be morally justified in treating humans 1.0 less well than humans 2.0, and treating both humans and transhumans less well than members of their own species. It would not necessarily follow that posthumans will behave in this way, but Nicholas Agar presents an inductive argument suggesting that this could well be the case.[34] It is based on how humans have treated and still treat sentient nonhuman animals in today's society. Cats, dogs, and pigs count morally, in their own rights, more so than stones and other inanimate objects, but less so than human beings. Sentient beings have moral status, but to a lesser extent than we do. One would make a moral mistake if one rescued a cat rather than a human from a burning building. The verdict would be the same if scientists in medical research exposed humans to suffering and death. But harm and

33 Francis Fukuyama, "Transhumanism: The World's Most Dangerous Idea," *Foreign Policy*, 2004, 144, pp. 42–43.
34 Nicholas Agar, *Truly Human Enhancement*. MIT Press, 2014, pp. 177–194.

even death inflicted on sentient beings to cure cancer or develop some medicine like insulin is typically taken to be morally justified. Given this ladder of moral status, rocks are at level 0, sentient nonhuman beings are at level 1, human beings are at level 2, transhumans are at level 3, and posthumans would be located at level 4. Given that we consider ourselves morally justified in treating sentient beings as we do, it is quite reasonable to assume that posthumans would take a similar stance toward us. Thus, radical enhancement may lead to a relative loss of moral status for humans compared to posthumans, exposing us to harm and even death. Therefore, he maintains that this risk makes pursuing radical enhancement dangerous and even irrational. We should not create posthumans.

The uploading and afterlife thesis is that we will one day be able to decide to upload our mind, that is, transfer our personal identity and cognitive and emotional life (what makes me, me and you, you) from our – augmented or non-augmented – organic minds to a different substrate all altogether, such as computers. Electronic chips will then replace our neurons as the seat of our self-consciousness and mental life. The idea is that just as we today can wake up with a new heart after undergoing surgery under general anesthetic and still recognize ourselves as you and I, in the near future, we can wake up as substrate-independent minds with completely artificial bodies or as parts of general AI. The light of consciousness and self-recognition will return, and we will be ready to try out our new bodies, which will possess superlongevity, superintelligence, and a radically enhanced emotional life. But why think that will happen and not think uploading will exchange our conscious mind for a completely mindless, nonconscious set of symbols or algorithms? If so, uploading would be experientially like death; the light of consciousness is out for good. You and I will be no more; only our memories will be preserved in digital form. What would be left would be merely a digital bibliography of our previous life and a trajectory of the life we would have continued to have if we had remained self-conscious and alive, and not decided to be uploaded; it would be a posthuman life simulated by a completely mindless, nonconscious set of symbols or algorithms. Why should we think scenario 1 is more likely to be actualized than scenario 2?

One likely reason might be that patternism or a similar theory of the self and its continuity over time is true. Kurzweil considers it a fundamental feature of his worldview, namely that he (and each of us) is "principally a pattern that persists in time."[35] Our self can survive outside the biological

---

[35] Kurzweil, The Singularity Is Near, p. 386.

body as long as there is a continuity between the memories of our "then-self" and our "now-self." One survives so long as specific information patterns are conserved, such as one's memories, attitudes, and dispositions, and as long as there is causal continuity so that earlier stages of oneself help determine later stages of oneself. Roughly, the idea seems that if a posthuman John* has John's memories and there is the correct causal psychological continuity between John and John*, that re-embodied person is John. They are the same person as long as John* remembers what John did, and there is a psychological continuity between them. One difficulty with this view is called *the duplication problem*. If patternism is correct, John's memories may be transferred to two future persons in exactly the same causal way. But identity is a one-on-one relation, and no person can be identical to two distinct individuals. However, I would like to highlight a different challenge. What is crucial is not merely that my memories or other information patterns are conserved but that my self-consciousness is transferred from my body in this life to the posthuman body in the afterlife. Otherwise, you and I will be no more, and merely our strings of memories will be digitized and causally extended into posthuman life. If so, patternism would not help us dodge Scenario 2.

Suppose we follow Lynne Rudder Baker and assume that a sufficient condition for being a person or a self is having a first-person perspective, that is, the ability to conceive of oneself as oneself. I, for instance, may wonder how *I* will die or whether *I* will survive an uploading. I then think of myself as myself, not of myself in any third-person way. Any being with the ability to think of itself as itself is a person or has a self. It does not matter whether it is made of biological or artificial stuff. Not merely organic beings like humans, but computers, silicon-based beings, or God (who traditional Western theists think is composed of no material stuff at all) could all have a first-person perspective. Notice that a being may be conscious without having such a perspective. Higher-level animals are conscious in this way. Some of them might have a rudimentary first-person perspective, but, for all we know, it is not robust enough for them to wonder how they will die. One has a robust first-person perspective if one has the "ability to conceive of oneself as oneself, from the first person, without recourse to a name, description, or other third-person referring device."[36] Such individuals know which particular individual they are without needing to pick themselves out from items in the environment.

---

[36] Lynne Rudder Baker, *Naturalism and the First-Person Perspective.* Oxford University Press, 2013, p. 31.

Rudder Baker believes that humans possess selves, a mental property in virtue of which a person is a person (having *a* first-person perspective), and that personal identity depends on having one unique first-person perspective (i.e., having *that* first-person perspective). By retaining one's unique first-person perspective, an individual in the afterlife can be identical to a particular person in this life. But we have seen that some worldviews – in my rational reconstruction, a scientistic worldview, and a Buddhist worldview – deny that selves or persons in this sense exist; it only *appears* to us that so is the case. It is an illusion, although it is not completely clear who is having this illusion. Therefore, if you embrace the no-self view, it may be completely rational to decide to be uploaded because you would lose nothing essential, only appearance. However, if you are uncertain and it is a real, unneglectable possibility that what appears to be the case is also the case, it would not seem rational to go through a surgical treatment to become a posthuman. It does not matter how superintelligent "you" might become because you are not there to enjoy these radically enhanced cognitive capacities. This is the *challenge of irrationality in choosing the posthuman life.*

The force of this objection depends to some degree on which worldview one embraces, but to the extent that transhumanism is a form of humanism, it is worrisome. We have reason to return to the distinction I drew in Chapter 3 between worldview-transcending and worldview-immanent arguments. A *worldview-transcending argument* contains premises or reasons that surpass people's different outlooks on life. Their force does not directly depend on whether we accept a theistic, Buddhist, spiritual, scientistic, humanist, or transhumanist worldview. Sometimes, these arguments have been referred to as "secular arguments" or "secular reasons," but this would not be possible within worldview studies, as in that framework, such arguments depend on the prior acceptance of a secular worldview. They would be the counterpart to religious arguments and religious reasons. Hence, both secular and religious arguments would be examples of *worldview-immanent arguments*, that is, arguments containing premises or reasons that depend, directly or indirectly, on the acceptance of one particular worldview or a subset of them.

Transhumanists like Young think, as we have seen, that a theistic opposition provides the greatest obstacle to creating a transhuman and posthuman world. One frequently raised objection by theists is that transhumanism entails that we play God and take God's role in creation and make it ours. But someone else is already God; therefore, we should not play God or make ourselves into gods. This is the *objection to not playing God.*[37] It seems that the core idea is that human nature is God-given, and therefore, major enhancements to human nature are forbidden. To abolish and remake human nature is to play God because God created humans as they are. This objection presupposes the acceptance of the belief that the universe and humans are the result of a divine plan, which we should not, but can, transgress. Hence, it is an example of a worldview-immanent argument. Still, it is an argument worth taking seriously because the world's theists outnumber the total number of people who embrace a secular worldview of one kind or another. If the former group obstructs bioliberal legal laws, the transhumanist vision of the future might never become a reality.

However, theists, as I have construed them, accept evolutionary theory. Instead, they disagree with naturalists or secular people about whether evolution was unguided or guided. Nevertheless, evolutionary theory suggests that humans have undergone several significant changes throughout their history. Primitive *Homo sapiens* first appeared approximately 300,000 years ago in Africa, with brains that were as large as or larger than those of modern humans. They were followed by anatomically modern *Homo sapiens* at least 200,000 years ago, and the brain shape of this species became modern at least 100,000 years ago. Current human nature evolved in the late Stone Age, approximately 10,000 years ago, to address the adaptive challenges faced by our hunter-gatherer ancestors in their environment. Evolutionists do not think there is evidence of any significant species-modifying changes in our nature since that time. Human nature is relatively fixed in this sense, but it could evolve in response to environmental or cultural changes. It is just that such a change takes a very long time. (Transhumanists maintain that these changes can go much faster in the future if we allow biotechnological enhancement.) If so, God never created a particular form of human nature. The notion rather entails biological variation to a significant extent. As long as the essential features of theistic anthropology remain – that transhumans and posthumans, like humans, are self-conscious, autonomous, and freely acting moral agents – the objection of not playing God should be, it seems, unconvincing to reflective theists.

---

[37] A discussion of this objection in both a religious and secular form is provided in C. A. J. Coady, "Playing God." In *Human Enhancement*, edited by Julian Savulescu and Nick Bostrom. Oxford University Press, 2009, pp. 155–180.

10

Choosing a Worldview

I have argued that we need to develop worldview studies – as a complement to religious studies – and the philosophy of worldviews – as a complement to the philosophy of religion – because a substantial number of people in the West, and also elsewhere, no longer identify as religious. We must study, both empirically and philosophically, what they consciously or unconsciously replace or seek to replace religion with and compare these secular worldviews with religious ones. I have picked seven contemporary worldviews, three clear cases of religious worldviews (theism, Buddhism, and the new spirituality), and three secular worldviews (scientism, secular humanism, and transhumanism). We have also seen that religious naturalism, at least in some forms, is a borderline case. But that just shows that there are no clear-cut boundaries, and sometimes it may be better to talk about semireligious or semi-secular worldviews.

I have presented the seven worldviews as distinct, opposing, and coherent views, although there are possibilities to combine them, at least to some extent. For many adherents of these worldviews, it is essential to emphasize that they take it to entail a rejection of other worldviews. On the other hand, some people think that scientism and secular humanism can be combined, and others believe that one can be a theist and Buddhist at the same time, to mention two combinations. For the latter options to be possible, rational reconstructions of these outlooks on life other than those I have provided are needed.

One downside to this philosophical study is that we do not know how representative these worldview options are. For this reason, we need more empirically oriented research, especially on secular worldviews. We have sociological studies of the group of religious nones. Still, these are not sufficiently precise to distinguish between those who have a religious worldview but have no affiliation with organized religious groups or organizations and those who reject religion and want to live completely secular lives. To take one step further and distinguish between different secular worldviews, questionnaires like the one provided by Petar Lukić and Iris Žeželj need to be developed and used. In their attempt to measure scientistic attitudes among the general public and distinguish scientism from science enthusiasm and anti-scientific stances, Lukić and Žeželj, in relation to the topic "Science and its relation to other ways of gaining knowledge," asked the participants to choose one option among the following:

5. Extremely scientistic – Only science can provide reliable knowledge of any phenomenon, any other way would be worthless.

4. Moderately scientistic – Science is by far the best way to reach reliable knowledge, all other ways have a lot less to offer.

3. Critical trust in science – Science is a good way to reach reliable knowledge in certain domains, but other ways are equally good for other fields such as law, ethics, or art.

2. Moderately anti-scientific – Science can offer some reliable knowledge, but you can learn about more things in other ways.

1. Extremely antiscientific – Science does not provide any reliable knowledge, all other ways of gaining knowledge are more valuable than science.[1]

To identify the number of people whose worldview approximates secular humanism rather than scientism, or religious naturalism rather than the new spirituality, similar questions need to be asked and similar questionnaires developed.

Hence, the downside of a philosophical study like this one is that it does not help us understand how many people would say that their worldview is or resembles one of the seven I have distinguished and analyzed. Still, it may provide us with insight into the questions we need to ask people to identify their particular worldview. However, one upside is that the individuals we have studied have devoted a great deal of time to thinking about who they are, where they come from, where they are headed, what is good and evil, and how they should live to thrive. These philosophical studies have focused on articulated and

[1] Lukić, Petar and Iris Žeželj, "Delineating between Scientism and Science Enthusiasm: Challenges in Measuring Scientism and the Development of a Novel Scale." *Public Understanding of Science*, 2024, 33/5, p. 574.

thoroughly reflected worldviews. We now have a better understanding of the worldviews that various philosophers, theologians, natural scientists, social scientists, humanists, and other professional thinkers articulate and defend, as well as how they think they can be justified. We know more about the worldviews some of the brightest people in society hold, why they embrace them, and how they view other competing worldviews. We have learned what beliefs, values, and attitudes these intellectuals consider essential to our identity and our place in the world, as well as what we should deeply care about in life. That, if nothing else, is truly exciting!

Chapters 3–9 have all been structured in a similar way. First, I have identified some core commitments of the worldview in question and developed them so that they became coherent with each other. In the process, I mentioned some reasons why its advocates believe their worldview should be preferred over others. Second, I have pointed out some challenges each worldview faces without suggesting that it lacks the resources to deal with them in a satisfying way. I left it there, so it has not been a part of my aim to say which one of these worldviews we should embrace. What I have been trying to show is that all have their fair share of problems. This is not surprising, if you, like me, believe that we live in a worldview-ambiguous universe.

However, we must live one way or another and believe that certain things are true rather than others. All of you who read this book have a worldview, whether you are fully aware of it or can articulate its content. That is to say, in what you say and do, you assume a particular view of who we humans are, of the larger world in which we live, and of what is valuable to strive for in life, and what is good and evil. Your worldview encompasses the beliefs and activities that are particularly important to your identity and the things you genuinely care about in life. It might be close to one of these seven worldviews or quite different in some or many respects. But how should you think further to develop an intellectually and existentially satisfying worldview, and how should you respond to the plurality of worldviews surrounding you? I will conclude the book by suggesting some things that you (we) could consider.[2]

---

[2] A more elaborated version of what follows can be found in Mikael Stenmark, "Choosing a Worldview," _AGATHEOS – European Journal for Philosophy of Religion_, 2024, 1/1, pp. 42–62.

HAVING A WORLDVIEW

At some point in their lives, many, perhaps most, people who live in a pluralistic society become aware that they have a worldview. That is, it becomes clear to them that their way of looking at the world and living their lives differs more or less radically from how others look at and live their lives. This difference is due, they realize, to other people having or expressing through their actions and their way of being a different understanding of who we are, the larger context in which we live our lives, and what is valuable to strive for in life. These people have a different worldview from their own, even if there are larger or smaller overlaps in content.

We cannot avoid being socialized into a particular worldview or accepting some outlook on life. We acquire it through our upbringing at home, our schooling, the communities we belong to, and the people around us, whom, without thinking about it, we see as "significant others." Therefore, we always have a worldview, but one we can be more or less aware of. In that sense, we cannot choose a worldview. It has already been given to us. This also means that what we consider good reasons for accepting or rejecting a worldview or some of its content are also initially given to us.

In another sense, however, we can choose our worldview. When we reach a certain level of maturity and self-determination, we can decide whether to remain the religious or secular people we are, change our basic orientation in life in any significant way, or even convert and adopt another worldview. With the emergence of a pluralistic society like ours, people can choose a worldview in a way they previously could not. As Smart points out, "in a society which is highly homogeneous, people do not meet other value-systems. They take their worldview for granted. But with the interplay between religions [and secular worldviews], new possibilities emerge. The question of judging worldviews becomes more existential: choice becomes just possible."[3] This also means that we can start reflecting on what we previously considered good reasons for accepting or rejecting a worldview or some of its content and adjust our view accordingly.

The talk of choosing a worldview presupposes that the range of actions we can perform that affect what we believe, assume, hope, and do about worldview matters has dramatically increased, so that I am, for example, well aware that I do not have to be a Christian. I may be a Christian today, but I can perform actions that make me become a Muslim or a

---

[3] Ninian Smart, *Choosing a Faith*. Boyars/Bowerdean, 1995, pp. 1–2.

secular humanist. No outlook on life seems inevitable anymore. The cultural diversity that characterizes our contemporary society entails that people's ability to choose between and within different worldviews has increased drastically.

But how should we choose? How should we think and act when we become aware that we have a worldview that is not as well thought-out or as comprehensive or coherent as it perhaps ought to be? How should we think about the content of other people's religious or secular worldviews, especially when they do not agree with what we believe, assume, or do? In this final part of the book, I intend to confine myself to presenting a proposal on how we, as reflective and rational people, should think about the choice and maintenance of a worldview in a pluralistic society, without having the space to argue its plausibility fully. So, I will inevitably lose a certain depth in the argument presented, but instead gain an overview of, at least, possible and hopefully plausible norms of worldview choice and management in real-life situations. We gain a holistic understanding of some intellectual and existential conditions for choosing and maintaining a worldview in a pluralistic society. We get an account of the bigger picture, even if the arguments for some of its details require further attention.

MAINTAINING A WORLDVIEW

I think that the worldview diversity that surrounds us is not sufficient in itself to force us to begin to doubt what makes us the religious or secular people we are. The reason is that we risk becoming cognitively paralyzed otherwise. Regardless of what you do, if you continue to believe, believe the opposite, or refrain from taking a stand, other intelligent, honest, and well-informed people have a different view from you. Regardless of what we believe, worldview diversity remains. Therefore, we cannot escape it simply by changing our minds due to this diversity. There is, so to speak, nowhere to go, and then it is just as well to remain where we stand until there are good reasons to change what we think about our life and our place in the scheme of things. The mere fact that some people hold beliefs different from ours is not a good reason to change our worldview. This stance has sometimes been called *epistemic conservatism* (or *presumptionism*) because it privileges the beliefs and values we already hold and says that they are okay – initially.[4]

---

[4] See, for instance, Hamid Vahid, "Varieties of Epistemic Conservatism," *Synthese*, 2004, 141/1, pp. 97–122. I have defended presumptionism in Mikael Stenmark, *How to Relate Science and Religion*. Eerdmans, 2004, pp. 89–103.

On the other hand, this diversity, or more precisely, the realization that many intelligent, informed, and honest people around us have a different outlook on life than we do, should make us less confident that we are right. This type of diversity is thus characterized by the fact that we realize that there are (a) many intelligent, well-informed, and honest people who believe other things than we do when it comes to choosing and shaping one's worldview, and (b) we meet them daily and socially interact with them more or less regularly. More precisely, the assumption in (a) is that these people are intelligent, well-informed, and honest concerning the points where they differ from us on worldview matters. Of course, they can also be assumed to meet this requirement more generally. Condition (b) goes beyond (a) in that these people are located in our immediate environment, not in other parts of the world. In such a pluralistic society, people with diverse worldviews, ethnicities, and lifestyles meet and talk to each other, eat together, and even marry each other. They do not live in sharply segregated communities and merely interact through economic transactions. In turn, this second condition is vital for what constitutes "live options" for us and not for other people in other places and situations; more on this later in the chapter. We can refer to this type of cultural situation as *significant diversity* and classify it as nonsignificant when one or both of these conditions are not met. In what follows, when I speak of "diversity," I will refer to such significant diversity unless otherwise stated.

This form of diversity, I claim, should reduce our epistemic confidence and make us aware that there is a real chance that we could have made a mistake. Nagel appears to react in this way when he writes that he is concerned about the fact that some of the most intelligent and well-informed people he knows are religious believers.[5] That fact removes some of the epistemic confidence with which he embraces atheism, and that God could exist is, for him, a non-negligible possibility. Plantinga embraces a Christian worldview instead but is well aware that many others reject such an understanding of life. His reaction to this plurality is as follows:

This is life under uncertainty, life under epistemic risk and fallibility. I believe a thousand things, and many of them are things others – others of great acuity and seriousness – do not believe. Indeed, many of the beliefs that mean the most to me are of that sort. I realize I can be seriously, dreadfully, fatally wrong, and wrong about what it is enormously important to be right.[6]

---

5 Thomas Nagel, *The Last Word*. Oxford University Press, 1997, p. 130.
6 Alvin Plantinga, *Warranted Christian Belief*. Oxford University Press, 2000, p. 437.

When it comes to most of what we believe or hold to be true, we may not reflect very much on the degree of conviction with which we embrace these beliefs. Instead, we likely become aware of it only when our beliefs are in some way questioned, for example, when other people express a different opinion. Generally speaking, it is only in such situations that people begin to think about how confident they are that what they believe is true. If the diversity we live in is significant, our general stance should be fallibilist in the sense that we should be less sure that we are right and realize that there is a real risk that we might have made a mistake. We should take the stance that the truth exists and is important, especially when choosing a worldview, but we must realize that we often have no secure access to it. Such a *fallibilistic principle of belief regulation* suggests that when we discover that other intelligent, well-informed, and honest people around us do not share, and may even deny, some of our most fundamental religious or secular beliefs, we have an obligation to consider the possibility that we may be wrong. As rational people, we should strive to remember that it is not obvious that we are right and that it is not obvious that others are wrong.

Moreover, if we adopt such an epistemic stance, it will have positive consequences for the possibility of creating more peaceful and less hostile relations between people – those who hold different, sometimes radically different, worldviews. Let me explain why I think it would make a significant difference. Suppose I am out walking in the street and meet someone who prevents me from going further. He stops me because he believes that just behind him is an invisible abyss. I shake my head and keep walking. If he insists on stopping me, I first tell him to move out of the way, and if that does not work, I may push him aside so that I can keep walking. I maintain that my approach to this man is strongly influenced by the fact that I can hardly imagine I am wrong and he is right. This assumption justifies my way of treating him. In other words, we have a justified tendency to ignore fools and sometimes even take the liberty to lock them up. We also often assume that we know better what is in their best interest than they do, even when they object.

My suggestion is that our views of people who hold a different worldview from ours are likely to be similar. Yours and my attitude toward and treatment of people with a different religious or secular faith will be heavily influenced by whether we assume that it is entirely out of the question that these other people could be right and we could be wrong. But the fallibilist principle of belief regulation I propose blocks the possibility in a pluralistic society to treat people who adhere to other worldviews as "fools" or as suffering from severe cognitive malfunction or something similar, and, thereby, justifies the view that one does not really need to respect their intellectual integrity, self-determination, and way of living. Note, however, that accepting this principle does not prevent us from maintaining that there are many cases of irrationality when it comes to other people's choice of worldview. To the same extent, we should not assume that everyone who endorses our religious or secular worldview, whatever it might be, does so rationally.

Thus, we should be guided by the principles of epistemic conservatism and fallibilism in our quest to understand and develop our worldview, as well as our understanding of people who hold a different outlook on life than we do. In a pluralistic society, we inevitably encounter people with different understandings of reality and what is meaningful and worthwhile in life. Typically, I do not abandon my worldview for theirs, and they do not surrender to mine, but we influence each other. Another consequence of such a meeting should be that we begin to reflect on what constitutes our core commitments and what constitutes more peripheral beliefs and values, on what is of great importance in our lives and what matters less. As rational people, we should reflect on what is "negotiable" for us in our critical and constructive dialogue with people we share social space with in a pluralistic society.

The answer to these questions about the center and the periphery also plays a role in how we should assess the objections directed against our religious or secular worldview. Not everything we believe affects us to the same extent. As I said, part of what we believe is more peripheral, and we can abandon such beliefs without much happening in our lives. For this reason, in a critical assessment, a rational person must consider the place that something she holds to be true holds in her life. It is not rational to treat everything we believe in the same way. For example, suppose you approach me and tell me that the train to Stockholm, which should have left the station at 1 p.m., is cancelled, and that I must take the train that leaves at 1:30 p.m. I might reply, "Okay," and immediately change my original belief. But assume instead that you approach me and tell me that Elon and Alice are not my biological parents. I would be much more hesitant to accept what you are saying. Why? The reason is that if the latter – in contrast to the former – were to turn out to be true, this would have profound consequences for my identity. Without much happening, I can give up the former belief but not the latter. We could say that different things have different "depths of concern" in our lives.

Also, regarding our worldviews, certain things are closer to people's hearts than others. Their degree of concern varies for us. For some people, God and their relationship with God are at the center; for others, it is the environment and the climate, women's struggle for equality, a fight against poverty and injustice, or, for that matter, getting rich and famous. For yet other people, hedonism, consumerism, or nationalism are at the center of attention. So, it is reasonable to assume that certain things that both religious and secular people believe and do are of great concern to them. If they are changed or abandoned, it will have far-reaching consequences for their worldview. Consequently, it is reasonable that we demand stronger reasons for abandoning something central to our religious or secular faith than if it were less important in our understanding of and approach to life. I, therefore, want to suggest that in our belief formation, we should be guided by what I previously called the *principle of deep concern,* which says that we should demand stronger reasons (or a larger amount of counter-evidence) for abandoning something that has great significance in our lives than for something that plays a more peripheral role and thus does not allow the outcome to be determined solely by the evidence we have access to.[7]

While the degree of conviction means that we can be more or less convinced of certain things, the degree of concern signifies that certain things affect us more or less. Some things in life affect us not only because they are at the center of our worldview but also because they are associated with strong (positive or negative) emotions, which affect our attitudes.

If, in our conscious reflection on our worldview, we realize that we should change or abandon something we believe in, how should we proceed? With the help of an everyday example, let me illustrate what I think is rational for us to do in such a situation. For example, suppose I think Peter is honest, but then I discover he lied to me. Should I then believe that Peter is a dishonest person, or should I revise my previous view more carefully so that I now believe that Peter is, overall, an honest person but that he sometimes lies? It seems that the latter proposal is more reasonable than the first. If there is reason to revise something we believe, we should not change the original belief more than necessary. I, therefore, suggest that we accept the following principle: When revising something we already believe, we should choose, among those alternatives that are available to us, one that is close to our original conviction. Let us call

---

[7] Stenmark, *How to Relate Science and Religion*, p. 106.

it the *cautious principle of belief revision*, because it suggests that we should not change our beliefs more than necessary.

Nagel can again be used as an example. He asks, "What, if anything, does secular philosophy have to put in the place of religion?"[8] and also writes: "I am resistant to the broad acceptance of scientific naturalism as a comprehensive world view. Theism is one form that such resistance can take, but I believe that there must be secular alternatives."[9] His way of reflecting on his worldview aligns with the cautious principle of belief revision. Presumably, as a young philosopher, Nagel may have been schooled into accepting scientific naturalism as the worldview he should embrace. When he begins to doubt that such a worldview is sound, the rational choice for him is not to start embracing any form of theism. Nagel should instead seek to develop a secular understanding of life that is closer at hand. Given his initial predicament, it is a naturalistic world-view that is different from scientific naturalism. The naturalism he, in fact, seeks to develop, which he hopes could replace both religion and scientific naturalism, entails a rejection of an epistemology in which science sets limits to what we can know. It also affirms an ontology that contains a natural teleology, according to which the existence of value is not a random byproduct of life, but rather seen as part of the explanation for why there is life at all.[10] Only when he no longer sees that such a modification of naturalism is reasonable should he consider converting to a theistic worldview.

We must also take into account that *worldview conversion* is not merely a gradual shift in beliefs, but a choice of a new way of perceiving reality and living. For this reason, it constitutes a significant break in a person's life and is not a gradual process of change. Conversion is a dramatic change, a fundamental shift in how the world is perceived and what we fundamentally care about in life. It is a Gestalt switch or a paradigm shift: The world is seen in a radically different way. In this situation, the increasing mismatch between our worldview and what we experience becomes too great, so we abandon our old worldview and convert to a new one.

My basic idea is that our level of epistemic confidence will affect our understanding of the prevailing worldview diversity we face and, thus,

---

[8] Thomas Nagel, *Secular Philosophy and the Religious Temperament*. Oxford University Press, 2010, p. 4.

[9] Nagel, *Secular Philosophy and the Religious Temperament*, preface.

[10] Thomas Nagel, *Mind and Cosmos*. Oxford University Press, 2012, p. 122.

our view of rational disagreement. However, we are surrounded by various alternative outlooks on life or different ways of living, so who should we engage with? What other worldviews are worthy of our attention and merit examining? I suggest that the answer is relative to your point of departure and the particular way you look at the world and live your life. Therefore, you should first more fully try to understand and critically explore the worldviews that, given your perspective on life, constitute real alternatives or what William James calls "live options."[11]

However, the worldviews that constitute live options differ among people. The stance I advocate has sometimes been referred to as *perspectivism*. Yet, I advocate a modest form of perspectivism because the assumptions, categories, beliefs, and values that make up our "perspective" or our "horizon" can, I believe, be rationally adjudicated. If all truths have been revealed, we would know which perspective is correct, but it is unlikely to happen during our lifetime. So, how should we act in the meantime? We have limited time and cognitive resources, and not the least other things to do in life than to think about the content of other people's religious or secular worldviews. Therefore, in our search for the truth concerning our existential questions, we should be primarily interested in those alternatives that constitute a live option for us. That is to say, we should pay attention to those worldviews that, from our particular perspective, seem to constitute a serious challenge or, for that matter, appear most promising or worthwhile. They are the worldviews we should enter into a critical dialogue with and – given the epistemic humility that should characterize our attitude in a situation of significant diversity – be open to so that we can learn something new that we did not know or previously have thought of.

The reasons we have discussed typically provide evidence to believe that it is true that reality is constituted in a particular way. But are only such intellectual or epistemic reasons relevant when we seek to understand reality and our place in it and choose how to live our lives? Should we not also consider other factors that have more to do with how it feels to live and find meaning in the world? Our choice of an adequate worldview is, after all, also *existential* (What creates meaning and what is worthwhile to strive for in life?) and not just *intellectual* (What is true?). The existential resources – how to deal with suffering and evil and meet our needs for love, meaning, identity, community, and personal

---

[11] William James, *The Will to Believe and Other Essays in Popular Philosophy*. Longmans, 1982.

growth – that worldviews provide can and do differ and are something we should take into account.

Kitcher criticizes those he sometimes calls "militant atheists" or "Darwinist atheists" (like Dawkins and Dennett) for completely neglecting the moral, existential, and social value of religion and relying, in their rejection of religion, solely on epistemic, preferably scientific reasons. He believes that such reasons are insufficient to demonstrate the superiority of naturalism (or, in his terminology, secularism) over, for example, theistic religions, because belief in God satisfies both an existential and a social need in people's lives; it gives their existence meaning and a context.[12] Therefore, a secular worldview must be able to provide people with a secular substitute for the meaning-making that religions have offered throughout the millennia; otherwise, it is "hardly unreasonable" for these people to remain religious.[13] Kitcher's embrace of pragmatic naturalism leads him to this conclusion. As rational people, we must consider pragmatic reasons when making choices about how we view life as a whole, our place in it, and how we live our lives to flourish as human beings.

What, then, are pragmatic reasons? We can say that pragmatic reasons are practically oriented and seek to justify our beliefs in terms of the benefits or utility we derive from acting (or not acting) in a certain way or assuming that certain things are true. Thus, unlike epistemic arguments, pragmatic arguments are benefit-oriented rather than truth-oriented. The benefit we are, perhaps, primarily interested in is the existential resources a worldview provides. How can it address our existential needs, including the desire to find meaning, belonging, personal well-being and growth, loving relationships, overcome angst, guilt, suffering, and alienation, create hope, and provide consolation in our lives?

I share the view of these philosophers that we should give pragmatic, not just epistemic, reasons a role in our choice of worldview. Nevertheless, the question of truth cannot be neglected, for a purely pragmatic argument opens the door wide to wishful thinking, where we believe what we want to be true, rather than what is actually true or what we should hold to be true on good grounds. For this reason, I suggest that we embrace merely a weak form of pragmatism. *Weak pragmatism* is the stance that both epistemic and pragmatic reasons are important when choosing

---

[12] Philip Kitcher, "Challenges for Secularism." In *The Joy of Secularism*, edited by G. Levine. Princeton University Press, 2011, pp. 31f.

[13] Philip Kitcher, *Living with Darwin*. Oxford University Press, 2007, p. 160.

what to believe in and how to live one's life. In James's classical under-standing of it, this means that if the evidence (i.e., the epistemic reasons) between two live options is approximately equal – in our case, whether we should embrace a religious or a secular worldview, such as theism or naturalism – then it is permitted to let pragmatic reasons or consider-ations prevail.[14]

Perhaps it would even be rational to let pragmatic reasons play a more decisive role than James thinks they should. After all, what is at stake when it comes to choosing a worldview is not only whether some beliefs are true or what conclusions we should draw regarding specific argu-ments but also *how we should live our lives*. It is not just a matter of making up one's mind; it is also a matter of choosing a way of living. If we cannot avoid having some kind of worldview, this choice cannot be postponed for human beings. We must live right now, one way or another. For this reason, people might be rationally justified in taking risks they would not be entitled to when a decision can be postponed. Choosing a worldview is foremost an instance of agent rationality, not spectator rationality.

I have proposed that when we become aware of having a particular worldview and start to reflect on its content, we should be guided by a set of intellectual norms. Ultimately, however, we as reflective people alone must take responsibility for the worldview we have, and if we are to do something as radical as convert and change our basic orientation in life, or if we, in critical and constructive dialogue with other people, are to continue to develop the religious or secular worldview that we already have.

[14] James, *The Will to Believe and Other Essays in Popular Philosophy*.

Select Bibliography

Baggini, Julian (2003). *Atheism: A Very Short Introduction*. Oxford: Oxford University Press.

Baker, Joseph O. and Buster G. Smith (2015). *American Secularism*. New York: New York University Press.

Baker, Lynne R. (2005). "Death and the Afterlife." In *The Oxford Handbook of Philosophy of Religion*, edited by William J. Wainwright. Oxford: Oxford University Press.

Baxter, Brian (2007). *A Darwinian Worldview*. Aldershot: Ashgate.

Bostrom, Nick (2003). "Transhumanist FAQ: A General Introduction." Version 2.1. https://nickbostrom.com/views/transhumanist.pdf.

Bostrom, Nick (2003). "Transhumanist Values." In *Ethical Issues for the 21st Century*, edited by Frederick Adams. Charlottesville, VA: Philosophical Documentation Center Press.

Bostrom, Nick (2013). "Why I Want to Be a Posthuman When I Grow Up." In *The Transhumanist Reader*, edited by Max Moore and Natasha Vita-More. Oxford: Wiley-Blackwell.

Bråkenhielm, Carl R. (2018). *The Study of Science and Religion*. Eugene: Pickwick Publications.

Bullivant, Stephen (2020). "Explaining the Rise of 'Nonreligion Studies': Subfield Formation and Institutionalization within the Sociology of Religion," *Social Compass* 67/1: 86–102.

Bullivant, Stephen and Michael Ruse (2013). "The Study of Atheism." In *The Oxford Handbook of Atheism*, edited by Stephen Bullivant and Michael Ruse. Oxford: Oxford University Press.

Burton, David (2017). *Buddhism: A Contemporary Philosophical Investigation*. London: Routledge.

Capra, Fritjof (2000). *The Tao of Physics* (25th ed.). Boston, Shambhala.

Chopra, Deepak and Leonard Mlodinow (2012). *War of the Worldviews*. New York: Three Rivers Press.

Clark, Kelly J., ed. (2015). *The Blackwell Companion to Naturalism*. Oxford: Wiley-Blackwell.

Copson, Andrew (2015). "What Is Humanism?" In *The Wiley Blackwell Handbook of Humanism*, edited by Andrew Copson and Anthony C. Grayling. London: Wiley-Blackwell.

Crisp, Thomas M. (2016). "On Naturalistic Metaphysics." In *The Blackwell Companion to Naturalism*, edited by Kelly J. Clark. Chichester: Wiley-Blackwell.

Crosby, Donald A. (2002). *A Religion of Nature*. New York: SUNY Press.

Darwin, Charles (1985). *The Origin of Species*. London: Penguin Books.

Dawkins, Richard (1986). *The Blind Watchmaker*. New York: W. W. Norton & Company.

Dawkins, Richard (1995). *River Out of Eden: A Darwinian View of Life*. New York: Basic Books.

Dawkins, Richard (2006). *The God Delusion*. Boston, Houghton Mifflin Company.

De Caro, Mario and David Macarthur (2004). "Introduction: The Nature of Naturalism." In *Naturalism in Question*, edited by Mario de Caro and David MacArthur. Cambridge, MA: Harvard University Press.

de Gray, Aubrey and Michael Rose (2007). *Ending Aging: The Rejuvenation Breakthroughs That Could Reverse Human Aging in Our Life-Time*. New York: St. Martin Press.

Dennett, Daniel C. (1995). *Darwin's Dangerous Idea*. London: Penguin Books.

Draper, Paul (2002). "Seeking but Not Believing: Confessions of a Practical Agnostic." In *Divine Hiddenness*, edited by Daniel Howard-Snyder and Paul K. Moser. Cambridge: Cambridge University Press.

Droogers, André and Anton van Harskamp, eds. (2014). *Methods for the Study of Religious Change: From Religious Studies to Worldview Studies*. Sheffield: Equinox Publishing.

Düwell, Marcus, Jens Braarvig, Roger Brownsword, and Dietmar Mieth, eds. (2014). *The Cambridge Handbook of Human Dignity: Interdisciplinary Perspectives*. Cambridge: Cambridge University Press.

Flood, Gavin (2020). *Hindu Monotheism*. Cambridge: Cambridge University Press.

Forrest, Jay N. (2018). "Buddhism and Religious Naturalism." In *The Routledge Handbook of Religious Naturalism*, edited by Donald A. Crosby and Jerome A. Stone. London: Routledge.

Fukuyama, Francis (2004). "Transhumanism: The World's Most Dangerous Idea," *Foreign Policy*, 144: 42–43.

Goodman, Charles (2014). "Buddhism, Naturalism, and the Pursuit of Happiness," *Zygon* 49/1: 220–230.

Hägglund, Martin (2019). *This Life: Secular Faith and Spiritual Freedom*. New York: Anchor Books.

Hammer, Olav (2016). "The New Age." In *The Cambridge Handbook of Western Mysticism and Esoterism*, edited by Glen A. Magee. Cambridge: Cambridge University Press.

Hanegraaff, Wouter J. (1996). *New Age Religion and Western Culture*. New York: SUNY Press.

Hanegraaff, Wouter J. (2013). *Western Esotericism*. London: Bloomsbury.

Harris, Sam (2010). *The Moral Landscape. How Science Can Determine Human Values*. New York: Free Press.

Harris, Sam (2012). *Free Will*. New York: Free Press.

Harrison, Victoria (2019). *Eastern Philosophy*. London: Routledge.

Hill, Thomas E. (2015). "Kantian Perspectives on the Rational Basis of Human Dignity," In *The Cambridge Handbook of Human Dignity*, edited by Marcus Düwell, Jens Braarvig, Roger Brownsword, and Dietmar Mieth. Cambridge: Cambridge University Press.

Inglehart, Ronald F. 2021. *Religion's Sudden Decline: What's Causing It, and What Comes Next?* Oxford: Oxford University Press.

Jeffner, Anders (1999). *Biology and Religion as Interpreting Patterns of Human Life*. Oxford: Harris Manchester College.

Jonbäck, Francis, and Carl-Johan Palmqvist (2024). "Between Belief and Disbelief, between Religion and Secularity: Introducing Non-Doxasticism and Semi-Secularity in Worldview Education," *British Journal of Religious Education* 46/2: 109–121.

Kateb, George (2011). *Human Dignity*. Cambridge, MA: Harvard University Press.

Kemp, Daren (2004). *New Age*. Edinburgh: Edinburgh University Press.

Kidd, Ian J. (2014). "Emotion, Religious Practice, and Cosmopolitan Secularism," *Religious Studies* 50/2: 139–156.

Kitcher, Philip (2011). "Challenges for Secularism." In *The Joy of Secularism*, edited by George Levine. Princeton: Princeton University Press.

Kitcher, Philip (2011). "Militant Modern Atheism," *Journal of Applied Philosophy* 28/1: 1–13.

Kline, David (2021). "Humanism against Religion." In *The Oxford Handbook of Humanism*, edited by Anthony B. Pinn. Oxford: Oxford University Press.

Kurzweil, Ray (2005). *The Singularity Is Near: When Humans Transcend Biology*. New York: Penguin Books.

Lama, Dalai (2006). *The Universe in a Single Atom*. London: Abacus.

Law, Stephen (2011). *Humanism*. Oxford: Oxford University Press.

LeDrew, Stephen (2016). *The Evolution of Atheism*. Oxford: Oxford University Press.

Lee, Lois (2015). *Recognizing the Non-Religious*. Oxford: Oxford University Press.

Lewis Hall, M. Elisabeth, and Peter Hill (2019). "Meaning-Making, Suffering, and Religion: A Worldview Conception." *Mental Health, Religion & Culture* 22/5: 467–479.

Lewis, James R. (2007). "Science and the New Age." In *Handbook of New Age*, edited by James Lewis and Daren Kemp. Leiden: Brill.

Linville, Mark D. (2009). "The Moral Argument." In *The Blackwell Companion to Natural Theology*, edited by William L. Craig and James P. Moreland. London: Wiley-Blackwell.

Lukić, Petar and Iris Žeželj (2024). "Delineating between Scientism and Science Enthusiasm: Challenges in Measuring Scientism and the Development of a Novel Scale." *Public Understanding of Science* 33/5: 568–586.

Lynch, Gordon (2007). *The New Spirituality*. London: I. B. Tauris.

Macarthur, David (2018). "Liberal Naturalism and the Scientific Image of the World," *Inquiry* 62/5: 565–585.

MacLaine, Shirley (1990). *Going Within*. London: Bantam Books.

Magee, Glen A., ed. (2016). *The Cambridge Handbook of Western Mysticism and Esoterism*. Cambridge: Cambridge University Press.

Midgley, Mary (1985). *Evolution as a Religion*. London: Methuen.

Nagasawa, Yujin (2018). "The Problem of Evil for Atheists." In *The Problem of Evil*, edited by Nick N. Trakakis. Oxford: Oxford University Press.

Nagel, Thomas (2010). *Secular Philosophy and the Religious Temperament*. Oxford: Oxford University Press.

Nagel, Thomas (2012). *Mind and Cosmos: Why the Materialist Neo-Darwinian Conception of Nature Is Almost Certainly False*. New York: Oxford University Press.

Palmqvist, Carl-Johan and Francis Jonbäck (2025). *Semi-Secular Worldviews and the Belief in Something Beyond*. Cambridge: Cambridge University Press.

Peterson, Michael L. and Michael Ruse (2017). *Science, Evolution, and Religion: A Debate about Atheism and Theism*. Oxford: Oxford University Press.

Plantinga, Alvin (2011). *Where the Conflict Really Lies: Science, Religion and Naturalism*. Oxford: Oxford University Press.

Plantinga, Alvin (2015). *Knowledge and Christian Belief*. Oxford: Oxford University Press.

Ricard, Matthieu and Trinh X. Thuan (2001). *The Quantum and the Lotus: A Journey to the Frontiers Where Science and Buddhism Meet*. New York: Three Rivers.

Rosenberg, Alex (2011). *The Atheist's Guide to Reality*. New York: W. W. Norton.

Rue, Loyal (2005). *Religion Is Not about God*. New Brunswick, NJ: Rutgers University Press.

Ruse, Michael (2017). "Naturalism, Evil, and God." In *The Cambridge Companion to the Problem of Evil*, edited by Chad Meister and Paul K. Moser. Cambridge: Cambridge University Press.

Sagan, Carl (1980). *Cosmos*. New York: Ballantine Books.

Schilbrack, Kevin (2014). *Philosophy and the Study of Religions*. Oxford: Wiley-Blackwell.

Scruton, Roger (2015). "Scientism and the Humanities." In *Scientism: The New Orthodoxy*, edited by Richard N. Williams and Daniel N. Robinson. London: Bloomsbury.

Searle, John R. (1995). *The Construction of Social Reality*. New York: Free Press.

Shafer-Landau, Russ (2024). *The Fundamentals of Ethics*. Oxford: Oxford University Press.

Smart, Ninian (1995). *Choosing a Faith*. New York: Boyars/Bowerdean.

Smart, Ninian (1995). *Worldviews*. Englewood Cliffs, NJ: Prentice-Hall.

Smith, Jesse M. and Ryan T. Cragun (2019). "Mapping Religion's Other," *Journal for the Scientific Study of Religion* 58: 319–335.

Stenmark, Mikael (1995). *Rationality in Science, Religion, and Everyday Life*. Notre Dame, IN: University of Notre Dame Press.

Stenmark, Mikael (1997). "What Is Scientism?" *Religious Studies*, 33/1: 15–32.

Stenmark, Mikael (2004). *How to Relate Science and Religion*. Grand Rapids, MI: Eerdmans.

Stenmark, Mikael (2009). "Three Theories of Human Nature," *Zygon: Journal of Religion and Science* 44/4: 894–920.

Stenmark, Mikael (2012). "Is There a Human Nature?" *Zygon: Journal of Religion and Science* 47/4: 890–902.

Stenmark, Mikael (2012). "Theories of Human Nature: Key Issues," *Philosophy Compass* 7/8: 543–558.

Stenmark, Mikael (2022). "Worldview Studies," *Religious Studies* 58/3: 564–582.

Stenmark, Mikael (2024). "Choosing a Worldview," *AGATHEOS – European Journal for Philosophy of Religion*, 1/1: 42–62.

Stenmark, Mikael (2025). "Worldviews and Science," *Zygon: Journal of Religion and Science* 59/4: 925–948.

Stone, Jerome A. (2008). *Religious Naturalism Today*. New York: SUNY Press.

Stone, Jerome A. (2018). "Defining and Defending Religious Naturalism." In *The Routledge Handbook of Religious Naturalism*, edited by Donald A. Crosby and Jerome A. Stone. London: Routledge.

Street, Sharon (2006). "A Darwinian Dilemma for Realist Theories of Value," *Philosophical Studies* 127/1: 109–166.

Swinburne, Richard (2010). *Is There a God?* Oxford: Oxford University Press.

Taves, Ann (2020). "From Religious Studies to Worldview Studies," *Religion* 50: 137–147.

Taylor, Charles (2007). *A Secular Age*. Cambridge, MA: Harvard University Press.

Valk, John (2021). *Worldviews*. New York: Palgrave Macmillan.

van Mulukom, Valerie, et al. (2023). "What Do Nonreligious Nonbelievers Believe In? Secular Worldviews around the World," *Psychology of Religion and Spirituality*, 15/1: 143–156.

Wildman, Wesley J. (2017). "Religious Naturalism: Oxymoronic Muddle or Future Spiritual Juggernaut?" In *A 21st Century Debate on Science and Religion*, edited by Shiva Khalili, Fraser Watts, and Harris Wiseman. Cambridge: Cambridge Scholars Publishing.

Wilson, Edward O. (1999). *Consilience*. New York: Alfred A. Knopf.

Index

Printed in the United Kingdom by TJ Clays Ltd.